THE COFFEE TEA OR ME GIRLS
LAY IT ON THE LINE

THE COFFEE TEA OR ME GIRLS
LAY IT ON THE LINE

Trudy Baker and Rachel Jones

GROSSET & DUNLAP
A National General Company
Publishers   New York

Excerpt from ENERGETICS by Grant Gwinup, M.D., © 1970 reprinted with permission from Sherbourne Press, Los Angeles, Calif. 90035.

Excerpt from HOW TO MAKE IT IN A MAN'S WORLD by Letty Cottin Pogrebin, © 1970 reprinted with permission from Doubleday & Company, Inc., 277 Park Avenue, New York, N.Y. 10017.

COPYRIGHT © 1972 BY GROSSET & DUNLAP, INC.
All rights reserved including the right to reproduce this book or any portions thereof in any form.

PUBLISHED SIMULTANEOUSLY IN CANADA
LIBRARY OF CONGRESS CATALOG CARD NUMBER: 75-183020
ISBN: 0-448-00819-X

Printed in the United States of America

DEDICATION

We offer this book up in sacrifice to Mary Ann, a friend and the only known virgin still flying for a major airline.

We also tip our wings to those valiant and forward-looking sex researchers who have managed to advise young girls on sexual happiness without knowing or being a young girl.

And finally, we bestow our blessings on Donald Bain and Eileen Rosenbaum, who live in the suburbs, and John Ott, who lives in the woods.

FOREWORD

There are those who will consider this a pornographic, lewd, obscene, licentious, prurient, smutty and altogether dirty book. That's all right with us as long as they don't work in the post office. People in the post office have made a dandy career out of reading erotic books and then deciding public morality will be threatened if these books are sent through the mail. Post office employees have the largest personal collections of pornography in the Free World, and entertain themselves on many a cold night rereading the books they've banned. We do hope, however, that single girls working in the post office will read this book. If *they* consider it pornographic, they need it more than the people getting it in the mail.

Other people will consider this an honest attempt to lend a helping hand to our fellow single girls who are having a dreadful time coping with the so-called New Morality. We don't claim any expertise in this field, just a firsthand knowledge of the problems facing today's single women. As stewardesses, we've come in contact with hundreds, maybe thousands of unattached girls who believe in the freedom of the day but haven't the foggiest notion of how to deal with it.

"How to deal with it?" you ask, eyebrows raised to the heavens. *"Any fool knows what to do with sexual freedom."*

Our answer to you, you smug and flippant bore, is

that knowing what to do with it and waking up in the morning after you've done it are two different things. Not only that, it isn't *what* to do that bothers many of today's young women, it's *how* to do it that throws them into a confused sweat. That's one of the areas we get into in this book—*how to do it*. You might consider it a home-repair tip book for the new sexuality.

Airline stewardesses represent a broad spectrum of young womanhood. We have all types serving coffee at 30,000 feet, and every one of them has to come down to earth each day and find pleasure, happiness and some semblance of sanity at home or in the crew motel. Some succeed, some don't. What we try to do in this book is relate the stories of some of the successes and failures so that you, you single female thing, can learn from the experiences. Young marrieds might learn a thing or two, too.

We offer only one suggestion before you read our book: Today's New Morality means nothing more than your freedom to do whatever it is that makes you *happy, secure and satisfied*. With that goal in mind, we invite you to read on.

TRUDY BAKER AND RACHEL JONES

Contents

I.	"You've Come a Long Way, Baby."	1
II.	"Where Am I Now That I'm Here?"	11
III.	Bubs, Backsides and Brittle Hair	26
IV.	"How Much Will the Brooklyn Bridge Cost Me?"	56
V.	All About SEX	79
VI.	"If You Do It More Than Once a Week, Your Hair Falls Out."	107
VII.	"An Orgy Is Two Couples in Bed with a Goat."	130
VIII.	"I'm New in Town ... Don't Touch."	144
IX.	"This Is the Nicest Affair I've Ever Had."	169
X.	Self-defense: The Pill and Karate	197
XI.	"If I Masturbate, Will I Become an Asexual, Incestuous Lesbian?"	219
XII.	"Marry You? All I Wanted to Do Was Go to Bed with You."	233
XIII.	"Go to Bed with Me? We're Married!"	264
	Epilogue	273

THE COFFEE TEA OR ME GIRLS LAY IT ON THE LINE

CHAPTER I

Confucius: "The woman's duty is to prostrate herself submissively before her husband in such a way as to have no will of her own, but to demonstrate a perfect form of obedience."

Chinese Stewardess: "Suggest you take honorable and ancient saying and stick it, you crazy old man."

"You've Come a Long Way, Baby."

It wasn't long ago that woman was merely a slave to man. We had our place and were expected to stay in it without whimpering. This was especially true regarding sex. You never dared react to the yearnings in your loins and become the aggressor with your high school hero, lest you pick up a bad reputation. Sure, you'd neck with him, but you had to be coy. If he ever thought you wanted it as much as he did, the locker room would soon have you branded as an easy mark, a round-heel, or worse.

So you played a little game as you fumbled around in the back seat of his car after a movie and pizza. While he huffed and puffed and you giggled, you said, "I can't, Harry. What would you think of me?"

"I'd think very highly of you, Cynthia."

"I've never done anything like this before."

"Honest? You mean I'll be the first?"

"Yes."

"I didn't know that. I'd better stop. I don't want to be the one who ruins you."

"Oh, shut up, Harry, and put your hand there again."

There's no need to be coy these days, but if you were brought up with a morality less liberal than today's New Morality, chances are you're having a devil of a time squaring away your new freedom with your upbringing.

It hasn't been easy for girls who grew up in the Forties, Fifties and Sixties. Here we are in the Sensuous Seventies and everybody's telling us we're FREE, free to compete for high-paying jobs, hold elective office, have abortions, buy the Pill, and enjoy sex for its own sake. But if you haven't been brought up to enjoy sex for its own sake, how can you enjoy it when it's suddenly thrust upon you?

Think of how far we girls have come in the matter of freedom. Eve, munching on a rotten apple in the orchard, was told, "And *he* shall rule over thee."

Shakespeare and Milton said things like, "Keep silent, be modest and accept a lesser place."

And most men agreed with Napoleon, that paranoid French midget, who said, "Woman is given to man to bear children; she is therefore his property as the tree is the garden's." We know a few Air France stewardesses who shake their tree every chance they get.

But they represent *today,* and Napoleon represents yesterday. How sad it is to realize that Napoleon's yesterday was as recent as the 1960s.

This is not a women's lib book. We don't believe in women's lib as it has been presented by the high-pitched shrill shrieks of the movement's beauties, one more unattractive than the next. Yes, we want job equality when it's reasonable. We want freedom from the mandatory housewife role. But we *like* being women. We like our role in life and sex. What we're looking for is a chance to go through our one shot on earth and enjoy it without recriminations, doubts or a lifetime contract with the local shrink.

The past is just that, the past, and we'd like it to remain there. But you should know a little about the long road we women have traveled.

Men, as you know, have always been the big shots in the man-woman thing. Fathers protected their daughters because any daughter who lost her virginity was less valuable on the marriage market. Husbands always looked after their wives' chastity because they didn't want to pay for children that weren't theirs. In a word, woman became man's *property,* and he protected his property as zealously as he protected his team of horses.

Aside from being *property,* women also have been considered one of two things:

1. *A Good Girl*—A virgin mother, untouchable and sexless, a pure and selfless thing.

2. *A Bad Girl*—Eve, a witch from the Dark Ages, a bloodsucking vampire or a harlot in search of adventure on the streets of the world.

Girls have also been expected to earn their keep. There was no sense in educating a girl; she didn't need an education to bear children. Better to save the money. (The average family in 1675 consisted of nine people.)

If a single girl in early New England was caught in the sack with a fellow, she might be whipped, branded, banished and maybe even hung. So she sat home and waited for some single guy to come along and pay her father for her hand. At least in marriage she could escape her father's protection. But, of course, she ended up with a husband's protection of her chastity, and God help her if she ever appeared to enjoy making love with him. Husbands were free, in those days, to beat their wives, provided "he used a stick no thicker than his thumb."

Once our eighteenth and nineteenth century girl married, she ceased to exist as a person, if indeed she ever had. The moment the ceremony was over her husband had gained:

1. Total control over her mind and body.
2. Total control over their children.
3. Total ownership of her personal funds and any property she might own.
4. Total right to the products of her labor.
5. Total control of how and where she lived.

A wife in those early days was classified with infants and idiots, according to the famous Commentaries of Blackstone upon which most of our laws are based. A wife could not make a will, inherit property, sue or be sued. Even if some local stud raped her she couldn't do anything about it unless her husband brought suit. He'd probably beat her before doing that.

If her husband died, the wife of the past was entitled to few of their joint possessions. Under early New York law, she was entitled to receive the family Bible, pictures, school books and all books not exceeding the sum of $50, spinning wheels, weaving looms, the stove, ten sheep and their fleece, two swine and their pork, wearing apparel, beds, bedspreads and bedding, one table, six chairs, six knives and forks, six teacups and saucers, one sugar dish, one milk pot and one teapot.

Good deal, huh?

But things started to happen. The women's liberation movement moved on three separate fronts: Legal, Social and Sexual.

A feminist group held a convention in Seneca Falls, New York, in 1848, and issued its Declaration of Sentiments. It said, in part: "We hold these truths to be self-evident; that all men and women are created equal. . . ." Nobody believed it but the ladies at the convention.

There was a fellow named Dr. Edward Clarke who, back in 1874, made his learned feelings known about equal education for women. Dr. Clarke theorized that the real trouble with middle-class women in America stemmed from any education they'd received. Catch this, now. Dr. Clarke said that when a woman's brain was forced to function in the process of learning, it took away blood necessary for menstruation. He claimed that uneducated women were much healthier than female students. Female students, he said, developed anemia and nervous disorders. Sweetheart that he was, Dr. Clarke even examined ladies in an Asian harem and found them to be "well developed, with skin rich with the blood and the sun of the East, their unintelligent sensuous faces glowing with dull good health."

But eventually colleges opened their doors to women. And pretty soon, females were allowed to vote. But we still weren't allowed to enjoy sex. In fact, in the late 1800s, women led the fight *against* sexual freedom for themselves. They claimed women were pure and morally superior. But the courts didn't recognize this so-called purity. Up until 1884 in England, a woman could be sent to prison if she withheld intercourse from her husband. Women were supposed to submit whenever their husbands demanded sex, but were not to enjoy it. An early sex researcher asked a staunchly Victorian British lady to describe her feelings during intercourse. She answered, "I lie on my back and think of England."

Those of you who read our previous books, *Coffee Tea or Me?* and *The Coffee Tea or Me Girls' 'Round-the-World Diary,* were introduced to Betty O'Riley, better known to her fellow stews as Betty Big Boobs. Betty lives for sex. "Ah just tingle all over whenever ah think of a fella doin' it to me," she says.

We asked Betty one night on a long flight what she thought about while making love.

"It depends. If ah like him and he's doin' it real good, ah lay there and think about what's doin'. But if ah don't care too much about the fella and he's not doin' such a good job, ah just lay there and think of Savannah."

"Savannah?"

"Sure. That's where ah was born. Sometimes when ah'm not tinglin' like ah should, ah think of Savannah and that makes me tingle."

You might call Betty a southern Victorian twentieth century woman. Then again, you might think of her as a southern mammary gland. Either way, the world is full of Bettys, and the stewardess corps has its share.

Today, we're all very aware of our sexual feelings. But in those days gone by, no one ever considered sexual gratification for the female. England's greatest authority on sexual matters, Sir William Acton, said, "Happily for society, the female species possesses no sexual feelings whatsoever." He obviously didn't know Betty.

Women, tightly corseted, repressed their sexuality before the New Morality allowed them to express it. But it was never too deep below the surface. Those puritanical years were, in a very silly way, sensual.

Suppressed sexuality was everywhere. People even

put skirts over such bulging sexual symbols as chairs, tables and lamps. Remember?

What was it really like to be a young woman of the Victorian era? If you could hop in your handy time machine and skip back one hundred years, you'd probably find young girls living a very different life from your own. Girls of that earlier era stood up straight, didn't dance, drink coffee, tea or other stimulating beverages, didn't lie on soft beds, sit in soft chairs or lean against anything for support. Socializing with boys at an early age was out of the question. If a Victorian young lass felt some urgings in her loins, she hopped in a cold tub. She didn't cross her legs, slept with her hands outside the bedclothes and never straddled a hobbyhorse or seesaw.

Your body was not to be explored, and steel ribs and whalebone corsets kept in any display of womanly flesh. Some finishing schools even demanded that a young lady sleep in her corset. Ouch!

Because you were a woman, you were expected to be sickly, frail and dependent. Women of the day constantly suffered from fainting spells, piles, pelvic disorders, headaches, bad backs, fatigued brains and weary central nervous systems.

Since you were always sick and ailing, there was little time or inclination for sex with your husband. When those few nights every month came around for a fling with the old man, you lay there like a piece of putty and allowed him to get relief. The rule, as a horrified nineteenth century gentleman pointed out to his enthusiastic bride, was that *women do not move*. Only sluts and prostitutes moved during lovemaking in those days.

But women started moving in bed and in the liberation movement. In 1911, Elizabeth Cady Stanton, an early and more digestible Betty Freidan, wrote, "The suffrage movement . . . logically if not consciously . . .

means social equality and, next, Freedom. Or, in a word, Free Love." She added, "Anyone wishing to get out of the boat should, for safety, get out now, for delays are dangerous."

By the 1920s many women had climbed in the boat and things looked better. Women had the vote, and to the despair of the leading women's libbers, they voted for most of the same things as did the men of the time. Girls established the period of flaming youth by raising their hemlines, fluffing their hair, drinking, smoking and, for heaven's sake, dancing. But that didn't mean women had come all the way. There was widespread resistance to this new female liberation. The State of Utah considered a bill providing fines and imprisonment for those women who wore "skirts higher than three inches above the ankle" in public. In Virginia, it was proposed that women be forbidden to wear blouses or evening gowns which displayed more than three inches of throat. Ohio was even worse, limiting the view to two inches. This same Ohio legislature was asked to prevent the sale of "any garment which unduly displays or accentuates the lines of the female figure."

With the Twenties came a wave of love and romance. Glamour, style and a flair for overstatement became important. This glamour blazed at us from the silent movie screens, and such magazines as *Vogue* and *Harper's Bazaar* sensed the public infatuation with it and handed it out in large monthly doses. Times were changing. Women's fashions showed more of the woman. Premarital intercourse became accepted among middle-class females, although they kept this acceptance secret and didn't condone it in public. Those Victorians concerned with the sexual double standard tried to destroy it by encouraging men to be as chaste and pure as women, but the gals of the Twenties attacked the problem by trying to be more promiscuous than the men. That challenge was too difficult to really pull off, but happy times were had in the trying.

Then, the Depression and the terrible Thirties came along, leaving everyone glum and saddened. There was neither time nor inclination to worry about such frivolous things as women's rights and sexual freedom. Putting food on the table took top priority and it was the men—the breadwinners—who took center stage.

You could probably classify the Forties as an age of responsibility. The wartime economy was insatiable in its need for goods and workers to turn out these goods. Women, wearing wide-shouldered fashions as perhaps a symbol of their responsibility, went into the factories and popped rivets to the tune of "Rosie the Riveter." Female legs were on display, but never above the knee.

The economy regained its health during the Fifties. Advertising became a national motivating force, and the little woman was glorified as a happy, unthinking user of everything the ads told her to use. You had to be blonde to be happy. You also had to be slightly overweight and stuffed into a girdle to avoid jiggling. "Creative Motherhood" was born as a concept, and happiness was a station wagon bursting with kids.

Welcome the Sixties with its accent on youth. Chubby, blonde, boopsy-boo females gave way to slender model types with tiny, firm breasts, shining natural hair, and mini-skirts. Twiggy became a sex symbol and airline stewardesses replaced movie actresses as the stuff dreams were made of. And, for the first time, it was okay to move in bed while making love. Sex was in, and we were as free to enjoy it as the men. Girl-watchers were treated to see-through blouses, no bras, the bikini, plunging necklines, plunging backs, micro-minis, topless and bottomless dancers and waitresses, and "X" rated movies showing everything you always wanted to know about intercourse. We've come a long way since our Victorian Grandma's day. And now that we're here in the Sensuous Seventies, we owe it to ourselves to find happiness and fulfillment. There are many traps into which a young girl of today can fall that will cause unhappiness. And there are the right roads to travel to achieve a full and happy life.

Can a girl really be happy in the New Morality?

We know the answer to be a resounding YES!

CHAPTER II

"A suburban nymphomaniac is someone who has sex the same day she's had her hair done."
—G. LINDAUER

"Where Am I Now That I'm Here?"

Here we are in the Sensuous Seventies. Our purses are filled with dispensers of the Pill, cans of feminine deodorant and large illustrated manuals of sexual techniques. We're free to join the Boy Scouts, show up on the F.B.I.'s Ten-Most-Wanted list, and go to bed with a guy we meet in a bar and not feel like a cheap pickup. But this doesn't mean automatic happiness. In fact, the changes that brought about this lovely freedom have spawned problems of their own. The Pill is an example. It will prevent conception but might give you blood clots. You take your choice, babies or blood clots. To make such a decision you have to know something about the Pill (see Chapter X).

Simply being free to enjoy sex doesn't make for a bed of roses. Before the New Morality became a reality, any guy who was fortunate enough to share your body would be delighted with plain old intercourse. Now, he might want to play a few variations on the old basic theme. Nothing says you have to accommodate him, but you'd better know what it's all about (see Chapter VII).

You also have to deal with a sizable segment of the male population that hasn't heard about women's freedom. Or they have heard about it but prefer to ignore it. That's one thing you must keep in mind. We've come a long way, but there's still a long way to go. They still regulate working hours for women in thirty-six states, and in many locations a single woman can't rent a hotel room or an apartment or go into a bar unescorted.

Sexual freedom has outpaced most other areas of women's liberation. Nobody says "NO" anymore. Each of us is very aware of our sexual feelings, and we're all part of what one writer has described as a "frantic search for orgasm." Orgasm has become a fashionable topic of conversation today, as have masturbation, pornography, homosexuality and all the varied sexual manifestations that deviate from the norm of Grandma's day.

The cult of the virgin has disappeared, too. Premarital sex is accepted as commonplace, and the increase in premarital sex is most significant among women. Present statistics indicate that the number of unmarried women who enjoy intercourse is just about equal to men.

But all this creates its own set of problems for many girls. We know a stewardess—we'll call her Sally—who is a neurotic wreck because she has never been sure she's experienced an orgasm.

"What does it feel like?" she often asks when a bunch of stews get together in someone's apartment for a bull session.

"It feels great," someone answers.

"I know it's supposed to feel great," she replies, "but I don't know if I've ever had one."

"Have you ever enjoyed making love, Sally?"

"Sure."

"Have you ever felt great when things came to a climax?"

"Sure."

"Then you probably had an orgasm."

"But maybe I didn't." Sally is usually chain-smoking at this point.

"So what, Sally?"

"So what?! I have to *know!*"

Sally has read dozens of books in search of an answer. We recall one night when Sally read us the orgasm description from the latest book. We were in the galley of a 707 drinking coffee and enjoying having our shoes off when Sally, half-glasses perched on the end of her nose, read: " 'Then it occurs, mutual detonation. The female begins with a series of tiny tremors, her heart races, her mouth goes dry and soon her entire body, bathed in the sweat of love, is buffeted with volcanic eruptions from her loins. The heavens open and the stars flash in her eyes. This is orgasm.' "

"Is that what happens to you?" Sally asked me.

"I think so."

"That's not what happens to me."

No matter how many times Sally has been told to stop worrying about orgasm and enjoy the simple pleasure of making love, she can't shake her feeling of inadequacy. Naturally, Sally will never experience the volcanic eruptions of orgasm in her present mental state. It's self-defeating, poor thing.

Technology and an enlightened view of abortion have meant a lot to today's single girl. And so have many of the victories won in the matter of equal employment. Young single girls now travel to large cities to take jobs and forge careers of their own. The automobile has made us more mobile, and the ability to earn a living has enabled many a woman, entrenched in an impossible, unfulfilling marriage, to strike out on a second life without fear of starvation or public condemnation.

These Sensuous Seventies have given us an increased interest in group sex, mate-swapping and group marriages. We've been exposed to a barrage of sexual stimuli. By the time a girl turns Sweet Sixteen she's seen many illustrations of how women behave before, during and after intercourse. It's all there on the TV and movie screens. There has also been mass merchandising of a sexually stimulating body. Toothpaste, deodorants, pimple creams, denture creams, hair sprays, cosmetics, suntan lotions and even antacid pills promise a sexier, more alluring you. The traditional courtship has given way to long sexual trials in which both partners enjoy sex while they decide if they wish to make it a legal commitment. The sexual liberation of the female is a very important liberation but, like other freedoms, it brings about problems. Today, a girl is made to feel she *must* engage in sex at the drop of a belt. And who's been telling her this? The sex consultants of the era, the writers and publishers who have made a classical buck from it. It is our opinion that most of them have done a disservice to today's single women.

There has been a great deal of controversy over women being sex objects. The most militant women's libbers picket *Playboy* because that publication, and its founder, Hugh Hefner, present the female as an object to be lustfully drooled over by male readers. So what? To try to deny that the undraped female form is sexually attractive to men is ridiculous. It's just biology when our male passengers stiffen as one of us reaches up into the overhead rack and our skirt comes with us.

We're perfectly aware of the fact that the sight of a bosom causes a man's heart to thump a little. It's not exactly news to us that a woman's body brings real pleasure to a man. To that extent, we suppose we *are* sex objects. But until very recently, it has been incessantly drummed into us that that is *all* we are. Under the Old Morality, we were bright little fluffs of down whose only possible means of self-expression was through a man. Our ideal was supposed to be romance. Our goal was marriage. Our life-style was dependence. Our status, our sense of self-respect, depended entirely on our husband's position, and not on our own accomplishments. Why on earth did we ever put up with it? Why did we willingly put ourselves in such a joyless, profitless position? Because we allowed ourselves to be sold a bill of goods, that's why. Because, ninnies that we were, we believed the myth of male superiority, or perhaps we were just plain cowardly and unwilling to accept the responsibility for managing our own destinies.

Besides, it's a self-fulfilling prophecy. If you tell a young girl that her total worth is located between her thighs, she'll begin to think very little of herself. She'll have no respect for her own abilities. As a result, women are more prejudiced against women than the most poisonous male chauvinist.

Not that we want, on that account, to deny our sexuality. Those grim-faced and totally humorless ladies in the women's lib movement—with apologies to Germaine Greer—aren't doing us any big favors when they insist there should be no distinction whatsoever made between men and women. Can't they see they're defeating themselves when they reason: (a) women have always been treated as sex objects; (b) we will not allow this state of affairs to continue; and (c) therefore, women must prove to men that they are not needed in any way, including sexually. Well, we happen to think that whatever the Brave New World of the future is like, it'll be nice to have men there with whom to share it. After all, it's their world, too. There's an old saying about cutting off your nose to spite your face that seems to apply to the more hysterical women-firsters we've been reading about lately.

But let's not go charging off trying to shoot flies with a cannon. In our opinion, Mr. Hefner and his magazine are both a bit of a bore, especially now that he's taken the whole thing seriously and smokes a pipe on his horrid television show and offers leather binders for his so-called philosophy. But the centerfold doesn't send us off in search of a picket line. We can't lose much sleep over the fact that the Grill Room of the University Club in New York City won't serve women. If we really thought these things were important, the next logical step for us to take would be to demonstrate against all Ladies' Room and Men's Room signs as being hatefully discriminating.

As stewardesses, we've been pointed to recently as prime examples of women being discriminated against. One case concerned the automatic retiring of stewardesses from flight duty after the age of thirty-five. We disagreed with this, and joined our fellow stews in fighting the rule. As you know, we won. To us, that *was* important.

The other use of airline stewardesses as examples of the trod-upon female is broader in scope. Lately women's lib leaders have been boarding flights and handing us leaflets that tell us to fight for equal opportunity in our airlines. We're told the airlines exploit us, use us only for sex-and-service jobs. It's pointed out that there are no women in control towers, or in the flight decks of jet airplanes. We don't know what they expect us to do. Are they seriously suggesting that we go on strike until the airlines we work for agree to hire and train us as pilots? Do they expect us to march to Washington and conduct a massive sit-in in the corridors of the Federal Aviation Administration until a suitable number of us are hired as air-traffic controllers?

We honestly don't know if women will ever be considered for such jobs, but there are two things we do know. The first is that neither one of us has the slightest inclination to do that kind of work. And, incidentally, we don't know of a single stew who does. Secondly, if women are ever to be given the opportunity for this sort of professional advancement, we know it'll never happen by way of the tactics being advocated by women's lib. They want instant solutions to some very tricky problems, and it simply can't be done. It'll come about slowly, and as the result of the development of a new honesty and frankness about the interdependent roles of men and women in our society. It will not come about by forcing either men or women into roles that seem liberated and new, but are in reality as repressive and self-serving as any ever preached by the most shortsighted Victorian.

Sex writers and women's lib leaders seem to make a habit of directing young girls into absurd positions. Take the case of Letty Cottin Pogrebin, former publicity gal for the New York publishing house, Bernard Geis Associates. In her book *How to Make It in a Man's World,* Mrs. Pogrebin describes her favorite bitch-witch lady boss: "Her eyes, her carriage and her voice were an open dare to anyone who might question her femininity. The wild-flower perfume, the clingy silk jersey dresses, the gracefully crossed long legs, the flirty yet ladylike off-color stories, the throaty laugh—all these could be turned on in a blinding flash to mask the brutal, emasculating, power-mad Prussian underneath."

That's fine to a point. Everyone knows a few of these bitch-witches and the description is accurate. But what sends us up the wall is that Mrs. Pogrebin tells her readers, presumably younger gals, to study these bitch-witch qualities and learn from them. This, she says, is the way to make it in a man's world.

Well, we think it's a sad message to pass along to today's younger women. Any message that tells us to be dishonest, in the home or out of it, in the boardroom, the motel room and in any other room where men are present, seems pretty distasteful to us. According to Mrs. Pogrebin, dirty pool is the only way for women to succeed these days, but we say that women who cheat in this manner really only cheat themselves. In the long run, the honest woman, honest about her womanhood, is the one who succeeds. We don't like being told to become frauds, no matter how much Mrs. Pogrebin enjoys this dark and questionable challenge.

This brings us to one point we feel stands above all others in achieving happiness and success as a single girl in this New Morality. It is expressed by Charles Reich in his very important and successful book, *The Greening of America*. He says:

"There is a revolution coming. Its ultimate creation will be a new and enduring wholeness and beauty—a renewed relationship of man to himself, to society, to nature and to the land."

Mr. Reich offers three commandments by which this revolution will be governed. Abbreviated, they are:

The first commandment—"Thou shall not do violence to thyself."

The second commandment—"Value what is unique and different in each self."

The third commandment—"Be wholly honest with others; use no other person as a means. It is equally wrong to alter oneself for someone else's sake; by being one's true self one offers others the most; one offers them something honest, genuine and, more important, something for them to respond to."

In other words, you must be *honest* with yourself

and with others to be happy in the New Morality. You must have sex because you honestly enjoy having sex. If you don't, don't do it and go through all the groans and grunts of false ecstasy because you think *he* expects it. Don't play the dreadful game suggested in *The Sensuous Woman* by authoress "J", who says that all you need to make a man happy is a jar of honey, some cans of whipped cream and "J's" manual at your side. We talk about honest appraisal of yourself elsewhere in the book, but you might as well accept right now the promise of total honesty if this book will be any help at all.

Before the New Morality becomes a reality in your life, either as a sexaul morality or as that described by Charles Reich, there is some burying to be done. There are ghosts who, although well-intentioned in some cases, have done more to stand in the way of a productive and happy New Morality than Hugh Hefner could accomplish in ten thousand years in his circular bed with all the Bunnies in the forest. These ghosts are Freud, Emily Post and Helen Gurley Brown.

Emily Post and her calling to teach all young women the correct ceremonial procedures they will ever encounter in life was, in effect, promoting dishonest behavior. As one writer put it, "It is sometimes difficult for a lady to grow, mature and develop to her fullest when she must spend most of her life learning what fork to use." The era of "white glove etiquette" is being replaced by an era of honesty, and we heartily approve. People who spend their lives searching for a manner of conduct determined to be "correct" by a small group of people leave us cold, stone-cold. We'd rather have a passenger use the wrong spoon for his soup and treat us like human beings than have one who does the whole table routine correctly but snarls at us every time we pass his seat.

Which brings us to Helen Gurley Brown. What

bothers us so much about Mrs. Brown is that while she's been writing books telling young girls what to do with their lives, she has done it without a speck of respect for her readers, the young girls of America. She contributed to the sexual revolution at the expense of the human revolution. She blasted the myth of the "Happy Virgin" and replaced it with the "Plastic Person." She suggests in her book *Sex and the Single Girl* that women redesign themselves, sharpen their wits and sharpen their claws so that they may be worthy of notice by the strong, all-important male. Mrs. Brown's attempt at honesty comes when she says she isn't beautiful, or even pretty. "Yet," she says, "I managed to sink into the consciousness and subconsciousness (*sic*) of an advertising tycoon, a motivational research wizard, two generals, a brewer, a publisher, a millionaire real-estate developer and two extremely attractive men who were younger than I." Helen Gurley Brown must keep a chart on her wall with red lines to indicate net worth, blue lines to indicate profession and orange lines to indicate the ages of her boyfriends. There is no line, however, to indicate the man's character, honesty and depth.

Over and over in her book, Mrs. Brown gushes about how she was able to remake herself so that these men talked to her, entertained her, gifted her and bedded her down. And what's so sad to us about all this boasting is that behind each conquest are intentions as vicious as a scorpion. We think she comes across as manipulative, phony and a great big tease of the worse variety. In everything except sex, Helen Gurley Brown strikes us as being a Victorian. Essentially, her message is: "You're not *married* yet?"

Well, Mrs. Brown tells us girls not to panic (panicky ladies are very unattractive). Try to appear relaxed, we're told. Polish yourselves up. Get pretty. Learn how to use sex as a *weapon*. After a while, if you follow this diet, you're bound to trap someone with credentials impressive enough for your wall chart. Then hang on, sweetie. It's a free ride from there on in.

Helen Gurley Brown enjoys perpetuating the tradition of the helpless, slightly stupid, trusting broad. She suggests we throw ourselves at the mercy of tradesmen, the theory being that if we are wide-eyed and trusting, a tradesman would no more cheat us than take advantage of an orphan. We deal with some shop owners who would cheat, plunder and rape a blind orphan just for practice. Besides, that role is old hat; wide-eyed, trusting, dumb broads end up with wide-eyed, trusting, dumb heavy equipment salesmen in town for a convention and wearing name tags.

What else is a woman according to Helen Gurley Brown? She is a sex dispenser, a pretty, neat, quiet, efficient and cheerful sex dispenser in a reusable tube. Man, on the other hand, is a favor dispenser. Young girls having an affair are advised "not to miss out on some of your justly deserved fringe benefits—wining and dining and buzzing around." After all, Mrs. Brown says, you have bestowed your most "precious gift." Any girl who thinks her vagina is her most precious gift to a man deserves to be cut off from all fringe benefits, including the time of day. *You*—all of you, not a particular part of your anatomy—are your most precious gift to man.

On the subject of sex being your most precious weapon, Mrs. Brown tells you that a girl can promise with a look, a touch, a letter or a kiss but "she doesn't have to deliver!" There's a word for girls like this, and it's a good deal more descriptive than bitch. You'll read it in Chapter V. The truth is, you don't have to deliver anything—except honesty. Remember?

From our vantage point, Helen Gurley Brown is not a promoter of the New Morality. Her morality is the Old Morality plus the Pill. But never sell Mrs. Brown short. Our reason for devoting so much space to Mrs.

Brown is that she has been the Number One influence on a whole generation of single girls. Her disciples are everywhere, teasing, exploiting and announcing how happy they are since they gave up their virginity and gained a pack horse to carry up their bundles. The stewardess corps is full of these Helen Gurley Brown creations, and they never rank very high on the crew's popularity scale. Fortunately, they're being replaced as younger girls come into the ranks and approach things with more honesty.

Finally, the matter of Sigmund Freud.

No one can deny that Freud has been one of the major intellectual forces of the twentieth century. His thoughts have been, however, the basis for much misdirected amateur psychology on the part of today's thinking man and woman. The terms *sick, neurotic* and *psycho* are used freely and without thought to their true meaning. We discuss each other's id and superego, unearth death wishes and talk of repressions and egocentricity. We *know* that every man wants to kill his father and possess his mother. We also *know* that every woman is filled and consumed with *penis envy,* and sees every hot dog and banana as a *phallic symbol.*

Freud felt that many of the problems of mankind stemmed from repressed sexuality. He preached that the way to improved mental health was to freely express sexual desires. When you consider he was working during the dark ages of the Victorian era, his thoughts and statements become even more startling and liberating. But when you get right down to the nitty gritty of Freud, you realize he was laboring under a few misconceptions about the female. Freud believed that a girl, as she matures, transfers all her pleasurable sensations from her clitoris to her vagina. He said that clitoral orgasm was immature, and that vaginal orgasm was mature (for more on this, see Chapter VI). The result of his teachings was to breed a generation of women trying vainly to achieve this magical vaginal orgasm. Masters and Johnson, today's prime sex researchers, have conclusively proved there is only one kind of orgasm.

Freud also believed that the female had little sexual energy, nature having discriminated against her. He assumes a pitying attitude toward women, which is what we don't need. We also don't need to be told that the minute we discover we don't have a penis, we dissolve into a traumatized heap. Not having a penis is not, despite what Freud says, such a catastrophic event as to haunt us girls all our lives. We are not driven by the sad fact that we are females, constantly in search of a penis substitute. We have babies, not because a baby is that penis substitute as Freud claims, but because we went to bed with a man and made love. And we love the babies that result because babies are precious and human, not because they give us the missing penis in our dreadful lives.

"The female's sexual role," Freud theorized, "defines her in life and in her family and has made her not only incompetent but necessarily hostile to intellect and high culture." Sorry, Dr. Freud, but we don't buy this. As far as we're concerned, we are as normal as the boys. We don't want their penises any more than they want our vaginas. You are, Dr. Freud, a partial Victorian. We reject your errors, accept your truths and proceed to the New Morality with equality, freedom and honesty.

What women basically have today under this New Morality is an alternate life-style. We have never had that before because men wouldn't let us have it. Some people love this alternate life-style concept. Others hate it, but everyone agrees on one fact—it's different.

Everything is different. Kids no longer *automatically* finish high school, *automatically* go to college and *automatically* take a job with the large corporation that pays the most. Girls don't *automatically* try to snare a guy and pick out the silver pattern together and announce the engagement and show off the ring and have a big wedding and take a safe job until they're pregnant and buy a house and move to the suburbs and buy a second house and a second car and so on and so on and so on. Sure, lots of people still do it that way, and if it makes them happy, that's great. But that isn't the pattern that has to be followed by today's girl. There are many people—probably your parents, too—who feel any deviation from the norm is terrible. It's a Revolution, they might say. They might even call it anarchy. Or Communist-inspired. But like it or not, today's young people, boys and girls, are on the road, living in communes (that's not our scene but they say it's great), working in ghettos for very little money and going to free schools and free stores and making free love.

What it all boils down to is that people aren't just working or becoming. People today are busy just *being*. We're not so goal-oriented. We want to take the time to see things and feel things and find out what we're all about as people.

We know lots of girls living the straight life, we know many who are living the hip life, we also know girls managing to live both. One of our friends is the picture of the demure, sweet stewardess during working hours. She's neat and clean and polite and quite proper. Off-hours, she slips into hand-embroidered blue jeans, a tie-dyed shirt and sandals and goes off as a volunteer worker in a free clinic in Harlem. She spends weekends in a commune and does her thing until the next flight of tired businessmen. Her other life doesn't appeal to us but we think it's absolutely great for people to have the freedom to live as they wish, think as they wish and love as they wish.

The point is you *choose* your life-style; it's not

dictated to you by Emily Post or anyone else. If getting dressed up for a date means a white chiffon cocktail dress to you, that's fine. It's also fine if it is a pair of blue jeans or a black leotard. A dinner date for one girl might mean chateaubriand at The Four Seasons. For another it's a beef stew cooked over a campfire in New Hampshire. For still another, it might be both.

Because there is a wide difference in life-styles these days, writing this book was a little difficult. How could we satisfy *all* females? Sex is the answer to that question, because sex is a common denominator. Sex as experience, sex as fun, sex as exchange of love—it doesn't matter. We *are* sexual creatures.

There are a few other common denominators besides sex, although the others are really requisites for happy sex. These include good health, sensible food and good exercise.

You choose your life-style. Choose it *honestly,* without ulterior motivations and phony goals. Forget Helen Gurley Brown, Emily Post and Freud. And let's get high together by happily enjoying being female.

CHAPTER III

"Fat is Fun!"
—TWIGGY

Bubs, Backsides and Brittle Hair

How do we begin enjoying the New Morality? The first step is to enjoy being ourselves, to start feeling relaxed about our bodies and the way we look with or without clothes.

What's that you say? Do we hear you wailing, "It'll never work. It doesn't make any difference what I do with my face or figure, I'm just not the *type* men find attractive." Well, if that's your complaint you really haven't been listening or looking around. There is no *type* today.

Back in the Twenties when Theda Bara ruled the silent screen, every girl in the neighborhood came home from the movies and practiced writhing around on an ottoman, pouting darkly at some imaginary lover as she puffed a cigarette through a yard-long holder. Then, just as everyone was getting the hang of it, along came bouncy little Mary Pickford and a whole generation of females obediently changed the way they walked, smiled, did their hair and dressed. They didn't mind having to change with the trends; it's the way it had always been, and the way it would always be—until now. Just as the ads keep telling you, you've come a long way, baby, and you're perfectly free to look and be whatever suits your mood. After years of being stamped out like animal cookies, American women have finally broken the die that molded them into someone else's notion of beauty or fashion. And if you doubt it, just think about the midi disaster. Ten years ago we would have meekly allowed the designers to dress us all as sisters of charity. But not today. We fought for the right to show our legs if we felt like it, and we won.

So remember, the only *type* that'll turn people on is the *natural* you. But this isn't as easy as it sounds. In fact, discovering the real you can be much harder then passively being told how to look and act. You've got to be ruthlessly honest with yourself, totally objective. All you need for starters is a pencil, a piece of paper, a full-length mirror (a three-way one if possible) and an hour, either alone or in the company of a close and trusted friend.

Take the paper and divide it into three columns. The first column will be where you list your good points. The second column is where you will note those faults that can be corrected. The third column is for weaknesses that you feel cannot be corrected, no matter how hard you try. Next, take off all your clothes and begin analyzing your body. The value of a friend at this point is that she can help you be objective. She can also be catty and bitchy, so choose her carefully. If your close friend happens to be a male and you can shed your clothes in front of him without embarrassment, then you can throw away the paper. You don't need help.

Take a hard look at your figure, your posture, your complexion, your hair, your facial features, nails and teeth. Note your good points, the things that need attention, and finally, the problems you simply can't correct. Now, get the worst over with first. Read down the list of things you hate about yourself but feel can't be corrected. Does it include entries such as "skin too pale" or "complexion too dark?" If it does, erase them. These are subjective judgments. You may wish you were fairer or darker, but it happens to be the way you are, and just because you don't like it doesn't mean it's a negative. The gals who fly for SAS may look different from the stews on Alitalia, but both get, and merit, appreciation from their male passengers. The kind of thing you ought to have in your can't-do-anything-about-it list is "short neck" or "big feet." But even these aren't hopeless. Okay, you've got a neck like a lady wrestler. No one will notice if they see you in a bulky sweater with a loose turtle neck. So, go easy with your list of uncorrectable flaws. Some of them may not be flaws at all, while others can be neatly camouflaged.

Unless you're some sort of sex goddess, your list of assets will probably be the shortest of the three. But even if it's made up of only one notation, like "cute nose" or "shiny hair," post it somewhere. Then, when you're feeling low and are convinced you don't have a single thing going for you, take a look at it. It's great for the ego.

Finally, we come to your list of things that need correction. Copy this one out on another piece of paper. It's going to be your blueprint for the days ahead. One last experiment and you're through for the moment: Before you get back into your clothes, reach up and take hold of a pinch of skin from the upper arm midway between shoulder and elbow. Take as much as you can. Measure it. If it's more than ⅜ of an inch, you're carrying more body fat than you need, and you'd better write the words DIET and EXERCISE in capital letters on your blueprint. There is one point to keep in mind, however, about diet and exercise. Because you happen to be a naturally stocky or plump girl doesn't mean you're doomed to a life of chastity. Do your best to tighten up where you can and lose those pounds of purely excess flab and then start thinking positively about your stocky, chubby natural frame. Remember, every man has his thing. There are leg men and fanny men and breast men. There are also men who swallow hard and perspire at the sight of a girl with good-sized thighs and a broad back. *Do your best* but be happy with what you have.

It's been said that a girl's crowning glory is her hair. It can also be a major disaster area. We'd like to tell you about our friend and fellow stew Harriet as an example.

Harriet didn't go to a hairdresser. She went to an architect who thought he was working with reinforced concrete. She'd come back from a three-hour twice-weekly session with her hair teased, baked, curled and molded into the most elaborate rococo statuary known to man. There was so much glop in her hair that touching it was like fondling a varnished football helmet. After years of this treatment, Harriet's hair had the consistency of leftover spaghetti. She seemed all head, one of those balloon entries in the Rose Bowl Parade.

Why did Harriet do this to her hair? Why do most of us do anything? It was to please a man, in this case a man named Doug. She told us this one night as we worked a flight together from New York to San Francisco.

"Doug is a management consultant in Los Angeles," Harriet said after we'd cleaned up the dinner trays. "I'm very much in love with him and he loves me. And I just think a girl has an obligation to look her best at all times for the man she loves."

"All the time?" Trudy can be blunt.

"Yes, all the time." Harriet was annoyed. She didn't like her womanly philosophy challenged.

"Even when you're in bed with him?" I asked.

"Yes."

We let it go at that until later in the flight. Then, over coffee and a fast game of gin rummy, Trudy asked Harriet how she managed to keep her hairdo in place . . . in bed . . . with Doug . . . when making love. I expected Harriet to tell my buddy to mind her own business, but she didn't. She turned coy, winked at us and said, "I have my own little technique." With that she packed in her hand and took a nap.

Naturally, Trudy and I speculated together over Harriet's mysterious technique.

"Maybe she wears a hair net," I offered.

"Don't be silly, Rach. No man would make love to a woman in a hair net."

"I know," I said twenty minutes later, "Doug has this box. It's lined with velvet and has an indentation that just fits Harriet's head and hair arrangement. She puts her head in the box when they make it together. The box has air holes so Harriet can breathe when Doug closes the box and makes love to her. Her body can move but the head and hair stay perfectly still. When they're through he opens the lid and out pops Harriet, every hair in place." This concept evidently tickled Trudy. She left right after I'd finished my hypothesis to answer a call from the man in seat 22A. She leaned over and laughed out loud in the face of the man in 22B. He might have laughed, too, except he'd been asleep. He snarled.

"Maybe Doug and Harriet do it differently," Trudy told me later. "Maybe it's all oral, you know? Cool and calm with very little movement."

"I'm tired of speculating," I answered. "Let's pin her down and ask her. All she can do is get mad and scratch our faces and pull our hair." We nailed Harriet as she emerged from the lavatory, and pushed her into an empty galley.

"Okay, Harriet, how do you do it?" Blunt Trudy.

"Do what?"

"Make love with Doug and keep your hair perfect." She looked away, so I added, "Look, Harriet, it's not that we're prying or anything like that. It's just that we might need to know ourselves someday. You don't have to give us all the intimate details. All we want to know is how you keep that elaborate hairdo in place while making love."

Harriet tried to escape but we blocked the galley entrance.

"Oh, for Christ's sake," she said, sighing and pouring a Coke. "When we get in bed my hair is neat. Doug is very gentle, at least when he starts. Then, after all the playing around, I put out the light and we go at it."

"And what happens to your hair?"

"It gets all messed up."

"And . . . ?"

"And we keep the lights out and Doug goes to sleep."

"What do you do?"

"I go to sleep, too."

"But what about your hair?"

"That's where the technique comes in. I always have my traveling alarm clock with me and I set it for an hour before I know Doug has to get up. Doug is a heavy sleeper and never hears the alarm. I go in the john and fix my hair. I've got it down now to where it takes me about an hour to make everything look right again."

Trudy and I looked at each other. "And when he wakes up in the morning there you are, like the heroine in a Rock Hudson silly flick." I'm afraid I sounded sarcastic.

"Doesn't he think it's strange," Trudy asked, "to see you there in bed in the morning with every hair in place?"

"He's never mentioned it," Harriet replied.

"He doesn't know that you get up every morning and go through an hour of preparation?"

"Nope. And I never want him to know."

We naturally had more questions for Harriet. I asked if they planned to get married. Harriet said she hoped they would, although Doug hadn't mentioned it. Could she keep her secret for a lifetime of mornings? Harriet said she thought she could. Didn't they make love in the morning? Doug wanted to but Harriet always managed to escape lest her hair go astray. It was all mind-boggling to a pair of girls who liked their hair and love-life to be free, natural and spontaneous.

Harriet's story has a happy ending, but only by chance. We ran into her again almost a year later. She was radiant, happy and in possession of a huge diamond on her left hand. But most noticeable was her hair. It was straight, natural, shiny and tied with a simple bow.

"Congratulations," Trudy and I said in unison.

"Thanks."

"Hate to pry again, Harriet," Trudy said, scratching the ground with a pointed toe, "but what happened to your hair and the routine in bed?"

Harriet laughed. "Well, to be honest, I got caught in the rain. Doug and I weren't getting along too well after I got transferred to L.A. He seemed to be losing interest in me. Anyway, I was working that flight that came back to L.A. because of a bomb scare. Remember that one two months ago?" We did remember. It occurred during a torrential rainstorm. Someone called the airline and said the flight that just left for New York had a bomb aboard. They returned to L.A. immediately and evacuated all the passengers.

"The damned evacuation slides didn't work," Harriet continued, "so we brought them all down by portable ramps out in the boondocks. I got soaked standing out there helping them down. I looked like a drowned rat. My hair made an eagle's nest look good. Marge, one of the girls working the flight with me, gave me a stiff bristle brush and I brushed until my arms dropped off. Marge tied it back with a ribbon and I headed out to find a cab and an all-night beauty parlor. But who's standing in the lobby waiting for me? Doug. He heard the news on the radio and drove out. I could have died. But his eyes lighted up and he gave me a big hug and he even ran his fingers through my hair. He'd never done that before. We went home and made love. He said the sight of my hair flowing over the pillow was the sexiest thing he'd ever seen. We even made it in the morning. In fact, he took off the next day from work and we just stayed in bed. He proposed that afternoon."

Harriet's case may have been an extreme one, but it illustrates the point that nothing influences the way you look more than your hair. So make sure the style you choose is part of the new you and not some artificial creation you see on the pages of the tonier ladies' magazines. Plush beauty salons are okay for plush beauties with lots of spare time and cash. But is that really *you*? Wouldn't you be happier going to one of the more casual hairdressers where the atmosphere is young, where you don't have to call two weeks in advance for an appointment and where nobody's got a hand out looking for a tip? Places like these will cut, wash, blow-dry and brush your hair in jig time. They will not, however, offer you a set made of Jello, which is the big thing at one elegant establishment we know of.

While style is important, and you should experiment until you're satisfied, even more important is the *care* you take of your own hair. One expert has estimated that three million women in America today are bald, and another four million are close to it. Considering the dreadful things women do to their hair, it's surprising that the entire female population doesn't look like Yul Brunner. Here's a list of things you shouldn't do to your hair.

DON'T tease your hair, unless you find split ends attractive.

DON'T spray. Most hair sprays contain varnish or shellac which interferes with normal skin function. Some sprays also can cause itching, scaling and cysts.

DON'T color your hair. Many hair dyes are potentially poisonous and can enter the body through the hair shaft. And don't be misled by those products that claim to darken your hair "gradually." Many of them contain lead. If you must color, check your labels carefully before you buy and apply or, better yet, go to a professional hairdresser. Bleaching is also destructive to hair. A temporary rinse, on the other hand, never hurt anybody. It's fun, kicky, and entirely harmless.

DON'T get a permanent wave, unless you like your hair dry and brittle.

DON'T straighten your hair, unless you like it very dry and so brittle you can almost shatter it.

DON'T set your hair with hair-splitting brush rollers, sharp pins or clips.

DON'T go too long in extreme weather without a covering for your head. Wind, cold and especially sun are very destructive.

DON'T swim without taking some precautions afterwards. Salt water and chlorine are bad for your hair. If you can't stand a cap (and neither of us would dream of wearing one—it makes an otherwise sexy girl look like a Navy Frogman), shampoo after swimming.

DON'T wear plain rubber bands. There are elastic-wrapped rubber bands on the market designed especially for hair.

DON'T use a nylon bristle brush. Natural bristles are more expensive, but they're worth it.

Now, here's a pair of do's and don'ts that will really throw you for a loss. DO shampoo every other day. DON'T shampoo every other day. Why the confusion? Because the experts themselves are confused. In doing the research for this book, we must have consulted more than a dozen authorities on beauty and hair care. Every one of them offered different advice on how often to shampoo your hair. So, instead of relying on them, we'll tell you what we do—we use our common sense. We wash it when it's dirty. We shampoo a little less frequently in the summer because we've been out in the sun a lot. We shampoo when our hair feels oily and is hard to manage. If we had to come up with an exact frequency, we'd guess that we shampoo about once a week. Also, for healthier hair, we use an herbal, vegetable or castile shampoo, and we've found that rinsing it with a mixture made up of one tablespoon of vinegar to a quart of warm water works wonders.

The experts may be divided about the shampoo issue, but there are a number of remedies they all agree upon. Here are some of the more common hair problems and what to do about them.

YOUR HAIR

Dry Hair:

Don't shampoo as often, but condition your hair frequently. Stay away from hot hair dryers, and never,

never use detergents. Brush vigorously every day with a natural bristle brush. And now, are you ready for this? Recondition your hair by applying a handful of mayonnaise. Rub it in, allow it to remain one hour, then shampoo and rinse.

Oily Hair:

Easy on the brushing and massaging. There are special, oil-reducing shampoos on the market. Use them. Watch what you eat. Cut down on butter, cheese, fried foods, chocolates, nuts and iodized salt.

Thinning Hair:

No home remedies, please. See a dermatologist. He'll take a hormone count and tell you if you have an estrogen deficiency. Then he can proceed to correct it.

Dandruff:

Some dandruff is normal. But if your shoulders look as if you've just come in from the blizzard of '03, you'd better see a dermatologist. Don't monkey around with any of those widely advertised dandruff shampoos. If you use them a lot, you may lose your dandruff, and maybe your hair.

Split Ends:

If you're bedeviled by split ends and are dying to grow your hair halfway down your back, you've got a problem, lady. The two simply don't go together. To get rid of the split ends, trim them every four or six weeks, and experiment with a shorter hairdo.

In passing along advice on how to take care of your hair, we've limited ourselves to basic, everyday things you can do in your own home or apartment. Not that there isn't a world of exotic treatment out there for you to try, but most of us prefer to eat our Jello, not smear it into our scalps. Still, here's one we couldn't resist telling you about. It's from Linda Clark's book, *Secrets of Health and Beauty*. To stop falling hair, mix four ounces of red cayenne pepper with one pint of 100-proof vodka. Every day for two weeks, shake the mixture several times. After two weeks, strain it through a nylon stocking, making sure the remaining liquid is clear of the pepper. Rub this mixture into your scalp and within five or six weeks there should be new hair on your head. Of course, if you drink it, there might be new hair on your chest.

YOUR SKIN

"The skin he loves to touch" is an advertising phrase we've all heard, and one that has made a certain soap maker rich. The reason it's been so successful over the years is because women instinctively understand that a clear, flawless complexion is not only a powerful lure for men, it's a sure sign of health and vigor. Most women, when they think of skin care, think only of oils and creams to apply on face and body. Actually, it's a little more complicated than that. Skin works two ways. It absorbs things into the body and also acts as a good indicator of what's going on within the body. So, diet is an important part of proper skin care.

To complicate things even further, skin can be affected by outside elements as well. It needs sun, air and water, but only in balanced amounts. Too much of any one thing will damage it.

More junk has been written about skin care than hair care, if that's possible, and American women, confused by all the things they've been told, spend millions of dollars each year for beauty aids they don't really need. Here's all you need to know.

Be sensible about the weather. Wind and sun cause dry skin. If you can afford one, buy an air humidifier for your home. Go naked for some period each day. Your skin needs to breathe. Wash thoroughly so that your pores are clean and open. Be careful about the kind of oil you use. Commercial products are usually made from mineral oil, and do nothing for your skin at all. The cosmetic industry will probably send us a bomb through the mail, but just plain unsaturated vegetable oils, like sesame oil, peanut oil or olive oil, are better for your skin and much cheaper to boot. Take care in your diet and include adequate amounts of Vitamins A, B, C and E. They all affect the state of your skin.

YOUR FINGERNAILS

DO use an emery board instead of a metal file when you give yourself a manicure. File each nail from the edge toward the center. Buff your nails frequently. Use protein cream, cuticle massage cream, superseal, proteinized nail conditioner or nail hardeners with cross-linked microfibers for weak nails.

DON'T use solvents and detergents, too much nail polish remover, or too much soap and water. Don't cut your cuticle or saw back and forth when you file.

If you have weak nails, they can often be helped by eating iodine in the form of seafood or iodized salt. Other hardening aids include Knox gelatine, foods rich in calcium and high doses of Vitamin A.

YOUR TEETH

Go to the dentist. Go to the dentist. Go to the dentist. And do it every six months. He'll clean your teeth, remove the unsightly brown tartar that collects on the teeth of anyone who smokes and put the dazzle back in your smile. In between visits, brush lots, massage your gums, try an electric toothbrush and buy a water pic. Water pics are groovy, and the dentists we know swear by them. By the way, don't let anybody talk you into using fluoride pills. If you're old enough to be reading this, you don't need them. Fluoride only strengthens the teeth of growing children. It does nothing at all for adults.

If we may be allowed a brief diversion, which has as much to do with sex as it does with teeth, have you ever noticed how people are fussy about using their own toothbrushes? Even the legendary Betty Big Boobs, who gladly shared everything she had with practically any man who asked her, would never allow him to touch her toothbrush. We know because one day the strap of Betty's purse broke, spilling its contents all over the floor of a hotel lobby in Chicago. We helped her collect her things and noticed a small yellow plastic bag.

"Is this where you keep your diaphragm?" Trudy asked, whispering in Betty's ear.

Betty didn't bat a lash. "Mercy no, honey. That's where ah keep his toothbrush."

"Whose toothbrush?"

"Whoever he is, that's who. Ah always carry a spare toothbrush in case ah end up enjoyin' a fella's company over night, if ya'll know what ah mean. Ah think there's nothin' worse and more immoral in this whole wide world than havin' a fella use your toothbrush. It's disgustin'."

Oh well, it's good to know Betty draws the line someplace.

YOUR SMELL

Smell is supposed to be one of the senses that has little to do with sexual arousal. If that's true, then the perfume industry has been barking up the wrong tree for a long time. Many women we know can practically be identified by the perfume they wear. That's because of their body chemistry. The natural oils in their skin mingle with whatever perfume they're wearing in a very special way. The same scent, worn by two different women, can result in two quite distinct fragrances. That's why you should never buy perfume merely by sniffing it in a bottle. Dab a bit of it on your skin and then decide if it's for you. And shop around. Try several different brands until you find one that seems best suited to your personality. Then stick to it. It'll be as distinctive as your signature.

There are other odors, of course, that are less pleasing. But if television and the magazine ads haven't instructed you how to deal with them, our message about deodorants will never reach you. Roll-on, stick or spray—it's all a matter of personal preference. Don't be upset if one brand tends to give you a rash. Again, it's a matter of your peculiar body chemistry. Just change to another one.

What about vaginal sprays? Do they work and should you use them? The girls we know are pretty evenly divided over this world-shaking question, but we happen to think they're a bore and a nuisance. If you're in the habit of bathing once a week or so, then perhaps you should consider them. But then you should also use lots of deodorants and douse yourself liberally with perfume. Most of us manage a shower at least once a day, and if we wash thoroughly, they're not really necessary. However, some girls have special problems.

And the sensitivities of an exploring lover might be a consideration.

A vaginal spray might be desirable during a particularly heavy menstrual period. But even then, if you change your sanitary napkin or tampon frequently, there shouldn't be any real trouble.

YOUR VOICE

One of the most difficult features for people to evaluate objectively is the way they speak. It is literally true that we do not hear ourselves as others do. We all know those loud, harsh talkers whose very presence makes us wince. Surely, if they could hear the way they sounded, they'd make an effort to change. But they can't and as a result, whenever they enter a room people edge away.

On the other hand, nothing is more pleasing than a soft, well-modulated voice. Maybe you've got one naturally. To find out, listen to your voice played on a tape recorder. If you've never heard yourself before, you're in for a shock. Is that *really* me, you'll wonder? It's you, all right. Now, note your faults, and make a resolution to do something about them. It won't be easy because changing the habits of a lifetime never is, but if you work hard, you can manage to lower your voice, to slow your speech, to perform other kinds of therapy. If your problem is severe, maybe a drama coach can help or a speech therapist. Yes, there's an investment of time and money involved, but it's worth it. Many a man has been turned on by a sexy voice.

DRESSING YOU UP

Fashions, as we're sure you've noticed, have a way of changing. But have you noticed the really fundamental change that has occurred in fashion over the past few years? For centuries, the way people dressed was a public declaration of "who" they were. The chief wore more feathers than the brave, the general more gold braid than the private, the queen more velvet and lace than the peasant. Sure, styles changed wildly. What was "in" one year was "out" the next. But the essential function of dress, other than to clothe the body, was to identify a person's role in life. The business executive told the world who he was by his conservative grey suit. The blue-collar worker wore . . . well, a blue collar.

The secondary role of fashion was to separate the sexes. No matter what the fashion happened to be, you could always tell the boys from the girls. But now, for the first time in history, at least in the western world, even this distinction is becoming blurred. And it's no accident. It can't be explained by calling it just another of those crazy fads. It's very definitely a reflection of the New Morality. It all has to do with a rejection of role-playing. Today, nobody cares about "who" you are. What counts is "what" you are. Fashion has become a means for expressing the way you feel.

Go to a sophisticated party. You'll see some women wearing lace, some wearing denim. You'll see skirts that sweep the floor, skirts that are mid-calf length, skirts that barely cover the thigh. You'll see hot pants, pantsuits, jumpsuits. You'll see African dashikis, Moroccan caftans, Indian saris. You'll see, in short, an incredible variety of style and fabric.

What this means is that there is no longer a single, accepted fashion "look." All the rules have been thrown out the window. One day you might feel like dressing yourself in boots, pants, shirt, a vest and a slouch hat. The next day you might prefer a ruffled shirt with a floor-length skirt. Both of these outfits are okay. It all depends on the way you feel and what your plans for the day might be. If a knit suit, gloves, a hat, purse and a strand of "good" pearls is your bag, then by all means wear it. But if that's the only costume you really feel comfortable in, then neither the New Morality nor this book is something you're going to enjoy.

For some, this new freedom is unsettling. They're anxious and insecure with no one telling them what to wear. Our advice to those of you who feel that way is to relax. It's not that important. Oh sure, you'll want to spend *some* time working on your appearance, but don't make a career out of it. Remember, you're not *just* a sex object. You don't have to spend hours dressing, making up, shopping, washing, brushing, plucking, polishing, shampooing, rinsing, buffing, shaving and combing. You're not merchandise that has to be attractively packaged before it can be moved off the shelf. All you need do is invest enough time to give yourself the confidence and self-esteem to free your mind for more important things. Create your own style. Develop it. Feel good about it. Use your imagination! And if you still can't break the habit of thinking in terms of what's "in" and what's "out," remember that the only thing that's really "in" is your body. The uncorseted, free, natural body is what it's all about.

YOUR MAKEUP

The natural look is the "in" look for makeup as well. Gone forever, we hope, is the day of the pancake mask. Again, it's a question of the New Morality. Females aren't painted, living dolls. We're individuals, proud of our individuality, so let's not hide behind layers of goo. For today's with-it girl, the right amount of makeup is usually the barest minimum.

Here's our makeup routine. It's simple and takes us about five minutes. We cover the shadows under our eyes with a cover stick. On goes a pale foundation or base, one that looks as though it isn't even there. Next comes a creamy eyeshadow followed by a soft brown pencil as an eyeliner. We draw a thin, even line across the upper lid and from the middle to the outer edge on the lower lid. A pale, pressed powder that matches the foundation is gently brushed with a damp sponge to set it and to remove any excess. The final step is the application of a very pale lip gloss. We've both given up using mascara, and I never bother with false eyelashes, although Trudy has fun with them occasionally. Trudy also uses blushers because she thinks it adds to her appearance. Neither one of us has ever cared for eyebrow makeup.

How did we develop our routine? We experimented. We played around and tried different combinations until we found what we thought was right for us. It had to be quick, easy and natural looking. Pursue *your* makeup with the same goals.

TO WIG OR NOT TO WIG

Stewardesses travel light, and since we're away from home base a good bit of the time, we've learned to pack what we need in a single, small suitcase. This pretty well eliminates the problem of wigs. There just isn't room for them. Even if we did have room, wigs, in our opinion, present more problems than they're worth.

Problem number one is expense. The wigs we can afford usually look awful. The wigs we think we could wear start at $300 and go up, and somehow we think we can find more interesting things to do with $300.

Problem number two is health. Frequent wearing can cut down circulation to the scalp and can cause destruction to the real hair underneath. Hair must breathe. Wigs smother it.

Problem number three is this: You've had a wonderful evening. It's late, and you're in his apartment having a nightcap. The romantic moment arrives. He pulls you close. You can feel his excitement, and your own heart is beating. It's clear to both of you you're not going to be satisfied with a kiss. You say, "Excuse me, I have to take off my wig." You leave the room. When you return, he looks at you blankly. You're not the woman he was holding in his arms a few moments earlier. You've changed. The magic is gone.

Even worse, suppose you just decide to go ahead and make love in your wig. You're lying together. His passion is mounting, and so is yours. Suddenly with a quick and uncontrolled movement on his part he's got what he thinks is your scalp dangling from his fingers. That can be an unsettling (we won't call it hair-raising) experience. WARNING: *Do not make love while wearing a wig.* They don't fit *that* tightly.

FEEDING THE NEW YOU

There you are, shiny hair, gleaming teeth, smooth complexion and a wardrobe full of kicky outfits. Now don't go and spoil everything by eating the wrong foods. What are the wrong foods? Unfortunately, the wrong foods are usually the least expensive and most widely available. Also, they're the ones everyone seems to like best, things like coffee and doughnuts, Danish pastries, hamburgers with a Coke and a plateful of greasy french fries, topped by a candy bar. They're the TV munchies, the pretzels, potato chips, pizzas, the late night peanut butter and jelly sandwich. They're items that are shoved under your nose wherever you go.

But even if you manage to avoid every temptation,

you're still not in the clear. You may think you're eating a balanced, nutritious diet, but food growers and packagers have seen to it that we all get more than our share of chemicals in the form of dyes, bleaches, emulsifiers, flavorings, buffers, fungicides, pesticides, sweeteners, drying agents, thickeners, preservatives, anti-foaming and anti-caking agents, acidifiers and moisteners. If we are what we eat, as one food expert suggests, then we're all subsidiaries of the Dow Chemical Company.

Is there no way, short of becoming a health food nut, to avoid a steady intake of junk food? If you're not absolutely mad about kelp, dulse, rice polishings, blackstrap molasses and wheat germ oil, there still is a way of managing a healthy diet, and you probably learned it in tenth grade but didn't believe a word. Here it is again: lean meat, fish, cheese, milk, eggs, fresh vegetables and fruit, whole grain cereals and breads. What does a bad diet consist of? Probably what you had for lunch yesterday.

THE FLAB WAR

Try this one for size. A prominent diet expert has estimated that Americans carry around five billion pounds of excess fat. No, that's not a misprint. We said *five billion*. So, you're thinking to yourself, "I'm only five pounds overweight. What's five pounds against five billion? Big deal." Well, it *is* a big deal because the five pounds you're talking about can make a huge difference to your health and your whole outlook on life. If you don't believe us, try this as an experiment. Buy a five-pound bag of potatoes from your neighborhood grocery store and walk around holding it in your arms for a couple of hours. For the first twenty minutes or so it won't seem so heavy. Maybe a little cumbersome, but nothing you can't handle easily. But wait.

By the end of the second hour, we guarantee you'll be arm-weary. That five-pound bag of potatoes will seem like a ton. And you'll be tired. Yet that's exactly the strain you're putting on your body by asking it to support that extra five-pound flab steak wrapped around your middle.

If you do your homework carefully, you'll discover a thousand different diets, each one of them with a champion who'll tell you it's the *only* way to get rid of your excess. You'll be told about high-protein, low-protein, low-cholesterol, all-fluid and no-fluid diets. At parties, people will talk to you for hours about steak diets, rice diets, grapefruit diets, egg diets, ten-day diets, thirty-day diets, banana diets, vegetable diets, cheese diets. Before you have a chance to try any of them, you'll be asked to consider pills, tablets, diet candy and wafers.

Others will try to convince you that the best thing for you is exercise. Try isometrics, energetics, aerobics, yoga, massage, exercise machines, reducing suits, reducing belts and reducing pants. How about sauna baths, steam rooms, jogging, barbells, and health clubs? How about just staying fat?

Well, we don't blame you for being confused. But bear with us for a little longer, and perhaps we can straighten you out. After thinking it over carefully and reading eighteen-zillion words on the subject of weight control, we have come to several conclusions.

The first conclusion is this: To lose weight, you must either cut down on the food you eat or increase your expenditure of energy. In other words, eat less or exercise more.

The second conclusion is that there is no such thing as a "miracle diet." You can't expect to lose your belly in a few days. Be wary of any diet that promises you an "instant weight loss." Diets like this look like they're doing a great job. But the vanishing pounds may simply result from a loss of body fluids. These will quickly be replaced within a few days and you'll be back where you started.

The third conclusion is that so-called diet foods are a waste of time. Here we go again. A few pages ago, we got the cosmetic industry mad at us, and now we're taking on the diet-food industry. Well, those are the chances you take when you set out to be honest. The reason we don't think diet foods are worth the trouble is because we've seen so many cases where they don't work. If a person is crash-dieting, popping diet wafers and lettuce all day long, it may be good for five, ten or even fifteen pounds. But who do you know who lives on diet wafers, and how long do you think it'll take before those pounds creep back on?

So how *do* you lose weight? Oh no, you're groaning—not exercise. I don't care what anybody says. I don't *want* to join the Royal Canadian Air Force. Relax, and listen to Dr. Grant Gwinup, who says in his book, *Energetics,* that "it has been repeatedly emphasized that exercise is a relatively poor way to lose weight." Feel better now?

Dr. Gwinup points out that you'd have to walk a mile to use up the energy in a single piece of bread, so you can see it's not a very effective way of cutting off the old flab. *But,* supposing you walk that mile anyway, and *don't* eat that slice of bread. Then you'd burn up the calories in the slice of bread you didn't eat. What the good doctor is saying is simply this. Don't bother with any special diet. Eat what you're eating today. But if you walked, say twenty minutes, each day *without* increasing your food intake, you'd lose one pound of body fat every month and a half, which works out to a weight loss of about eight pounds a year, provided you kept up the good work for the entire twelve months.

For those who are really serious about weight control, Dr. Gwinup advises opening what we call a flab account. This is similar to a checking account in that you have to keep it properly balanced. On the debit side, you keep track of the number of calories you consume. Most bookstores, by the way, carry little paperbacks that tell you the number of calories in an average portion of the foods you're most likely to eat. On the credit side of your flab account, you list the calories burned up by the activity you undertake. If you're eating more calories than you regularly use, then you'll get fat. If the two balance, you'll stay as sweet as you are. In other words, there'll be no change. However, if you throw off more calories than you take in, you'll reduce. Guaranteed. There's nothing mysterious about it.

Now you'll want to know how many calories are burned up in the things you ordinarily do. Okay, here they are, as Dr. Gwinup has calculated them.

ACTIVITY	CALORIES (per hour)
Sitting (little movement)	50
Talking on telephone	50
Bathing	100
Dressing and undressing	50
Typing	50
Reading	25
Routine housework (leisurely)	100
Cooking	100
Watching TV	25
Walking (moderately fast)	300
Skiing	450
Jogging	600
Running	900
Wrestling	800

This whole method of weight reduction made so much sense to us we posted Dr. Gwinup's table of calorie expenditure on the bulletin board in our kitchenette. In fact, having it posted there was responsible for Anita, a stew friend, telling us of her great adventure in sensuous weight reduction.

Anita was a fat virgin. We're not calling Anita names. She *was* a fat, flabby girl who'd never been to bed with a man in her young life. This was all before she discovered the weight reduction possible through caloric sex.

We met Anita when she moved into our apartment building. She was a new stew with another airline which, because of its low standards in stewardess recruiting, shall remain nameless. Suffice it to say that Anita, even in her slimmed-down state, would never find employment with our line. Anita was what you might call a member of Fat Anonymous. She would sit in our place, eyes riveted on the potato chips and peanuts and pastries, and actually shake with yearning. Every time we offered her something, she'd adamantly refuse. It was the same with alcohol. Anita never touched a drink, although she obviously wanted to. We never gave it much thought until one evening when she stopped in. She seemed in a state of shock.

"You look dreadful," I said.

"I feel dreadful, Rachel. I just had a fight with Ralph and he told me he never wanted to see me again." Ralph was a gangling flight engineer Anita had been seeing. Trudy offered her a drink. She accepted, to our surprise.

"Maybe she's AA," I muttered to Trudy in the kitchenette. "I'd hate to have us cause her to go off the wagon." Trudy nodded, but gave Anita the drink anyway. Anita downed it and went into the kitchen to make another. More followed. Anita got drunk, babbling-bumbling drunk. We were about to cut her off when, from the kitchen, came a loud, piercing laugh. She came back into the living room with Dr. Gwinup's chart in her hand.

"What's so funny?" Trudy asked.

"This chart," she said with a thick tongue. "It's missing the best exercise of all."

Trudy laughed. "Oh, I know what you're talking about. Working a full 707 on a short trip with full meal service burns up 8,000 calories. Right?"

"I don't know. I was talking about *fucking.*"

Anita's statement sobered the room. Words are words, and we all use the choice four-letter beauties from time to time, but Anita's statement seemed so blunt and out of context. Trudy responded by saying, "Oh." I took a handful of peanuts, the dry roasted variety, and stuffed them in my mouth. I don't like peanuts, but I figured they'd keep me from laughing.

Anita sat down and cleaned all the potato chips out of a bowl in seconds.

"Thought you were on a diet," Trudy said.

"The hell with it," Anita slurred, attacking the cheese goodies next. "It was all for Ralph. That's the only reason I lost the weight. The hell with it."

We didn't press Anita for more details on her lost love and resulting dieting decision. We didn't have to. Anita began to talk as freely as she ate. And after she began her tale, Trudy flicked the switch on a Sony cassette tape recorder that had been given to us as a gift. We'd used tape recordings in our first book, *Coffee Tea or Me?,* the tapes made at parties and stewardess bull sessions when our fellow stews were letting their hair down and letting it all hang out. Naturally, we never used any of the recordings in the book unless given permission by the person on the tape. We later asked Anita if we could use the tape we made of her and she agreed, providing we didn't use her last name. That's only fair.

"When I met Ralph I was a big fat ugly girl. A lot of people think we met after I became a stewardess . . . *crunch* (potato chip) . . . what a laugh . . . he's from my home town. That's where I knew him from . . . *crunch* (popcorn). We used to date sometimes back home. Ralph was always kind of a jerk to the rest of the kids . . . you know? Big and tall and clumsy. So he dated me even though I was fat . . . *crunch* . . . *crunch*. When he went away to work for the airline I figured he'd find some pretty stew and that'd be the end of Ralph . . . but he didn't . . . he'd come home sometimes and call me up and we'd go out . . . and you know what? . . . we never made it together . . . I was a virgin and so was Ralph . . ."

(Trudy and I thought this was a good time to take a break from this live soap opera and refill the chip dishes. The task completed, Anita continued.)

". . . so, I kept getting fatter and Ralph kept getting . . . well, more frustrated."

"Didn't you get frustrated, too?" I asked.

"Sure . . . so I ate more. Pretty soon I was like a balloon . . . I know I'm no Twiggy now, but I got down slim enough to apply to Ralph's airline and get hired."

"But how did you slim down if you were frustrated and kept eating?" Trudy was leaning forward, all ears.

"Well, one night, after going to the movies Ralph told me he couldn't stand to be with me any longer and neck in the car without getting some relief. I asked him why he hadn't gone to bed with the stewardesses and he said he was too shy to try . . . but he knew me and wanted to take me to a motel. We went and made love . . ."

"How was it?"

"Not too good, I guess. Ralph didn't know what to do very well and I was . . . well, just so damned fat I was too embarrassed to be good at anything . . ."

(Anita started crying and made herself another drink.

Trudy took a phone call from her latest "favorite fella," and ended the conversation just as Anita had finished making her new drink.)

". . . and then . . . then . . . oh, I don't want to talk about it any more . . ."

"Talking is the best thing, Anita," Trudy said with motherly conviction. "Get it out."

"It's all so damn silly, I guess . . . we lay in bed after it was over and started talking. Ralph told me he loved me . . . I told him I was disgusted with myself for being so fat. I'd tried this diet and that diet but never stuck with them. I even started exercising but all that did was give me a bigger appetite. Finally, Ralph asked me to marry him. I just went all to pieces . . . I told him I'd never burden him with a fat pig for a wife. He kept telling me it didn't make any difference. Finally, I jumped out of bed, flipped on the overhead lights and stood in front of him, my big flabby belly jiggling and hanging down over my crotch and my fat legs bulging together and my fat arms drooping and my damned big fat tits hanging like a pair of melons. It was so disgusting to me I started laughing, got dressed and told him to take me home. I kept laughing until he dropped me at my house . . . then, I went inside and cried until the sun came up. . . ."

By this time Trudy and I were weary of the story and wished Anita would go home and continue it some other evening. But she'd gotten over any hurdles that might have been before her and was ready to roll on. We cut her off from further drinking for fear she'd fall down and we'd be stuck with her for the night. I asked her what happened next.

". . . what happened then? . . . I kept eating and got fatter. I didn't have a date for almost a year. I got so low I even thought of suicide a few times and then I got a hold of one of those calorie charts, like the one in your kitchen. I'd tried to diet so many times but never kept with it for more than a day or two. I remember reading the chart and realizing I didn't do any of the things that really burn up calories, like jogging or skiing. I got even more depressed when Cynthia, my only girlfriend, got talking to me about the chart. She used to be overweight, too. You know what she told me? She told me she never had any luck with a diet until she started working with the calorie chart. Only she added one item . . ."

"What item?"

"Making love . . . just plain simple fucking, like I said before. Cynthia told me that making love burns up about 500 calories. What she did was find a steady boyfriend, and every night instead of making a snack and going to bed alone, she made love and skipped the snack. She figures she saved 500 calories by not eating the snack and burned up 500 by making love. That's 1,000 calories every night. She really slimmed down. . . ."

Trudy and I were thinking the same thing. Had Anita used Cynthia's technique to lose weight? We didn't have to ask.

". . . I did it. I managed to interest a local guy in dating me and we made love every night in his room behind the gas station . . . It was summertime and we sure did sweat a lot. Pretty soon I was down to the weight I've been since joining the airline. That's when Ralph and I started going together again . . . it's all been so great, so beautiful. . . ."

"So what's the problem?"

"Ralph found out . . ."

"Found out what?"

". . . that I had this affair with the gas station guy. I told Ralph I only did it to lose weight. I told him I did it for him but he won't believe me. . . ."

She cried again, this time in uncontrollable sobs. We tried to comfort her but it was no use. We let her cry it out, turned off the tape recorder and tucked her in on the couch.

There's no sense in prolonging this story. Anita went on an eating binge. And, unlike us, we interfered in her romance with Ralph. We called him, had him over for dinner and laced into him, Trudy from behind the salad bowl and me over the standing ribs. We told him he was a bastard, an insensitive bore and an ungrateful pig.

"After all," Trudy said, "it could be worse. What if Anita was sleeping with guys for money. I can point out a few dozen of those."

"Not only that, Ralph, you're sending her back to her former fat self. You'll be responsible for whatever actions she takes. She might even take the dive or stick her head in the oven."

"One last thing, Ralph. Think of it in positive terms. How many men have a wife who needs it every night just to keep her waist trim?"

That seemed to do it. Ralph called Anita and asked her to dinner. They got married and, at last count, had three children. Anita has put on some weight but not much. It's so cute to see them together and comment on how Anita is staying slim. She always turns to Ralph and gives him an intimate smile. Ralph never fails to blush.

CHAPTER IV

"You can't go home again."
—THOMAS WOLFE

"How Much Will the Brooklyn Bridge Cost Me?"

Mary Lou was nineteen. She was graduated from high school a year earlier and was living at home with her mother, father and twelve-year-old brother. Mary Lou was bored. About half the girls she'd been close to in school were off at college. The ones who remained had settled down to jobs that kept them busy, or to husbands and new homes that kept them busier still. Most of the guys, the ones that were fun to be with, were either down at the State University or doing their military service. What was left wasn't very exciting.

But Mary Lou had a dream that kept her from total insanity during the endless hours she labored as an indifferent assistant bookkeeper in Becton's Wholesale Plumbing Supply Company. The dream was to shake the dust of the dull town she had always known and head for the adventure and excitement of a big city.

To Mary Lou, it didn't matter which city, just as long as it was big and far away. It would take money, of course. Mary Lou knew that, and saved every penny she could spare. She read her savings account passbook as if it were a love story, knowing each ten-dollar deposit brought her a step closer to her dream.

At first, it was a dream she shared with no one. But then, unable to keep it in, she confided in her mother. Instead of the encouragement she expected, she was criticized. Instead of finding a partner who delighted in her delicious conspiracy, she found someone who betrayed her. Mary Lou's father was told. He said he would not permit her to leave home. There was a frightful scene, and Mary Lou slammed the door of her room, trembling with anger and frustration.

During the long hours of the night, as she stared up at the ceiling, she made her plans. She would leave as soon as possible. Each day, when she left for work, she'd take along an article of clothing, sneaking it out of the house so that no one would notice. She planned to hide these behind some dead-storage files at Becton's. No one would think of looking there. Then, when she had collected her wardrobe and her personal things, she'd march down to Patmo's General Store, buy a cheap cardboard suitcase, pack her things and catch the afternoon bus to Oklahoma City. Once there, she knew she could make connections with a Greyhound to New York City where freedom awaited her. She had over $400 in her bank account, and she figured that would be enough to see her through the first month. After that, with a job and a place of her own, she'd be on easy street. Eleven days after the scene with her family, Mary Lou left home.

The Port of New York Authority Bus Terminal, the scene of New York's and Mary Lou's first meeting, is located in one of the dingier parts of town. It's an area of cheap hotels, pornographic movie houses and open prostitution on the streets. But Mary Lou had no way of knowing that. To her, this was New York, and she set about trying to find a niche for herself among the pimps, dope pushers and hookers that crawled along the dirty streets on either side of Eighth Avenue. Mary Lou didn't try to find a more respectable neighborhood where she would have been safer because she didn't know where such a place might be. Besides, she was tired after her long journey and bewildered by the size, noise and confusion of the city life that throbbed around her. She chose a small hotel near the bus terminal and took a room.

The wiry young man with sharp eyes behind the desk told her she could have one for $8 a day. She agreed. He put down the magazine he was reading and Mary Lou felt a shock that jolted her stomach. The cover showed two men and a woman openly engaged in a sex act that seemed so unnatural to her it almost made her ill. She stared at the picture in horrified fascination until she caught the clerk leering at her suggestively. He led her up some stairs and along a corridor covered with threadbare linoleum to a dingy room directly alongside the hotel's neon sign. The room's furniture consisted of a bed, a chest of drawers, a straight-backed chair and table and a sink in the corner. A cracked linoleum mat completed the amenities. After letting her in, the young man seemed reluctant to go away. Mary Lou wearily wondered what he wanted, and then realized he was probably expecting a tip. She fished a quarter out of her purse and handed it to him with a murmur of thanks. The clerk pocketed the coin, but still lingered. Finally, he made her a proposition. He'd steer her business and keep only 25 percent of the take. Most guys wanted half, but he liked her, and anyway, he was just starting out. Was it a deal? He'd guarantee her $25 a hustle for each John he sent up.

Mary Lou wanted to scream at him but was unable

to speak. Her face must have reflected the pain and loathing she felt, for now it was the clerk's turn to look uncertain. They stared at each other in total silence for a moment, and then he shrugged and backed out, closing the door after him. Mary Lou leaped forward and slammed the lock home. She was desperately afraid.

The next day did little to boost her morale. After an early breakfast at a nearby cafeteria, she went to a newsstand and bought a copy of *The New York Times* to look at the classified ads. But there was no place she could read her newspaper in comfort or privacy. She couldn't face going back to the hotel and there didn't seem to be any parks in New York, at least none that she could see. She had heard about Central Park, but didn't have the slightest notion where it might be. She leaned against the side of a building and began turning the pages.

Just as she had found the classified section, she felt a man standing next to her. She moved away from him, but he pressed even closer. She heard him mutter something about $20, and panic gripped her again. She folded her paper and walked away quickly. But where could she go? She was beginning to feel like a hunted animal. Then she thought of the cafeteria where she had had breakfast. She could have privacy there for a ten-cent cup of coffee. The counterman said there was a twenty-five cents minimum during the breakfast hour and suggested she have a Danish, too. She did as she was told, took her food to a table and opened her paper again.

The number and variety of jobs available absolutely staggered her. So did the wages they were paying. There was a secretary's job going for $145 a week, but Mary Lou knew she didn't have the qualifications for it. She didn't know how to take shorthand, and typing was never her strong suit. She searched for the listings under Assistant Bookkeeper, and to her delight, there seemed to be dozens of them. Maybe things were looking up after all. She settled down to decide which one she would take. Finally, after much deliberation, she determined she'd try for one at a brokerage house in the Wall Street area. There was only one hitch. She didn't have the faintest idea of how to get there.

A policeman, she realized, would certainly know, and there was no question in her mind that he'd be a safe person to ask. She emerged from the cafeteria and began searching. At last she spotted a blue uniform and approached it. As she had expected, the cop was helpful. He pointed out the subway, and told her which train to take.

Even so, she managed to get on the wrong subway line. She finally made it to Wall Street and the address of the brokerage firm. Once there, she was subjected to a cold, businesslike interview by a lady from personnel, who wanted to know about her education. When she was forced to admit that she had never taken any commercial courses in high school, and had never, in fact, been given any formal training as a bookkeeper, the lady terminated the interview. Mary Lou walked out in a daze. She had been counting on that job.

Back on the street, she pulled herself together, and told herself this wasn't the only job in New York. Now that she was in the Wall Street area, she might as well try a few more places. She hadn't thrown away her paper and there were several other possibilities to explore. But they all washed out. It began to dawn on Mary Lou that her experience at Becton's was never going to cut any ice here in New York. It began to look as though she had overestimated herself. But if she couldn't get a job in the only field she knew anything about, what could she do? Become an usher in a movie house? Get a job as a waitress? Slinging hash in some greasy spoon wasn't part of her dream. Her dream was a good job in a busy office where she'd meet interesting people. It was her own cozy apartment where she could entertain her new friends, or retire alone to spend a domestic evening washing her hair and reading a good book. Her dream included theaters, museums, art galleries, parties. But without a job, none of these would ever become a reality. They were as unreachable in New York as they were back home, a thousand miles away. Mary Lou felt defeated, lonely and bitter. She had gambled so much, and she had lost.

Do you think we made up the story about Mary Lou? Do you think she's the exception rather than the rule? Mary Lou is the first cousin of a friend of ours. We heard Mary Lou's story one night over dinner, and we shook our heads. It was an old, familiar one. Whatever happened to Mary Lou? She stuck it out exactly eighteen days. She was down to her last $20 when she finally threw in the sponge and called home for money. There was a good bit of stern moralizing from her family, but they finally came through, and Mary Lou returned to her father and mother and her twelve-year-old brother with her tail between her legs.

Actually, Mary Lou was one of the lucky ones. Each year tens of thousands of innocent young girls pour into the big cities of the country, anxious to try their luck, eager to test their wings. A surprising number of them simply disappear. Some are touched by horrors they never knew existed.

We're not telling you all this to discourage you from striking out on your own. We're all for independence. In fact, we're firmly convinced that there comes a time when a young girl *must* leave home. We know that it is traditional for boys to cut their apron strings before they're considered men. Well, we think that rule applies to girls, too. But it's not a thing to be done on the spur of the moment. It requires determination and, above all, careful preparation. Here's an eight-point battle plan we've devised for any young girl who's thinking about setting off for new horizons. It's not a list we threw together in a slapdash manner. We've talked to a lot of girls who told us, "How I wish I'd known about that before I left home." So read it carefully, and think about it.

1. **Decide where you're going:** Mary Lou made the mistake of just wanting to get away—anywhere. That's not a good reason for leaving home. You should be headed for a destination, not escaping from what you consider to be a trap. Consider a variety of places where you might want to live, the variety of life-styles that are available to you. If sand and surf are essential to your happiness, Kansas City is not the place for you. If you shrivel up in the cold, avoid Chicago. Perhaps the single most important factor that will determine your new home is what you want to do when you get there. If you're absolutely determined to get into publishing and nothing else will do, New York will be your first choice and Boston your second. If you're interested in a career in retail merchandising, then the field is wide open. There are department stores in every large city.

In any event, try to find out as much as you can about *your* city. Don't just lie there and daydream about life in San Francisco—find out about it.

2. **Get to know your dream:** If you can't visit the cities you're considering, buy the local newspaper. Get the paper's name and address in your library. Then write for a month's subscription. When you do, be sure to ask the subscription department to include their Help-Wanted and Apartments-for-Rent sections. Sometimes they are omitted in out-of-town editions.

When the newspaper arrives, read it cover to cover. Pay particular attention to the two sections we just mentioned. What kinds of jobs are available? How much do they pay? Check out the apartment. Can you afford to live there?

3. **Finding your way around:** Write to the Chamber of Commerce for a city map and any other information about the city. When it arrives, study it. Try to pinpoint some of the addresses listed in the Help-Wanted and Apartments-for-Rent sections. Knowing that Manhattan is laid out like a checkerboard with the avenues running north and south and the streets running east and west, or knowing that Washington is laid out like the spokes of a wheel, can help a lot on that lonely moment when you're standing on a Manhattan or Washington street corner, late for an appointment and lost.

4. **Local transportation:** We know many stewardesses who transfer to New York from Los Angeles and bring their cars along with them. You need a car in Los Angeles, but in New York it is a liability. One stew buddy finally sold her car after realizing she was paying as much for garage rent, insurance and upkeep as she was paying for her studio apartment in Manhattan. Check the area in which you're interested and determine how much transportation will cost you.

5. **Money:** Don't take off for a strange city figuring you'll land a job within a few days. It usually doesn't work that way. Don't leave home with less than $600 in your purse. And *please,* not in cash. Traveller's checks are honored everywhere. Even a restaurant will cash one. Why do you need so much? Well, you'd be wise to count on at least a month before you find a job. Otherwise, the pressures on you will mount and you may grab a dull job out of desperation. And during that month, you'll need money for rent, food and transportation.

6. **Get to know someone:** Write to everyone you know who lives in the city of your choice. If friends

at home tell you they have friends in the city, write to them, too, even though you've never met them. Mention your mutual friends. Tell them you are moving to their city, and give them a general idea when you'll arrive. Ask if you may call. The first few nights in a new city can be very lonely. Just having a few phone numbers often helps.

7. **Where to stay:** Decide in advance where you're going to spend your first few nights. Don't make Mary Lou's mistake and trust to luck. A hotel can be lonely and expensive. A women's residence is less lonely and very proper. A friend's apartment feels more like home, but how does your friend feel about it? Get it straight *before* you arrive how long you'll be staying. If you're there for more than a few days, insist on paying your share of the rent and groceries. Nobody likes a sponger. If you're a charity case, you'll be losing a friend just when you may need one the most. We have a mutual friend, a stewardess who flies for United Airlines, who assumes that every one of her friends can't wait for her to visit them. When this gal, whom we'll call Martha, came to New York after attending United's stewardess college, she camped in with two high school chums who lived together in the upper Eighties. Martha stayed there six weeks. We got to know her through a fellow named Tim. Tim dated one of Martha's high school friends and told us of the final confrontation between the girls and their six-week guest.

"Look, Martha," one of the girls said, "we hate to be nasty or anything but you've been here six weeks. Not only that, you've never even offered to pay for a slice of bread or a lemon or *anything.*"

Martha looked hurt, according to Tim. Her eyes filled up and she said, "I guess this is a good lesson to learn." She started sobbing. One of the girls put her arm around her shoulders and tried to comfort her.

"Look, Martha, we didn't mean to upset you. It's just that we decided you should be told how we feel. I know you're new to the city and haven't traveled much and probably just didn't think of it."

Martha looked up and said through clenched teeth, "Some friends. I'm crying because now I know you can't trust anyone, even your friends." With that she threw her clothing into suitcases and stormed from the apartment.

We asked Tim where she went.

"Went right out and camped in with a couple of stews she'd met in training. They threw her out after a couple of months and she bunked in with somebody else."

"Hasn't she ever gotten a permanent place of her own?" Trudy asked Tim.

"Not that I've heard of."

That was two years ago. Martha eventually did find a place to live, a small studio apartment in which two other girls live. But Martha still travels a lot and stays with friends in every city of the world. As we said, Martha assumes every one of them is waiting with baited breath for her arrival. We're sure that's true, but the breath is baited in apprehension, not joyful anticipation. One other note: Martha has been known to flatly refuse to allow anyone to stay in her studio apartment unless they help with the rent from the first day.

Don't you be like Martha.

8. **Are you equipped:** Do you have the necessary training to hold down a job? If you can't type, take shorthand, never worked in an office, had no experience in a work situation, then you're in for trouble. Put yourself in a prospective employer's shoes. Why on earth *should* he hire you? You can't do anything. So before you leave home, acquire some marketable skill. You may not get the most fascinating job in the world,

but nobody's binding you to it for life. Once you've got a paycheck coming in regularly, you've got the ambition to find ways of training yourself for a more interesting career. Right? If you don't, skip it. Stay where you are.

But let's assume they thought of you when they invented the words "ambition," "optimism" and "determination." And let's assume you're so thoroughly briefed on your destination that you can find your way around the city blindfolded. You've packed your bags and made the big move. You're on your own at last. What's the first move? An apartment or a job?

Unless you have unlimited funds, it'll have to be a job. That's because when you take an apartment, it's customary for the landlord to require one or two months' rent in advance. There may also be deposits to pay to the phone company and to the gas and electric company. Besides, how can you decide what kind of apartment you can afford until you know your income? So buy the next day's newspaper every night, and plan your campaign.

FINDING A JOB

Some girls are lucky enough to have known what they want to do for years and have trained accordingly. Knowing where to look isn't really a problem for them. But for every one of these fortunate creatures, there are tens of thousands of females whose only strong points are their energy and eagerness. How do they break in? Here's a suggestion they might consider. Try temporary office work. There are several things to be said for this kind of free lancing. It will give you an opportunity to acquire firsthand knowledge of various jobs and different companies. At the same time, it will finance your search for *the* job. Then, in your travels from one office to another, ask yourself these questions:

Does the job challenge, excite or intrigue?

Is it a dead-end job? Sometimes that's hard to know and sometimes you can make your own promotions. But if you find yourself in a typing pool with thirty other drones, you can expect to be there for a while.

Does the job give you access to the kind of people who interest you? And we don't just mean men.

Is your boss a talented, interesting person? Is he or she the sort who will honestly help you in your career?

Finally, this piece of advice. If you've picked a field that interests you, and have zeroed in on a company within that field that seems to suit you, don't wait for them to advertise an opening. Apply, and apply and apply again until you're practically on a first-name basis with the people in personnel. Many a great career has been started in this fashion. Don't allow yourself to get discouraged. Things may be desperate but remember, they're never hopeless.

YOUR APARTMENT

You've got the job you've been after, and it looks like it's going to work out. Wonderful. What did you say you were going to do now? You're going to rush out and find a permanent place to live? Oh no, you're not! Not until you make out a budget. A hard look at the available dollars and cents will determine a few crucial things like where you'll be able to live and if you can afford to live alone. Budgets are tricky things to draw up. We all tend to be a little too optimistic about the economies we think we can manage. So a good rule of thumb is to make what you think is a realistic estimate—and then up it by 10 percent. Here's a sample monthly budget for a single girl living in a large city.

ITEM	ALLOTMENT
FOOD (You may be taken to dinner often, but remember to include the times you'll invite people to have dinner or a snack with you.)	$ 50
LUNCH AND COFFEE BREAKS (You forgot all about these, didn't you?)	25
TRANSPORTATION	15
CLOTHES (Come on now, be realistic.)	100
ENTERTAINMENT	25
SAVINGS (Rainy-day department)	10
UTILITIES	6
TELEPHONE	7
LAUNDRY AND DRY CLEANING	15
COSMETICS	10
READING MATERIAL (There'll be *some* nights you'll want to be alone.)	10
MISCELLANEOUS	35
FURNITURE (Get it by degrees.)	20
TOTAL	$328

The one big item that's not on the budget is rent. But the whole point was to find out what you can afford. So, let's work backward. Suppose your weekly take-home pay—that's the amount on your check *after* all your deductions—comes to $107. Multiply that by four, and you get an income of $428 for the month. Since you're already spending $328, that means you can afford an apartment that costs no more than $100. That's the top. At this point, the question of whether or not to have a roommate answers itself. If you can't possibly afford an apartment in the neighborhood of your choice, you'll either have to find another neighborhood or a roommate.

What to Look For

In either case, there are a number of things to look for when you're apartment hunting. Don't fall into the "right address" trap. Remember, if the building has an elegant lobby with a crystal chandelier and music in the elevator, you can be sure it's the tenants who are paying for it, not the landlord.

One girl we knew couldn't resist a crack at an apartment with a particularly snappy address. Whenever she had an opportunity, she'd let it drop where she lived, and expected people to be impressed. They were. But then stories began circulating about her odd behavior. She'd never allow dates in her apartment. She'd insist on meeting them downstairs in the plush lobby and would say goodnight to them at the elevator door. The more we asked around, the more evident it because that nobody—male or female—had ever been inside her home.

Trudy and I have never been able to abide mysteries, so we decided to find out what was in that apartment. One evening, when we knew she was home, we paid her a visit. We sweet-talked our way past the doorman, who wasn't supposed to let anybody in without calling upstairs first but did when we told him we were old friends and wanted to surprise her. Actually, it turned out we were the ones who were surprised. She was simply embarrassed. Short of being unbelievably rude, she couldn't very well keep us out as we stood at her door. She reluctantly let us into a magnificent three-and-one-half-room apartment that contained a mattress, a Salvation Army table and chair and an old packing case she used as a dresser. There wasn't another stick of furniture in the place. She kept herself so broke paying the rent that she couldn't afford anything else.

So discard the elegant-lobby idea and keep looking.

Married folks are all right. In fact, you may hope

to become one of them yourself some day. But do you want to live in a building that's inhabited solely by young families? That cute looking guy in 3-G is absolutely no good to you if he has a wife to come home to. Check for baby carriages and tricycles parked outside doors and in storage rooms.

If you can possibly get away with it, demand to see a floor plan. Does your living room share a common wall with the bathroom next door? If so, you can expect to hear a not-so-distant waterfall every time your neighbor takes a shower or flushes the toilet.

Don't rent a furnished apartment unless you have no choice. The things around you won't be *yours*.

Avoid ground-floor apartments. They're short on privacy and safety.

Extras like terraces and fireplaces sound very appealing when you read about them in the newspaper, but they add to the expense of the apartment and often you can't use them anyway. Many fireplaces in New York are strictly for show. You can't even burn a letter in many of them without filling the room with smoke. And have you ever tried relaxing on your terrace just as the incinerator in the apartment house next door cuts loose? Five minutes of that kind of treatment and you and your friends all end up looking like Smokey the Bear after a forest fire. Our advice is to save your money and look for large, light rooms instead.

Measure the size of the rooms, particularly if you're planning to have a roommate. Is there enough space for two beds and two dressers? In the first apartment Trudy and I ever shared, the bedroom was so small we had to move a bed every time we wanted to open the closet. Oh, it was a great joke all right. The first hundred times.

Study the neighborhood. How safe will you feel coming home at night?

The Lease

You will probably be expected to sign a lease. One or two years is the average. In addition to paying one or two months' rent in advance, you'll be asked for at least a month's rent for security. Security is the landlord's protection against damages. If there are none, it should be refunded to you in full when you move. Should you move before your lease expires, you are technically responsible for the rental until the lease is up. What happens if you get a job in another city and want to try it out for six months without losing your apartment? After all, you might want to come back. The ideal solution is a clause in your lease that allows you to sublet. You can always ask, of course, and good luck to you. In some cities, landlords will write in such a clause with no pressure. But it's almost unheard of in New York, except in the case of luxury apartments. There is one thing you can expect, however, and that is a clause giving you the first right to renew the lease. It doesn't mean you *have* to, but it does mean the apartment can't be rented out from under you without giving you a chance at it first. Note that some leases renew automatically unless you notify your landlord *in writing* a specified number of weeks before it expires.

If all this sounds confusing, it is. And in cities where the apartment market is right, it's also unfair. That's because landlords use a standard, printed lease form, and that is probably the most prejudicial document ever drawn up. Under its terms, a tenant has virtually no rights whatsoever. Still, a landlord can make it even worse by adding some ruffles and flourishes of his own, so *read the lease before signing,* no matter how fine the print. And keep a copy. Then one night when you're fixing dinner for that young lawyer you just met, ask him to explain each clause to you. You'll have a good cry together.

Decorating with Imagination

No matter how you decide your living arrangements, you'll want to fix up your new home. Remember when we talked about fashions, we said the important thing in choosing your dress is to express the way you live and how you feel. It's an equally good rule to follow when you're dressing up your apartment. As a young, single girl working in a city on a shoestring budget, you're not expected to decorate your living quarters with Queen Anne sofas, wing chairs and side tables. Besides, that's not the kind of life you're living. For you, life should be kicky, fun and casual. And so should the things around you.

Decorate inexpensively, but with a flair. Canvas director's chairs? Sling-back chairs? Why not? That ancient sofa in the secondhand shop down the street might look just fine if you drape it with a vivid, rich fabric and throw a few pretty pillows over it. One imaginative stew friend has a sofa made of an old claw-footed bathtub. She had one side sawed out, painted it, made pillows for the bottom and back and now has the most marvellous $25 sofa we've ever seen. Yes, it *is* comfortable.

Another friend without much money and in need of chairs carted home two old automobile seats from the scrap yard. They were in excellent condition, but the man at the yard had no use for them. Then, to complete the ensemble, she put a table between them constructed from a pile of brightly painted tire rims with a wooden slab on top.

Plants add life and texture to a room. But not the single, spindly, little cactus you had on your windowsill when you were a little girl. A big, luxuriant display of green is far more interesting than a dozen tiny pots in a row.

Wall decorations can be objects whose shapes intrigue you. They can be something as simple as a piece of fabric, a Mexican tapestry, even swatches of wallpaper.

Lighting is important. Overhead bulbs, no matter how well shaded, tend to be cold and unflattering. Scatter inexpensive lamps all over the place.

One last tip: Ask your guy to help you shop and put together an apartment. It's fun, togetherness, and you'll learn lots about each other.

ROOMMATES

What about roommates? Having a roommate can be economical, practical and fun. It can also be pure hell. In fact, living with another female can be trickier than living with a man. So why not live with a man? Well, it's a thought. Having a male roommate is not what it used to be—absolutely out of the question. A girl who's spent four years in a co-ed dormitory is unlikely to be aghast at the idea of sharing an apartment with a man. Sharing his bed may be another matter, however. And don't think the question will never come up, no matter how clear the understanding is. If you share the same mailbox key with a man, sex will rear its lovely head, you can depend on it. So before you say you think it's a perfectly swell idea, make sure you know in your own mind how you feel about it.

If you can contemplate the idea without breaking up into a million tiny nerve ends, there are still a few things you'd better agree upon. Is your relationship going to be sort of a trial marriage, or are you both free to go out with other people? Even if you earnestly assure each other that neither of you will ever, ever prevent the other from having a good time, do you really believe that? We know you're terribly sophisticated and all that, but we also know that females tend to be possessive (so do males). So don't let yourself in for a hurt you can't handle.

On the whole, we feel that a girl shouldn't live with a man simply on the basis of convenience and economy. No matter how hard you try to convince yourself otherwise, he is or will eventually become your lover. And that's a different arrangement altogether. Of course, if that's what you're after, go ahead. But at least understand what it is you're doing.

And so, if you're not yet ready to live with a man, and if the apartment you've set your heart on costs about twice as much as you can afford, you're going to have to settle for a plain old, garden-variety female roommate. But before you two move in together, you'd better have several long sessions where you both let your hair down. You'll want to know absolutely everything about her habits, tastes and morals. And be prepared to be just as frank as you want her to be. If you've been known to bring men home to spend the night, tell her. If you're thinking of adopting a Russian wolfhound, warn her. If rock music's your style, and she won't listen to anything but madrigals and Bach, you're in for trouble. Does her ambition to play the trumpet in an all-girl band cause her to practice half the night? You'd probably want to know.

Think realistically of what living with a roommate is going to mean to you. Living comfortably with one means consultation and compromise. You may not be able to paint the living room in green and black squares as you've always wanted. But, on the other hand, she'll be deprived of the joy of keeping an alligator in the bathtub. Both of you will have to give up many of your eccentricities and, unless the place is bigger than most, you can both say goodbye to your privacy.

THE NITTY AND THE GRITTY

Here are a few things every young girl should know about living in a big city but was afraid to ask.

Open a checking account. That way you won't have to carry large sums of money and you'll have an accurate record of where it's all going. There's a difference between regular and special checking. Get the facts at your bank, and you decide which suits you best. It's not a good idea to bounce checks, so balance your checkbook every month.

Make sure you're well covered by insurance. Arrange for household insurance, auto insurance if you have a car and health insurance if your job doesn't provide it. Remember to add these costs to your budget.

Loans, credit cards and charge accounts are dynamite if handled irresponsibly. Before you indulge your whim, remind yourself that *the bill is going to arrive.* Okay, if you've simply *got* to have that zebra rug, go ahead, but don't say we didn't warn you. One absent-minded friend ran up a department-store bill of $1,500 which she absolutely could not pay. The letters from the credit department got sterner and sterner. Finally, the store threatened legal action. Out of desperation, she married the first guy who asked her. He paid all right. But so did she.

Find a doctor. Call the local medical society or any local hospital for the names of various specialists in your neighborhood. It's a good idea to have one before you need him, so, even if you're not sick, set up an appointment and reach an understanding that you're going to be his patient.

Find a lawyer. Any problems relating to your legal rights warrant a consultation with an attorney. And that doesn't mean that cute law student your roommate is going with. The Bar Association in every city has a list of lawyers available at a reasonable fee.

FEELING AT HOME

You look great, you feel great. The job's fun, and you wouldn't trade your studio apartment for the plushest penthouse on Park Avenue. Life is just a bowl of cherries. Or is it? Do you have all these things going for you, but you're still not entirely at ease in the city? Do you find that you're wearing a rut back and forth between your office and home? Do you envy the gay young sophisticates who seem at ease in any situation, who can handle just about anything that comes up? Well, at one time, they were probably just as shy as you are. But they learned. They learned by doing. And so should you.

Get up off your duff, and go into the terribly smart little art gallery down the street. Ask the man in the antique store why that porcelain snuff box with painted flowers is going for $2,000. Don't ask him belligerently, as if he were out of his head to be demanding such an outrageous price. Ask him because you want to know. You'd be surprised at how easily he'll talk to you, and how much interesting information he can give. You just might get a short course on eighteenth century French enamelware.

Your date takes you to a restaurant where the menu is hand-written in French, and you can't read a single word. "Do you care for cervelles?" he asks. How do you know? You have no idea what cervelles are. But then why should you? It's not a crime *not* to know something, but it is a crime not to ask. Saying, "Why, I adore cervelles," when you don't have the foggiest notion if they're animal, mineral or vegetable is just plain dumb. It's also not honest.

Headwaiters, especially those at the fancier restaurants in town, all go to a school where they're taught to look down their noses at people. It's a fact of life. Accept it. Don't be intimidated by them.

Do you panic when you find yourself in a situation where you're expected to tip? Here's a schedule we've drawn up for ourselves:

Taxi drivers and waiters get 15 percent of the bill, and never less than 20¢.

If you're checking into a hotel, give the doorman who unloads your luggage 50¢ to $1. The bellboy who takes you to your room deserves at least 25¢ for each bag. If you're traveling light and have only a single overnighter, splurge and give him 50¢.

Set fees per bag are the rule at many airports, bus or train stations. Ask the porter, then add 25¢ or 50¢ to that. If there is no set fee, a tip of 25¢ per bag is plenty.

In bars, the general rule is 25¢ a drink.

The doorman in front of your apartment building will expect a quarter if he hails a taxi for you. You'd better give the elevator man something if he accepts and holds a delivery for you, and *always* stay on the right side of your superintendent. The people who provide services for you in your apartment house expect to be remembered at Christmas. A holiday remembrance is also in order for the mailman and the newspaper delivery man.

At the beauty shop, 15 percent of your bill, divided one-third to the person who does the shampooing, and two-thirds to the stylist, is about right.

Some of our readers might consider these details boring and unnecessary. Perhaps they are, but we've known too many girls who have been thrown by them. They fret and worry so much about doing the right thing that there's no time to relax and enjoy life. Recognize them for what they are, details that you can learn to handle without a thought. That way, you can concentrate on the business of being alive and free in the Sensuous Seventies.

CHAPTER V

"Real intimacy takes place between real people and usually progresses more or less quickly to sex."
—ERIC BERNE

All About SEX

Judy is a high school history teacher who lives and works in Cambridge, near Boston. She summers at a camp on Cape Cod where she teaches kids how to sail. During the winter, she and eight other singles share a ski lodge in Vermont. Judy gets to use it every other weekend. Being naturally curious, Judy has explored practically every inch of her adopted city. She's wandered all over Boston and is as much at home down on the waterfront where the *S.S. Constitution* is docked as she is up on Bunker Hill. Lately, Judy has developed an interest in Chinese cooking. However, not content with merely following recipes in a book, she has made it her business to get to know most of the best cooks in Boston's Chinatown. The secrets they revealed so intrigued her that she is now working with a friend on a Chinese cookbook which she hopes to have published.

The cooks and restaurant owners know about her project and are amused by her enthusiasm. More than once, she has been personally invited into a kitchen to see how a particular dish is prepared.

Judy is not beautiful, but she is fresh, vibrant and full of energy. She has built an interesting life for herself, and doesn't feel she's merely marking time until marriage. She's living and loving every minute of her existence, and has developed a widening circle of friends that range from her fellow school teachers to H'sien Tang, who is probably the best noodle-maker in New England.

Several weeks ago at a friend's house, Judy was introduced to Bart, a graduate student at Harvard. Later, they spent an hour at a coffee house, and then he took her home. Before leaving, he invited her to a production of the Brattle Players the next evening in Cambridge. She accepted. As she was undressing for bed she thought about Bart and decided she liked him very much. Even after being with him such a short time, she knew there was going to be something special about their relationship. She was, she realized, about to enter a new phase of her life. Far from feeling alarmed, she was warmed by a wave of pleasurable expectancy.

After that first meeting, Bart saw Judy regularly over the next few weeks. It turned out he was quite interested in the theater, but not as a profession. He was studying for a degree in Clinical Psychology, and had no time to continue his career as a talented, amateur actor. Still, he kept up his contacts and enjoyed seeing old friends who were seriously trying to make a name for themselves in what Judy soon realized was one of the most fiercely competitive businesses in the world. Bart also introduced her to Boston's art galleries and to a host of struggling young painters and sculptors.

For her part, Judy initiated Bart into the mysteries of skiing, and they laughed together at his first awkward attempts to get down the beginners' slope without pitching headlong into the snow. She brought him around to sample H'sien Tang's noodles, which he pronounced to be the most delicious he had ever eaten. This, of course, earned him H'sien Tang's full approval, and Judy could see a questioning look in the old Chinaman's eyes when he smiled at her.

The time spent with Bart was effortless. Neither one of them made any attempt to force developments. They were content to be happy in each other's company. Not that there was no physical contact between them. They had kissed many times, and passionately. She had quickened to the feel of his hand on her breast. Her nipples had responded to the gentle caress of his fingers, and she had felt her knees tremble. But Bart never pressed. They both knew unconsciously that they would recognize the moment to make love, and they both wanted it to come quietly and naturally.

Lingering over dinner one evening in an Italian restaurant they both enjoyed, Judy knew the moment had come. They had planned to take in a movie that night, but Judy suggested they return to her place. Bart put down his cup of espresso, and sought her eyes. They were direct and frank. Wordlessly, he signalled for the check, left some money on the table, and they rose.

Hand in hand, they made their way leisurely to Judy's apartment. She turned the key in the lock, and the next minute they were standing in Judy's living room, looking at each other. Bart held his arms open, and Judy came to him. For a moment, they simply stood there, faces pressed together. Then Bart led Judy to the sofa, and drew her to him.

They began by kissing, gentle and deep, which they had often done before. Judy kissed Bart about the ears and on his neck. He stroked her hair, and kissed her eyes. Bart's hand dropped from her shoulder, caressed her neck, and settled on her breast. Through her blouse, he felt her nipple become hard and erect. Judy's eyes were closed. "Oh yes, Bart. Yes," she murmured.

Tentatively at first, Bart maneuvered the top button of her blouse out of its buttonhole. When he saw she made no objection, he quickly unhooked the next two. Then he slipped his hand under her blouse and felt her naked breast. Judy couldn't help an involuntary shudder as he touched her. The excitement was almost more than she could bear.

The hand on her breast was firmer now. He alternately squeezed and fondled. Bart dropped his head and began to explore her breast with his tongue. Finally the tip of his tongue found her nipple, and he sucked hungrily. The sight of her breasts, the smell of her skin, the taste of her nipples gave him intense pleasure.

As for Judy, the feeling of his face and mouth against her skin aroused her to a degree she never thought possible. She felt his hands circling her waist, drawing her blouse up over the band of her skirt. Gently, she pushed him away.

"Here," she whispered, smiling at him reassuringly. "Let me."

Gravely, he watched her finish unbuttoning her blouse. Quickly, she undid her cufflinks.

"Don't you ever wear a bra?" Bart's voice was low. His breath was coming in shallow gulps.

A smile played at the corners of her mouth. "Aren't you glad I didn't tonight?" She found to her surprise that she, too, had difficulty controlling her voice.

At last her blouse was free. "Hmm," Bart nodded. He parted her blouse slowly and touched her two breasts with a tantalizing softness. He ran his fingers lightly across her nipples, and just as she was sure she couldn't stand another moment of his all-too-careful handling of her body, he gripped her firmly, brought his arms around her back and pressed her to him. The texture of his sport shirt against her body stimulated her, and she found herself moving rhythmically. His lips sought hers and, as she tasted his tongue, she drew it deeper into her mouth. What had been a comfortable warmth in her groin now became an almost unbearable heat. More than anything, she wanted his hand between her thighs. She wanted to feel his strength inside her vagina.

For the second time, she struggled free of him. They sat on the couch, she half-naked and he fully clothed, staring at each other in an unbelieving way. Then she held out her hand for his.

"Come on," she urged. "Let's go into the bedroom."

They stood together, still staring at each other. She looked at his tall, muscular body and thought to herself that in a moment she'd see it in its full nakedness. Then she noticed the erection that his trousers couldn't hide. It seemed so natural for her that she moved without thinking. She came close to him, put an arm around his neck and kissed him. Her other hand slid down his trousers and gently stroked the hard bulge below his belly. She felt him contract his muscles suddenly.

"My God," he whispered hoarsely. "Let's go."

She led the way into her tiny bedroom and switched on a soft bedside lamp. This, too, was an automatic action on her part. But later she had to admit to herself that she had done it because she didn't like groping in the dark. If they were going to make love, then Judy felt every one of their five senses should be brought into play.

Standing quietly by the bed, Judy watched as Bart kicked away his shoes and stripped off his shirt.

"Don't you ever wear an undershirt?" she asked him.

He grinned and stepped near her. "Aren't you glad I didn't tonight?" They both laughed, and then Judy felt his hands at her shoulders, pushing off her blouse.

She stood quite still and let it fall to the floor. Then with a quick movement, she unzipped and unsnapped her skirt, and she stood before him, wearing only the briefest pair of flowered bikini panties. In a moment, Bart was entirely naked. His penis was enormous. For a second, she wondered how it would ever fit inside her, but then she forgot everything to give herself up to the pleasures of the moment.

They sank together on Judy's bed, exploring each other's body with their hands and lips. She ran her fingers along his chest and back, down his sides. She searched his mouth with her tongue, and against her belly, she could feel his penis, huge and rigid.

His hand traveled down her back, and he massaged her buttocks with a rotary motion. She felt him tug at her bikini, and she lifted her body so he could slip it off easily. She felt his hand and its passage down her thighs, past her knees. With one foot, she kicked her panties free and lay there as Bart propped his head on his hand and gazed at her body. They examined each other, his hand gently stroking her face, she kissing his fingers.

Then, as if upon some prearranged signal, they fell into each other's arms. His hands were on her buttocks, moved up her sides and finally slid down to her belly. Judy opened her thighs, inviting the touch of his hand, and at last she felt his fingers enter her vagina, soft and moist. The ball of his middle finger gently caressed her clitoris, the focal point of her entire sexuality. Judy groaned with unabashed delight. As he continued to stroke her, she reached for his penis and closed her fingers along the shaft, rubbing it gently.

Deeper his fingers probed the walls of her vagina, each motion providing inexpressible pleasure. Cupping her hand, she moved beyond the base of his penis, and gently fondled his testicles.

It was Bart's turn to moan. "No," he said with a quiver in his voice. "Don't, I..."

Judy was aghast. "Did I hurt you?" she inquired.

"No, it's not that," Bart said. "I can't stand it... Oh, yes, I can."

She found his penis again, and began a rhythmic stroking that matched the way he was exciting her clitoris. Now they were both locked into the same rhythm. They could feel their passion mount. The time for release was near. Neither one of them could hold back the flood much longer. With a firm pressure, Bart pushed Judy's shoulder to the bed. He scrambled to his knees and knelt over her. She spread her legs and prepared to accept him. He leaned down gently and, as he covered her face with kisses, she could feel him slowly enter her. Her entire body seemed filled with his presence. Gradually, at first, he began to move his penis in and out of her vaginal opening. She responded to his thrusting with her own movements. Then, to ensure her approach to orgasm, he shifted slightly to his side, lay quietly inside her while he played with her clitoris. Judy's movements increased in tempo. Soon her pelvis rocked steadily, and then Bart was on top of her again, ramming his penis home with a force that was an unendurable joy.

Bart could feel the walls of her vagina contract spasmodically, gripping his penis down its entire length. He sensed Judy's uncontrolled movements heralded her climax, and he was right. Suddenly, she gave a small cry, and her body rose and fell with a remarkable intensity. Then she stiffened and began trembling.

"Oh Bart, oh Bart, oh Bart," she murmured over and over again.

He quickened the pace of his own movements, and underneath him, Judy responded. She felt his fingers grip her back, his arms tighten around her body, and then it was his turn to move in quick, pumping motions.

She heard him give a long, shuddering sigh, and she felt him relax. Totally spent, he remained deep inside her, their bodies still pressed together. After a moment he withdrew. They lay side by side, allowing a drowsy warmth to spread through their arms and legs.

At last, Bart held out his arms, and Judy nestled her head on his shoulder. They talked sleepily for several more moments, kissing each other, trying to put into words an experience that no one has ever succeeded in describing adequately. Finally, without even bothering to turn off the lamp, they slept.

In their first intercourse, Bart's and Judy's approach was simplicity and honesty. They were neither worried nor were they disappointed when their orgasms were not simultaneous. They neither expected too much, nor too little. Above all, both of them were absolutely ready to share sex. They had grown to it together, as naturally as a pair of flowers seeking the sun. How does a girl know she's ready for sex with a particular man? Jane, a surprisingly grave yet lovely English girl, who is a stewardess with BOAC, told us this.

"I always ask myself six questions," Jane said, one night when she was entertaining us in her London flat. "I ask myself, 'Are my feelings and actions completely honest? Will it leave me feeling good about myself? Will it do the same for him? Do I trust him fully?' The answers to those questions must be yes without any reservation. Then I ask myself, 'Will our having sex do harm to anyone?' And finally, 'Does it involve risks I can't handle?' The answers to those two questions must be no." Jane looked at us with a clear, no-nonsense expression on her face. "Think about them for a minute. They offer a pretty good guide for a girl who's uncertain, don't you think?"

We certainly did agree that they made a good guide, and we still think so. If there's a speck of doubt concerning a single one of these questions, then stay away from the guy. You're not ready to have sex with him yet.

When is a girl ready to have sex for the first time? Or the forty-first time, for that matter? We wish we could supply you with a nice, sure-fire formula, but we can't. And neither can anybody else. But we *can* tell you when not to have it. (1) When you don't come up with the right answers to that little quiz our English friend thought up. (2) When you think you're going to get something—and that goes for anything from a wedding ring to a weekend to Acapulco. (There's a name for girls like that and it isn't nice.) Or (3) When you simply want sex, and the guy happens to be available and willing. Sex under those conditions may be physically satisfying, but afterwards, you're both likely to feel cheap and unfulfilled.

The reason for this is quite simple. People tend to forget that you don't *get* sex from anybody, and you don't *give* sex to anybody. Sex is sharing. Sex is the ultimate togetherness. It is not, as so many manuals would have you believe, simply a mechanical act. Good sex does not depend on what you do to him and what he does to you. It can't be diagramed like a football play.

On the other hand, a fear of the unknown, an uncertainty about what to expect, has kept many a girl from the deep pleasure of the most profound intimacy life can offer. It is for this reason that we're going to sit down with you now and tell you in the frankest way what is involved, emotionally and physically, when you go to bed with a man. We're not going to give you a clinical analysis of the physiology and psychology of the sexual act. We're not sex researchers, and long white laboratory coats never suited us. We're girls and what we want to share with you is girl talk—the kind we've had hundreds of times with friends and our fellow stewardesses in apartments and hotel rooms in dozens of cities around the world. If you think there's something a little strange about your all-absorbing curiosity about sex, you can relax. In Paris or Rome, in Buenos Aires or Tokyo, wherever we've traveled, we've discovered there's a universal interest in the subject. So please fasten your seat belts. We're about to take off.

WHAT ARE THE ELEMENTS OF SUCCESSFUL SEX?

1. **Skilled and tender foreplay.** In a sense, everything that Judy and Bart did together in the first few weeks they knew each other was foreplay. Early foreplay may involve nothing more than a mutual exchange of looks. Two people may sit across the room from one another, fully clothed, and find themselves highly aroused. Unexpected things turn people on. It can be the shape of a wrist, a line around the mouth. Sitting together at the restaurant that night, Judy and Bart were both ready to make love. He had an erection, and Judy was fully lubricated. They could have torn off their clothes the instant they walked into her apartment, and reached a climax in two or three minutes. But, despite their excitement, they instinctively knew that even greater pleasure would be theirs if they engaged in still more intimate foreplay before coupling.

The purpose of foreplay is to grow exquisitely aware of bodily sensations, to concentrate intensely on your feelings and the feelings of your partner. Judy and Bart used their mouths and tongues extensively during their foreplay. They used them for nibbling, nipping, licking and sucking those parts of each other that are known as the erogenous zones. Which parts of your body are your erogenous zones? For both sexes they are the lips, ears, breasts, particularly the nipples, the inner surfaces of the thighs and legs, buttocks and entire genital area. Caressing or kissing these parts will usually serve to heighten sexual excitement. But these contacts must be gentle and delicate.

2. **The use of all the senses.** Sexual excitement is triggered by all five senses. Judy wanted the light on because she wanted to see Bart and because she knew the sight of her body would give him pleasure. The taste and smell of Judy's skin acted as a powerful stimulant for Bart. Even hearing has a part to play. We once heard a "dirty" record, even though there wasn't a word spoken throughout its entire length. It consisted of the sound of clothes being removed, the rustle of a sheet, the sighs of pleasure, the rhythmic creak of a bed spring, the sobs of passion. There were four of us in the room, and we listened with rapt attention. When it was over, we all agreed that it was one of the most provocative experiences we had ever undergone. Sexually, it was far more arousing than a stag film. So don't discount hearing as an important element. The sounds of sex contribute to enjoyment, too.

3. **Attention to your partner's wishes and responses.** Nothing is more of a turn-off than a caress which for some reason irritates or causes discomfort. Nothing is more disappointing than a caress that's almost right, but not quite. The freedom to exchange cues is an important element of foreplay. When Judy said, "Yes, yes," to Bart, she made it plain he was touching her in a way that brought her pleasure. Similarly, she was sensitive to the way he reacted when she fondled his testicles. So don't be shy about telling your man what feels good to you, and encourage him to express his own feelings. After all, it doesn't make much sense to be coy with him now. You're in bed with him, aren't you? Not that verbal communication is the only kind. When your guy touches you in a way that sends a throb of pleasure

coursing through your body, your physical reaction will stimulate him. And it works in reverse, too. A woman derives much pleasure herself from arousing a man, and, unless she's incredibly insensitive, she won't need his assurance that she's doing the right thing.

4. **Awareness of the changes in your own and your partner's body as sexual activity proceeds.** After Judy's blouse was unbuttoned, Bart touched her breasts and nipples very gently. This was very exciting to Judy—up to a point. Then she wanted him to hold her firmly, and Bart responded because he was aware of her new need. The human body goes through some very definite changes during the sexual act (more of this later), and what might be a powerful stimulant at one point could be simply irritating at another. Be aware of the variations in your partner's body and react to them.

5. **Knowledge of a wide variety of pleasure-giving activities.** You may think you don't know any, but our sexuality is so deeply rooted that you can safely let instinct take over. You'll be surprised at how much you know. Besides, wide experience in sexual techniques is really not important. You're interested in giving your guy what is pleasurable to him, and you want him to reciprocate. You already know how to accomplish this—by communicating with him.

6. **Free expression of feelings and desires.** A girl we knew—we'll call her Jeannie—had been having sex with a man for months, but she never seemed satisfied. She always seemed excited about the prospect of spending a night with Jack, but from little things she'd say, small hints she'd drop, we didn't think she really enjoyed it. Although the situation had her depressed, we didn't feel it was our business to poke our noses into her affair—until one night when she sat moodily in our living room and confessed her relationship wasn't as good as she wanted it to be.

"If it's no good," Trudy advised, "break it up. Don't keep on going with him just out of habit. Believe me, it won't get any better."

I was about to agree with Trudy, but Jeannie broke in. "But it's not his fault," she cried. "It's me. I'm the one who's to blame." We sat waiting for her to explain, but whatever it was she wanted to say was difficult for her. Finally she looked at us both earnestly. "I've never told anybody this, and I wouldn't now . . . except I just *have* to have somebody to talk to."

It seemed that Jack and Jeannie got along beautifully in every way. They enjoyed doing the same things, and they shared the same sense of humor. They were completely turned on by each other all the time—except in bed.

"And that just doesn't make any sense, does it?" Jeannie asked us plaintively. We had to agree.

"The trouble," Jeannie explained, "is that we make love the same way each time. I don't know how many times we've gone to bed together, but I know this. There isn't a thing we're doing to each other now that we didn't do the very first time."

"The point is," Trudy interjected, "whether or not it's any good."

"Oh sure," Jeannie replied without much enthusiasm. "It's great. We each have our orgasms. I've even had multiple orgasms. But when it's over, I lie there and think to myself is this *all?*"

I couldn't suppress a smile. "I really don't see your problem, Jeannie. What more do you want?"

"I know, I know," Jeannie said, and there was despair in her voice. "He's gentle and kind, and he makes love to me beautifully. But there's so much more I want to do." Jeannie dropped her eyes and began fidgeting with her handkerchief. "But I . . . I just can't."

"Do you want to tell us?" Trudy asked. "I mean, don't think you have to, but maybe we can help."

Jeannie continued to stare into her lap. She was obviously struggling with herself. When she finally spoke, her voice was practically a whisper. "I want," she began, "I want to go down on him. I want him to go down on me." She looked up guiltily, as if she had said something frightful and was expecting to be punished for it. When she saw we didn't look as horrified as she thought we were going to be, she found the courage to continue. "But you see, I'm ashamed to suggest it to him. I'm even ashamed of wanting to do it. Why can't I be satisfied with natural sex?"

"What's unnatural about it?" Trudy wanted to know.

Jeannie looked surprised. "Well, isn't it? How would you define an unnatural sex act?"

Trudy looked at her coolly. "I'd say that an unnatural sex act is one that could cause mental or physical harm. And I can't see," she went on, "where using your mouth on a man is going to do him either kind of damage. Quite the contrary," she concluded. "It'll give him enormous pleasure."

"But how can I be sure?" Jeannie asked.

Trudy made a face. "Ask him," she said.

It turned out later that Jack had been just as dissatisfied with their lovemaking as Jeannie. But he, too, had strong inhibitions, and felt she wasn't ready to try any variations to their intercourse. As a result, Jeannie's suggestion opened an entirely new dimension to their relationship. They were, Jeannie told us later, like a couple of kids who had just discovered a brand-new, fun game.

When Jeannie asked us about a month later if we had ever tried making love in the shower while standing up, we knew they had found a way of freely expressing their deepest feelings and desires to each other.

7. **A strong erection on the part of the male.** Obviously, without an erection, normal intercourse will

never take place. But don't think the responsibility for a full erection lies only with the man. If his penis is so limp he can't enter you properly, perhaps you haven't aroused him sufficiently. On the other hand, it may have nothing at all to do with you. Maybe he's under a strain. Maybe he's had a few more drinks than he should. Alcohol can be a sexual depressant. Above all, don't berate him for his lack of performance. He feels badly enough as it is. However, if the condition persists, try to persuade him to see a doctor.

8. **Adequate lubrication of clitoris and vagina.** The moisture a woman secretes through her vaginal opening when aroused is a reaction designed by nature to facilitate the entrance of the penis. Without proper lubrication, penetration can be uncomfortable or even downright painful for a woman. The causes for this condition are roughly similar to the reasons a man fails to have a complete erection—exhaustion, preoccupation, excessive alcohol. If it happens frequently enough to have you worried, see a doctor.

9. **Muscle relaxation and deep, full breathing during foreplay.** "Relax, you'll enjoy it more," seems to be a good motto governing foreplay. The climax is where you're heading, of course, but the current advertising campaign for the Cunard Line says it all: "Getting there is half the fun."

10. **Gradual concentration on genital area.** During the first stages of their lovemaking, Judy and Bart explored many different parts of each other's body. It seemed to Judy that no matter where Bart touched her, he gave her delicious pleasure. But later, she wanted his hand between her thighs. She ached to feel the sensation of his fingers in her vagina. Instinctively, she knew he, too, wanted his genitals fondled, and so she stroked his penis. This gradual focus on the sexual

organ is a natural progression, and one that signals the most intense period of foreplay.

11. **Control and use of sexual muscles by both male and female.** It probably never occurred to you that you have muscles whose primary purpose is to afford you and your partner greater pleasure during the sexual act. Some of these muscles are involuntary, that is to say you have no control over them. But others can be consciously brought into play. The muscles you use to shut off your urinary stream are an example. Deliberately contracting and relaxing them around his penis after he has entered you will increase his excitement and this, in turn, will fuel your own passion.

12. **Awareness of your partner's progress toward climax.** When does foreplay give way to the sex act itself? At what signal do both partners recognize they are approaching climax? With most couples, there is an unspoken understanding that the time has come. Each is acutely aware of the other's needs and reacts accordingly. They have both learned how to interpret each other's movements and understand the importance of communication and sharing.

13. **A full, satisfying orgasm for both.** Enough said. Sex without a climax is an unfulfilling, frustrating experience. How do you know if you've ever had one? Here's what we finally told Sally. We advised her to forget all the exotic descriptions of orgasm. We told her that if she felt at peace and fulfilled after making love, it would mean that she had had an orgasm. We still think that's a pretty good definition. Sally, of course, refused to believe us and is, to this day, continuing her search for definite proof that she has had that elusive, ultimate experience. We hope you'll be more sensible.

14. Attention and mutual affection following orgasm. To have your partner grunt over to his side of the bed after making love, and then fall instantly asleep without a word or a touch can leave a girl feeling lonely and cheated. Bart and Judy both knew this, so they continued their intimacy in ways that were warm and reassuring.

15. Complete relaxation and a sense of well-being. Nothing so shatters the mood of deep contentment that follows good lovemaking than the necessity to make an abrupt departure. There should be time for both partners to savor the experience they have just shared. Ideally, a couple should choose a safe and comfortable place to engage in intercourse, somewhere removed from any chance of being disturbed. That's why making love in the back seat of his car is *not* a good idea.

At this point, you're probably dying to ask dozens of questions. Let's see if we can't anticipate a few of them. What happens to that list, you're wondering, if Judy had been a virgin? It wouldn't have gone so smoothly then. Well, it happens she *was* a virgin. Her relationship with Bart had included occasions of petting to climax. During that time, he had, by placing first one finger, then two, inside her vagina stretched her hymen so that on first intercourse, she felt no pain at all. Many girls take on this responsibility themselves. Quite a few of them don't have this problem because their hymens break naturally as they engage in normal, physical activity. Occasionally, it's true, a hymen is so thick and resistant that it requires minor surgery. If careful stretching does not make it possible for two fingers to be placed inside the vagina without pain, a girl should consult her gynecologist. If this is your problem, a word of advice: DON'T allow a boy to break through, either with his fingers or by penile thrust.

Since we're discussing sex, we should probably get into some definitions. Just about every book on the subject of sex does, and we hate to be an exception. We will, however, try to avoid the textbook approach.

The *vagina* is that passageway into which the male places his penis during intercourse. Obviously, there is an outside opening, and the passageway leads to your uterus.

The *uterus* is also known as the *womb*. After the male penis has entered the vagina and penetrated deeply, it ejaculates, or discharges *sperm,* a white, creamy liquid. The sperm may fertilize one or more of the female's eggs. If this occurs, the fertilized egg or eggs implant themselves on the wall of the uterus where the baby develops.

The vagina is protected by layers of skin known as the *vulva*. These layers of skin are on the outside of the vagina. There are two layers. The outer fold of skin is known as the *labia majora*. If you place your fingers gently on your vagina, you'll feel this outer layer. The inner layer is known as the *labia minora*. Don't worry about terms. It's all skin.

The *clitoris* is very important to sexual pleasure. It is a tiny bump located in the center, upper part of the vulva. This bump has no biological function, but sex researchers claim it is the center of a female's sexual pleasure. Orgasm often can be attained by massaging the clitoris. Most women masturbate this way, and deft lovers will massage the clitoris to bring a woman to the point of orgasm, or to actual orgasm.

The male sex organ is the *penis,* a hose-like organ that projects from his pelvic area. When a male is sexually aroused, his penis receives a flow of blood and swells to two or three times its normal size. It becomes hard and rigid, thus enabling it to enter the vagina.

Men have what is known as *testicles,* or testes, which are two small, oval glands that manufacture sperm.

They are located in a sack of skin known as the *scrotum,* which hangs from a man's body to the rear of the base of the penis.

Excitement is the early and middle part of foreplay. During this time, this is what will be happening to your body:

Your nipples will become erect and increase in size.

Your breasts will swell and become larger.

The outside lips leading to your vaginal opening will thin outward and flatten. You have absolutely no control over this natural opening.

The inner lips also expand, clearing the way for subsequent penetration. You can see now that foreplay, in addition to providing pleasure, performs a real function in preparing your body for intercourse.

A "sweating" phenomenon develops on the walls of your vagina. These drops form a smooth coat which allows the penis to slide more easily into your vaginal passage.

Your clitoris may become enlarged. (It doesn't happen to all women.)

While you are experiencing these changes, here's what is going on in a man's body:

His penis becomes erect. This is caused by a widening of the arteries within the penis. The blood supply enters and fills tiny reservoirs. Small valves in this organ shut automatically, preventing the blood from escaping and forcing the penis to remain in its erect state. This is such a reflex action that it can happen when a man is asleep, under anesthesia or even when he's paralyzed.

His scrotum constricts, and his testes become elevated.

The second stage of sexual intercourse is the *plateau* stage. You are now at the height of your sexual arousal, which can only find release through orgasm.

Your nipples are still erect and your breasts remain enlarged.

A pink mottling known as "sex flush" may appear on your breasts and belly, and may spread over your entire body. This condition is generally more evident in blondes and redheads.

Your muscles will grow tense, and you may experience muscle spasms.

Your heart beat and breathing rate will increase. Your blood pressure will rise.

Your outside lips will stretch as far as they can go.

Your inner lips will go through a dramatic color change, from pink to bright red to a deep wine shade. A woman's inner lips, or labia minora, are often called the "sex skin." Its color will be determined by the extent of your arousal. No woman approaches orgasm without this color change.

Your clitoris will draw away from your vagina.

Your vagina will dilate and will undergo a distinct color alteration. The outer third of your vagina swells, becomes distended, and forms what is known as an "orgasmic platform." You are ready to proceed to climax.

During this time, the man is experiencing similar muscle tension and spasms. His heart rate, breathing rate and blood pressure are also rising. He may or may not develop a "sex flush" of his own. This varies widely.

All of the body changes of the plateau stage are now at their peak. Then, at the moment of your *orgasm,* you will feel a sensation of suspension followed immediately by a thrust of intense, sensual awareness centering in your clitoris but radiating upward into the pelvis. The feeling can range from mild to shock level. There is numbing loss of sensation in other parts of your body.

The exact feeling has never been described precisely. Some women report a sense of bearing down or expelling. Others say they experience a sense of openness.

But one reaction is universal. You'll undergo involuntary contractions called "pelvic throbbing" localized in the "orgasmic platform." These are fairly vigorous and are spaced a fraction of a second apart.

During male orgasm, his pelvic muscles will contract to literally hurl his penis deep inside your vagina. An involuntary arching of his back will drive his entire body forward. At the time of release, some men momentarily lose consciousness. About a quarter of an ounce of seminal fluid is pumped through his penis in approximately six separate jets or spasms. These are under such pressure that the fluid, if allowed to come out freely, would form a spray a foot or two in length.

We mentioned earlier how important it was for good sex to share a warm, relaxed intimacy after intercourse. It not only results in a fine feeling of well-being, but, like foreplay, it performs a necessary function. As you can see, both of your bodies have undergone incredible changes as you made love. The organs involved need time to return to their normal shape. During this *resolution* stage, your heart and respiration rate and your blood pressure slowly subside. Your tightened muscles relax. Your sex organs gradually return to their usual size and color, while his penis will shrink almost at once. After about ten or fifteen minutes, your body will show no physical trace of the tremendous forces it had released a few moments earlier. Unless, of course, you've gotten pregnant, but we'll get into that in Chapter X.

We've gone into such detail about what happens to you when you make love because we've found most girls simply aren't aware of what goes on. Our old friend Betty Big Boobs, for instance, was amazed to discover how complicated it was.

"Ah declare," she said after she had read the foregoing section. "Ah nevuh knew that. Now ah know why ah tingle so." Betty never was scientifically inclined, but she did make a point that was worth considering.

"Now ah admit that's sure interestin'," she said. "But

what ah wanted to know when ah was sixteen was what he was goin' to do to me, an' what ah was s'posed to do to him."

For those of you who share Betty's concern, here then is what you can expect a normal man to do to your body when he makes love to you.

He will probably want to kiss you on the mouth. He will probably want to enter your mouth with his tongue, and he will try to suck your tongue into his own mouth. He will certainly want to cup your breasts in his hand, and he may want to stand behind you, caressing both of your breasts simultaneously as he kisses your neck and shoulder. He may want to undress you, or he may prefer watching you undress in front of him. In any event, he wants to see your body. All of it. He wants no modesty. And he'll want to touch your body. All of it.

He will want to kiss, lick and draw your breast into his mouth. A great many men are highly aroused by breasts. They want to see and feel them in a variety of different positions. Not content with just feeling your breasts with his hands or kissing them, he may want to rub various parts of his body against them—his arms, his chest, his belly and even his penis. He may enjoy putting his penis between your breasts and stroking it with them.

He'll want to hold you close to his body, feeling every part of you against every part of him. He will caress and kiss your legs and thighs. He will explore your genital area with his hands, and introduce his fingers into your vagina, feel your labia and stroke your clitoris. He may want to stimulate your vaginal area by rubbing it against various parts of his body. He may wish to kiss your genitals and slide his tongue in and out of your vaginal passage, sucking at your clitoris. This genital kissing is known as cunnilingus. Finally, he will want to slide his penis into your vagina, whereupon he will stroke and thrust until orgasm is reached.

During this time, what are you likely to do to him and what will bring him the most pleasure? He will certainly expect you to respond. You will be a disappointing sexual partner if you merely lie back passively.

Generally speaking, he will want you to kiss and caress him as he does you. The one exception might be his breasts and nipples. Some men are not turned on by female attention there. Ask him. He will definitely want you to fondle his penis, and probably his testicles. You may, like our friend Jeannie, want to go down on him, to kiss his penis, to take it in your mouth. This is known as fellatio. It is one of those forms of foreplay which gives most men great pleasure. They report that having a woman kiss, lick or suck, combining lips, tongue and hands in a general stimulation of the genital area is perhaps the surest way to full arousal.

You many want to perform simultaneous mouth-genital stimulation, known in slang as "69." Many people feel this provides maximum sensory stimulation prior to intercourse.

Finally, you will want to accept his penis into your vagina and, by using the several sets of muscles surrounding the vaginal area, squeeze, stroke and caress the penis while it is in your vagina. This movement, coordinated with pelvic thrusting on your part and on the part of your partner, will provide a combination of exquisite sensations which should culminate in orgasm for both of you. Usually, his orgasm will occur before yours. If orgasm has eluded you, and his penis is no longer firm, then you will want him to stroke your clitoris gently and rhythmically until you reach climax. If he is uncertain or unsure, guide his hand with yours, and put his finger on the proper place. Tell him what feels good to you. Advise him on ways to hasten your orgasm. Don't, for heaven's sake, let false modesty keep you from experiencing full enjoyment. He'll do what you say because he'll want to please you. If he doesn't and ignores your needs, you've made a terrible mistake.

Although we don't think we can be much clearer on the subject of what to expect when the two of you go to bed together, there is one area that still may puzzle you. We've told you that the climax of the sexual act begins when he inserts his penis into your vagina. But you're not sure exactly how this is done. How do you arrange your body so he can enter you most easily? How does he maneuver his? The answer is that there is no one, single way. Recently, a sex researcher using a computer calculated that 3,780 positions are possible. That boggles the mind a bit, so would it be too much of a disappointment if we detailed only fourteen?

1. **Male superior.** This is the most common position in our culture. The female lies on her back with her thighs spread, her knees drawn up on either side of the male or her legs wrapped around his middle. The male lies on top of the female. Although, as we said, this is the most widely used variation, some experts feel that this position is the most difficult for men to control their ejaculation, as well as the most difficult for women to come to orgasm.

2. **Male superior, Variation I.** The female lies on her back with the male above, but she brings her legs together between his. In this position, the penis is not fully into the vagina, but is in greater contact with the overall female genital area. Some girls like it that way.

3. **Male superior, Variation II.** The female lies on her back with legs raised and resting on her partner's shoulders. In this one, the penis is deeply in the vagina,

but the female has little range of movement. If you don't feel like moving much, this one's for you.

4. **Female superior.** The male lies on his back. The female straddles him, resting on her knees. The female has full range of movement, and the position is said to be the best to curb premature ejaculation. Despite these virtues, many men object to it. They can't stand the idea of a woman being on top.

5. **Female superior, Variation I.** Same as above, only the woman's position is reversed. The male is on his back. The female straddles him, her back toward him. Good if you have an especially pretty back.

6. **Lateral coital.** The male lies on his back, one leg bent at the knee. The female lies atop him and slightly to the side, her opposite leg bent at the knee.

7. **Side, face-to-face.** The female is on her side, knees drawn up, her thighs separated. The male is facing her, resting between her thighs. You're really eyeball-to-eyeball during this variation, and that can have its drawbacks. One friend reported she had done it that way with disastrous results. Her partner's face looked so comical as he went through contortions of passion, that she burst out laughing in the middle. That's considered bad form.

8. **Side, face-to-face, Variation I.** However, if you're the serious type, you can try it this way, too. The female is on her side, knees drawn up, alternating legs with the male. His leg is on the bottom. There should be four legs stacked up in a row. Count them. If there are more, you've gotten mixed up with group sex.

9. **Side, reverse.** The female lies on her side, knees drawn up, her thighs spread apart. The male enters her from the rear, This one's great if he's had garlic for supper and you haven't.

10. Seated. The female is on the edge of a chair or bed, with the male leaning over her. If you use a chair, make sure it's a sturdy one.

11. Seated, Variation I. The male is seated, with the female straddling his thighs with her own. The big bonus here is extremely good clitoral contact. Girls we know recommend it highly.

12. Rear. The female is on her hands and knees. The male enters from the rear. Called the "dog" position, it often appeals to men, less to women. In case you're wondering, no, he does *not* enter the anus. If the woman spreads her legs a little, the man can easily penetrate the vagina.

13. Rear, Variation I. Same as above, but with the woman doubled over, knees to chest. Since there's more tension involved, the male sometimes experiences difficulty entering.

14. Rear, Variation II. Perhaps this should be a variation on the basic seated position. The seated man takes his partner on his lap with her back to him. The man separates his thighs slightly, the woman opens hers as wide as possible. There's a fine opportunity here for manual stimulation of the clitoris, but it's rough on the muscles.

These fourteen positions are about all you're ever likely to encounter unless you happen to be like our friend Rosalie, who had a passion for sexual athletics. If Rosalie had known about the researcher with his computer and the 3,780 positions, she would have been green with envy. Even Rosalie had never tried it so many ways. It was Rosalie's ambition never to have sex twice in the same way. This dogged determination to increase her repertoire may have provided her with kicks, but on one occasion, at least, it led to grief.

"Listen to this," Rosalie breathed excitedly to us one day, as she read from an illustrated sex encyclopedia. " 'The man and woman take their positions, seated at opposite corners of the bed. . . .' "

"And when the bell rings, they come out fighting," Trudy interrupted.

Rosalie shot Trudy a disgusted look and continued. " 'They slide toward each other on their backs. As they make contact, the woman turns a quarter of a circle, and both partners spread their legs. They maintain this position until the man has entered the woman and they are firmly locked together. For maximum effect, the woman should have one leg against the man's chest, and the other against his back, holding him in a kind of scissor grip. The man should do likewise to the woman.' "

"I told you," Trudy said triumphantly. "It's a contest after all."

But Rosalie was not to be stopped. " 'Then, slowly, the man raises his legs and performs a headstand, with the woman still in place. After a few moments, they change positions as the woman gracefully performs a headstand.' "

"Gracefully!" Trudy snorted. "That's a laugh."

" 'At no time,' " Rosalie concluded, " 'should the couple lose sexual contact. If this is done properly, the variation can be unforgettable and mutually rewarding.' " She put down the book and stared into space. "Wow," she sighed, "wait till I tell Martin about this."

We don't know how mutually rewarding the experience was, but we do know it was unforgettable. We bumped into Rosalie a few days later and had a chance to sign our names on the cast she was wearing. It seems that in the middle of their acrobatics they slipped off the bed. They hit the floor with a thump and Rosalie ended up with a fractured wrist. We offered our condolences but asked if maybe she hadn't learned a lesson.

"I sure have," she said firmly. "Never try that variation on a bed. Spread a mattress and do it on the floor."

Rosalie was incorrigible.

CHAPTER VI

"Some sex researchers know as much about sex as Al Lottman knows about performing one-liner comedy."
—LONG JOHN NEBEL, WNBC

"If You Do It More Than Once a Week, Your Hair Falls Out."

There is no subject that carries with it such a crushing load of misinformation, fear and guilt as the matter of sex. Some of the things we've heard repeated to us as truths have been so incredible that they defied the imagination.

We overheard one small eight-year-old solemnly explain to his companion where babies come from. "They come," he said, "when you kiss a lady real hard and rub her titties." His friend took in this information and nodded with equal solemnity. His question was now answered and, as far as he was concerned, the matter was settled.

It may be all right for an eight-year-old to accept this kind of intelligence without inquiring further into the question, but you don't have that excuse. So, let's bury a few of the most commonly believed myths that cloud the whole subject of sex. We present them in no particular order. We've put them down as they occurred to us.

Men are ready to make love any time, but women can only be aroused on specific days of the month.
Both men and women are capable of sexual arousal at any time. However, it is true that women are more likely to want sexual activity during the days just before menstruation. This is probably due to the increased pooling of blood in the tissues and pelvis area.

The bigger a man's penis, the more likely he is to satisfy a woman.
More men believe this one than women. Women know that size has nothing to do with gratification. In making love, as in all the fine arts, it's quality, not quantity, that counts. Penis sizes vary widely. The unofficial world record reported by one manual is fourteen inches long and three inches in diameter during full erection. The normal range, however, extends from four to eight inches. That's more than enough to do the job very nicely, thank you. We wish we could convince men of this, but they seem obsessed by the size of their sexual organs, relating them somehow to their virility. This is a beautiful example of a sexual myth that will not die.

Certain sexual "supermen" can make love all night, every night.
That's another myth that's kept alive by men. Why they should want to spread this word is beyond us, for it leads women to expect too much. After orgasm, the

normal male, under normal circumstances, can't have another erection for at least twenty minutes. Actually, an hour is more like it. While it's not unusual for a man to want to make love twice in one night, if he tries for a third time, he's just a big show-off.

Having intercourse more than twice a week is unhealthy.

We don't know who thought that one up. Some killjoy, we suppose. Both men and women can have sex as frequently as they wish without running the risk of any physical injury.

An uncircumsized male makes a better lover because he takes longer to come to climax.

Male babies are born with a fold of skin covering the tip of their penises. It is common practice, most generally for sanitary reasons, to surgically remove this skin when the baby is a few days old. This operation is called circumcision. Some men never undergo it. They are supposed to be better lovers because their foreskin is supposed to protect the extremely sensitive tip of the penis, providing greater control over ejaculation. The fact is that during the thrusting action of intercourse, the skin, known as foreskin, is pulled back, exposing the penis tip in the same manner as the circumcized male. There is no difference whatsoever.

Too frequent ejaculation leads to loss of physical strength and possible emotional instability.

An old wives' tale. On second thought, maybe a tired old wives' tale. Your 175-pound he-man is not going to melt down to a 97-pound weakling just because you make love frequently. Neither will he suddenly break into mysterious crying jags. Too frequent sex has nothing to do with a man's physical or mental well-being.

Ejaculation is detrimental to the physical condition of men in athletic training.

An old coach's tale. Completely untrue, as was convincingly demonstrated to us by the story of Mollie and Frank. Mollie and Frank were childhood sweethearts. He went on to State University, and she followed him two years later. By the time she got to the campus, Frank had become something of a legend. He was the only sophomore on the varsity football team and, as a wide receiver, had set new records for the number of passes caught and total yardage gained. By the time he graduated, he was on everybody's All-American list and an early draft choice by a professional football team, which shall be nameless. Despite all the attention, Frank remained basically a nice guy, still as devoted to Mollie as ever, even though, as she told us, he had to fight off the advances of countless admiring females. When Frank joined the ranks of the pros, he and Mollie had a decision to make. With the nice bonus he was given, they could afford to get married immediately. But Mollie still had two more years of school to go. They decided to wait until she finished college. However, by the middle of July, both of them knew they couldn't stand being apart from each other any longer, and agreed that marriage was the only answer.

But this presented a problem. Frank was in training camp, grunting and sweating through two-a-day practice sessions, and couldn't get away. If there was one thing the coach was fanatical about, it was women. They corrupted his boys, sapped their strength and took their minds off the serious business of football. Women were taboo. Still, Mollie went down to the camp, checked into a nearby motel and waited for Frank to contact her. This he did the evening of the day she arrived, and they arranged to meet at a local tavern for a few beers. He couldn't have dinner with her, he explained, because he was expected to eat at the training table along with everybody else. But the hours between eight and ten were his to do with as he liked. At ten, he had to return to camp because there was always a bed check at ten thirty, and if you weren't in the sack, you were slapped with a fine. Mollie thought training camp sounded like a boarding school for retarded boys, but kept her opinion to herself, and agreed to meet him.

They were seated in a corner booth at the tavern, holding hands and totally absorbed by each other when Mollie felt a presence standing near their table. She looked and there stood an enormous man, dressed in a sport shirt, glowering down at them. Frank followed her gaze, and then dropped her hand guiltily. She later said he acted exactly like a schoolboy who had been caught cheating on an algebra test. He got to his feet hastily, nearly spilling his drink.

"Oh, hi, Coach," he began nervously. "I'd like you to meet. . . ."

He got no further. The coach never once glanced at Mollie. Instead, he concentrated all his venom on Frank. "A woman," he hissed furiously. "You're out with a woman." Mollie said he made the word sound dirty and shameful.

Frank flushed. "But, Coach," he explained, tumbling his words out in a rush, "she's my fiancée. We're going to get married."

The look of disgust on the coach's face took on awesome proportions. "Married?" he said in a voice thick with loathing. "You want to play football, or do you want to get married?"

"Both," said Frank. "What's the matter with doing both?"

"Not in my club, you don't," came the answer. "Not during the season. I know too many guys who start playing house when they should be reading their play books. Then they show up on the field the next day, and not only do they get their plays mixed up, they can be knocked over by a feather." The coach's face softened as he decided to take the fatherly approach. "Listen, son," he said, gripping Frank on the shoulder. "Broads are bad news in this business. They'll suck the strength right out of you. I've seen it happen too many times."

Mollie, who had a temper, flared. "Who are you calling a broad, you big dummy?" she demanded.

Ponderously, the coach turned and looked at her for the first time. He stared at her in silence for a moment. "You," he finally announced flatly. "I want you to stay away from my guy, here."

"He's my guy," Mollie said heatedly. "He's not yours."

"His body belongs to me while he's on my team. And I'm going to make it my business to see to it that you can't touch it."

So Mollie found herself with a rival, someone who was more possessive and jealous than any female could ever have been. Keeping Mollie and Frank apart became an obsession with the coach. At first, he tried working Frank to the bone, hoping he'd be so tired at night he wouldn't have the energy to go out. When that didn't work he'd follow them, or arrange to have them followed by a pair of hired gumshoes.

After a while, it got to be quite a game, trying to find a few moments of privacy together. Mollie and Frank worked every trick they could think of. Once Frank tried the age-old stunt of stuffing pillows under a blanket to give the impression he'd gone to bed. It took the coach nearly an hour to catch on to that one before he took off in hot pursuit. Another time, Mollie, aware that she was being shadowed, went into the ladies' room of a restaurant, and climbed out the window. That gave her a fifteen-minute headstart, and they never did find them that night.

Finally, after more than a month of this cat-and-mouse routine, training camp was broken. The exhibition season was over and the regular season was about to begin. Frank had survived all the cuts and was a full-fledged member of the squad. At this point, team discipline was more relaxed. Wives were free to join the players and resume normal housekeeping.

But the coach couldn't bring himself to trust his rookies. During practice for the opening game, they were sheltered in a hotel and subject to bed checks every night. However, it was understood that even this surveillance would stop on Saturday, the day before the first game. Evidently, the coach thought that no rookie in his right mind would endanger his professional debut by doing something foolish like getting married right before his big moment.

But he underestimated Frank. Somehow, Mollie and Frank had managed to get their blood tests and marriage license, and were planning to have the ceremony performed Saturday afternoon. Their only problem was where to go for their wedding night. Neither one of them knew the city, and they were afraid that if they tried to check into a hotel, the coach's private eyes would find them out. That was how we came into the picture. Mollie and Frank had both known Trudy in high school. We got a call on Thursday from Mollie, who filled us in on what was happening.

"I've got the perfect solution," I heard Trudy say. "Rachel and I have a night flight to Mexico City on Saturday, and we won't be back till Tuesday. We'll be leaving the apartment about seven. Why don't you two come here at six, we'll open a bottle of champagne to celebrate—of course, we won't be able to drink any of it, but you understand—and then the place is yours."

I guess Mollie spent about fifteen minutes thanking Trudy before she hung up. When Trudy gave me the details, I agreed she had done the right thing, and we set about making a cozy nest for the two lovebirds.

"You know," I told her on Saturday afternoon, as we were making up the bed with fresh linen. "I feel like one of those bawdy madams from an old English novel."

"Don't be silly," Trudy replied, slipping a pillow into its cover. "They're married." She glanced at a clock that read three fifteen. "They've been married fifteen minutes by now."

"At four they can celebrate their first anniversary. What's the proper first-hour anniversary gift?" I wondered.

"A kiss," was Trudy's guess. "It has to be."

But at four o'clock, Frank and Mollie were in the back of a taxi, careening through midtown traffic. Behind them was a private car, containing two private detectives and the coach.

"Faster," urged Mollie. "Can't you go any faster?"

"Listen, lady," the driver told her, "we're six inches off the ground as it is."

"How do you think he found out?" Mollie asked her new husband.

Frank shrugged. "I don't have any idea." The coach had stopped them just as they were emerging from the judge's chambers after exchanging vows. He was choleric with anger.

"Aha!" he had cried, triumphantly. "Gotcha!"

Frank had grabbed Mollie by the hand and dashed with her down another corridor, with the coach and his minions in heavy pursuit. They flew out of the building, found a cab and hurled themselves inside. Moments later, the chase began.

At four thirty, Trudy and I had just finished packing our bags, and were sitting down for a cup of coffee, when our doorbell began ringing like a fire alarm, Mollie and Frank weren't due for another hour and a half. But when Trudy opened the door, there they were.

"Quick," Mollie said to Trudy. "Hide us."

Trudy was a little slow on the uptake. "Hide you?" she said. "Why?"

Mollie didn't bother to reply. She slammed our front door shut and ran to our bedroom. "Trudy, you remember Frank, don't you?" she called over her shoulder.

Trudy nodded vaguely. Frank smiled and waved a hand. "Hi, Trudy, how've you been?" Mollie whisked Frank into the bedroom and closed the door.

It had barely clicked shut when the pounding started on our front door. Trudy and I stared at each other in amazement. "This," Trudy announced marching up to the door, "is getting to be like a Marx Brothers movie." With that she flung the door open and in spilled a figure. I have seen big men, and I have seen angry men, but I have never seen a big man so angry before.

"Where are they?" he shouted hoarsely.

Trudy stared at him calmly. "How do you do?" she said. "My name is Trudy Baker, and this," she said, indicating me, "is Rachel Jones. Who are you?"

The coach didn't seem to hear her. His eyes kept darting around our living room. Then he spotted the door leading to the bedroom. "Aha!" he cried, leaping toward it. But Trudy was too fast for him. She put herself between him and the door and forced him to look at her.

"I don't think we've had the pleasure of meeting you," she said levelly.

But all he could say was, "Are they in there?"

Trudy still refused to lose her cool. "Rachel," she said to me in her most ladylike voice. "Would you be so good as to call the police. Tell them a strange man has forced his way into our apartment and won't leave."

That took the wind out of his sails. "Forced my way. . . . What are you talking about?"

"Well, we haven't invited you in, have we? While

you're at it, Rachel, why don't you call the newspapers. They'll be interested in the story. 'Pro Coach Named Would-be Rapist' will make a nice headline."

For the first time, the coach looked concerned. "Wait a minute," he sputtered. "Wait just a minute. Nobody's trying to rape you."

"Oh." Trudy replied. "Then what *are* you trying to do?"

Now he seemed confused. "I'm . . . I'm looking for someone." Then his eyes narrowed with suspicion. "Say, how did you know I was a coach?"

"Oh," Trudy said demurely. "I've seen your picture hundreds of times. You're a famous man."

The coach grinned. "Oh, not so famous as all that."

Then Trudy plunged home her harpoon. "You will be tomorrow. After the newspapers print their stories. Rachel, haven't you made those calls yet?"

"Now wait a minute," the coach said hastily. "I can explain everything."

"That's what they all say, isn't it, Rachel?" Trudy asked me. "But you know," she said, looking at him steadily, "I don't think I'm really interested in your explanation."

The coach gulped, like a little boy. Trudy has always had a way of handling difficult passengers. If they get too bad, she manages somehow to intimidate them. And this was no exception. Here was a man who was six-foot-four, at least, and who must have weighed 265 pounds. Yet Trudy, about half his size, was telling him that he was being very naughty indeed and ought to learn to behave himself.

"Yes, ma'am," he gulped.

"The only thing I'm interested in is seeing you walk out of our apartment. You understand that? You had no business charging in here like this."

"No, ma'am."

"So you'll leave now."

"Yes, ma'am."

"And you promise me you won't come back?"

The coach nodded his head. It was obvious he wanted to get away from this formidable female as soon as possible. "I promise," he said.

"Goodbye."

The coach mumbled something and backed out of the room. We could hear his footsteps clump down the hallway. In a moment, the elevator swallowed him up and there was silence. Then the bedroom door opened, and out came a radiant Mollie and a grinning Frank.

"You were fabulous!" Mollie cried. "Absolutely fabulous. Wasn't she, Frank?"

Frank nodded his head admiringly. "If I hadn't heard it myself," he said, "I wouldn't have believed it possible."

"It's a little bit early, but let's break out that champagne. Rachel and I will stick to coffee."

The four of us sat around our living room and toasted Mollie's and Frank's marriage. At first the conversation was quite animated but, after half an hour, it became quite evident that they were barely aware of our existence. Finally, Trudy and I exchanged looks, and we both got up.

"Well," Trudy said. "We're going to have to be going now."

"Oh, must you already?" I didn't notice too much disappointment in Mollie's voice.

"Yes, I'm afraid so. We've stocked the refrigerator. I think you'll find everything you need."

Mollie couldn't stop staring at Frank. "I'm sure we'll find everything we need," she said mechanically.

I was beginning to have the uncomfortable feeling of being an intruder in my own home. "Let's go, Trudy," I said abruptly. The last thing we saw as we closed the door was the sight of Mollie slowly moving into Frank's arms.

"Two will get you five they're in bed before we hit the street," I said to Trudy as we walked down the hallway.

"Before we hit the elevator, you mean," Trudy shot back. I thought it over and decided she was right.

Being in Mexico City for three days, we missed Monday's papers, but Mollie had saved us the clippings. You can get some idea of what they said by one of the headlines that went: "Rookie Receiver Makes Sensational Pro Debut." Frank, it seems, had caught eight passes, two for touchdowns, and had gained 194 yards.

"And you'll never guess what the coach said," Mollie told us. "He shook his head and said to Frank, 'Just think what you could have done if you'd been in bed by ten thirty.'"

"What did Frank say to that?" Trudy wanted to know.

Mollie laughed. "He told him he was."

Moral: An athlete's best athletic supporter is his woman.

Without ejaculation there can be no pregnancy.

A foolish girl's tale. Remember, it *can* happen. And here's how. A small gland inside the penis secretes a few drops of liquid shortly after erection. That drop often remains on the tip of the penis long before orgasm. And in that drop there can be as many as *50,000* sperm. Even placing the penis near the vagina without actual penetration can sometimes result in a surprise pregnancy. Surprises are nice. But not that kind.

Many women are naturally "frigid" and generally less interested in sex than men.

Women deliberately turn away from sex? Are you disinterested in it? This may have been true in the past, but the reasons lie with her training, not with her biology. In fact, there is evidence to support the statement that women are more highly sexed than men.

Women are slower in their sexual response than men.
At last, an observation that's not a myth. It seems to be true. Women generally take up to thirty minutes to achieve orgasm, while men can often get there within two or three minutes. But here again, evidence indicates that there's no biological reason for women to be slower. It seems to be more a matter of cultural conditioning. Some observers feel that women may be "sexually anesthetized" from childhood by the attitudes of society. Others say that girls, even now, deny their sexual feelings in order to conform to the generally acceptable image of "proper" female behavior. This sometimes makes it impossible for them to feel *anything* with regard to sex. Cultural conditioning, too, apparently accounts for man's reputation as a speedy operator. The notion has been put forward that it comes about as the result of training themselves to reach climax as quickly as possible during early masturbation in order to avoid parental discovery. Also, many men have had their early sexual experience with prostitutes, and these ladies, for obvious reasons, encourage their customers to complete their business in short order. On the surface, it would seem that the wide disparity in the speed of sexual response would make satisfactory intercourse virtually impossible. Actually, though, a couple quickly learns to accommodate each other by effort and practice.

There is a difference between vaginal and clitoral orgasm.
This myth, as we have seen, can be put directly on the doorstep of Sigmund Freud. It has been with us for too long, and it has driven several generations of women

wild with doubt and frustration. Fortunately, it has been conclusively proven that the two orgasms are identical. Unless the clitoris is stimulated, either directly or indirectly, orgasm does not take place. What *is* true is the fact that the sensation is often greatly increased when the penis is in the vagina at the moment before and during orgasm.

Simultaneous orgasm is important to successful sex.

Another myth that has driven several generations of men *and* women wild with frustration. The search for simultaneous orgasm often creates so many problems that free and natural lovemaking becomes impossible. A more realistic goal is satisfaction for both partners. In fact, many people prefer separate orgasms so they may enjoy their partner's as well as their own.

Intercourse during menstruation is harmful.

On the contrary, there is evidence that intercourse during menstruation may help to lessen menstrual cramps. There's no reason for a couple to avoid it if they want to have sex together. Menstrual blood is neither dirty nor taboo.

Intercourse during menstruation will never result in pregnancy.

Almost true, but not quite. There *is* a chance, although admittedly a very small one.

Intercourse during late pregnancy is harmful.

Harmful to whom? The baby? Absolutely no ill effects. The mother? Normal pregnancy will proceed. There is only one caution. If a woman has had a history of spontaneous abortion, perhaps it's not a good idea.

When a woman takes the lead in initiating sex, the relationship is in trouble.

It's this kind of misconception that makes a gal want to join the women's lib movement. Well, almost.

Saying a gal shouldn't be the aggressor in sex is like that old Victorian attitude that women shouldn't move during intercourse. In fact, the only trouble in a relationship in which the female initiates things is if she isn't able to successfully lure her man into bed. If the TV has a greater hold on him than your feminine charms, there is trouble, indeed.

But we must throw in a word of caution. Many men were brought up to believe that males chase and females submit. It might be difficult for a man to accept your advances. It might scare him. There is a girl who flies for Continental Airlines named Phyllis who told us a very amusing tale one evening at a party. Phyllis found herself head over heels in love with a fellow who lived in her building. His name was Peter and he was in his mid-thirties. Phyllis was twenty-two.

They'd see each other in the building lobby or on the elevator and exchange chit chat, but it never progressed. She sensed he wanted to make a pass but had a feeling he declined to do so for fear of being rebuffed. Many men avoid approaching a girl for just this reason. Their egos won't stand the blow of rejection. This is especially true of American men.

Phyllis decided to put into practice her inner feelings about being a sexually free human being. *She* would make the pass, a very obvious and open sexual pass. She waited for the right moment. It came one evening as she was returning from shopping and Peter was returning from his job at a midtown ad agency. They entered the elevator together.

"You look beat," Phyllis said with a smile. "Tough day?"

"Very. Insanity."

"Gee, I hate to ask you before you even have a chance to sit down, but I need a favor. Would you give me a hand with something in my apartment?"

"Sure. You're on my floor, aren't you?"

"Yup. Right down the hall."

Phyllis led him to her apartment, opened the door and preceded him inside. "Have a seat, Peter. I'll be out in a minute."

As Phyllis tells it, she knew Peter wanted to see the situation develop into something sexual. She was confident he wasn't gay, and even noticed his pants begin to bulge when she brushed past him on her way into the bedroom. He took a seat and Phyllis whipped off her clothes and slipped into a very sexy, black lace nightgown. She untied the ribbon holding together her long, brown hair and let her hair fall loose over her shoulders. After a quick check in the mirror, she came back into the living room. Peter was looking through her record collection when she entered. She came up behind him, wrapped her arms around him and kissed his ear.

"Hi," she cooed.

"What?" Peter jerked around. Phyllis kissed him and pressed close against him. He managed to pull away from her and walk to the window.

"Come sit down," Phyllis beckoned. Peter didn't look at her. He peered through the dirty window panes and seemed to pull himself up to full height as though getting ready for battle.

"Look, Miss . . ."

"Phyllis. And come sit with me."

". . . look, I don't know what led you to think I was this type of guy, but I'm not. I'm sorry and I find you very attractive and all but. . . ."

"I wasn't thinking of you as anything but an attractive man whom I wanted to be with. That's all."

"Yes. Well, I do have to be going. I . . . I . . . I left something on the stove."

"You couldn't have. You haven't been home."

"It's a timer. Yes, that's what it is. A timer. I leave a timer on for the stew to start before I get there."

"Don't be silly." Phyllis got up and allowed the top of her nightgown to fall, exposing her breasts. Peter gulped, headed right for the door and left.

"Did you ever see him again?" I asked Phyllis.

"Sure. But he always looked the other way. I sure learned something from that. Men want sex but a woman who takes the lead just scares them to death. I think they are afraid you'll ask for money when it's over. Besides, I guess it does take away from them their so-called manly role."

Phyllis knew she went overboard in her open invitation to Peter. She never again made such an overt pitch, although she does initiate sex, but in a subtler way. Younger men, brought up in this age of freedom, might not react as Peter did. But the moral is, we suppose, that there is still a long way to go in woman's freedom as an equal partner in sex. Even in marriage, men are apt to be put off by too direct an approach. But it's something to work for in a relationship, an open and equal acceptance of both partners having sexual needs and the right to take steps to fulfill those needs. Just make sure the fellow you choose to pull a Phyllis on hasn't left anything burning on the stove.

You will go crazy if you masturbate.

If that's true, then 99 percent of the population is certifiable and should be locked up immediately. A survey reported that this was approximately the percentage of people who have masturbated. Perhaps the other 1 percent is lying. Nobody ever went crazy because they masturbated, although a lot of people have been nearly torn apart by fear and guilt. Recent researchers seem to feel that masturbation during childhood and adolescence is absolutely necessary for good psychosexual development. Masturbation without guilt or shame, they say, is the foundation for healthy sex without guilt or shame.

You will go crazy if you masturbate too much.

That's what the guy said when he heard about a man who masturbated three times every day. "That's way too much," he declared flatly. "Twice a day is plenty."

Masturbation will prevent you from enjoying sex.

The exact opposite seems to be true. People who develop their sexual feelings and their ability to come to orgasm through masturbation have a better chance of fully enjoying sexual intercourse. The only exception seems to be young boys who practice masturbation in such a way that they ejaculate very quickly.

Even though you're a virgin, you should have no trouble in finding immediate satisfaction in sex.

Maybe. Some do, some don't. Everything takes practice, including sex.

Masturbation after marriage is an insult to your mate.

How uptight can you get? We can think of dozens of reasons why one partner would be in need of sexual release and the other not. Illness, stress and separation, just to name three. Of course, if masturbation replaces intercourse, then you might think about your relationship a little.

If a woman needs manual stimulation of her clitoris or if her orgasm is later than her partner's, she is doing something wrong.

What she's doing wrong is thinking wrong. Most women need and enjoy manual stimulation. And, as we've said, women generally respond more slowly than men. Don't worry about it.

Creative people should indulge in sex sparingly because frequent intercourse limits their productivity.
Janice Weems quit her job as a stewardess with Pan Am to marry Bud Shumingrue, an up-and-coming novelist. Bud was in his mid-thirties when he married Janice, but looked at least fifty. He'd gone prematurely grey, and had dyed his beard grey to match his hair. He drank a lot, disappeared for weeks at a time and loved bumming around with fellow writers. This was upsetting to Janice, but she loved Bud and chalked it up to the peculiar pressures placed upon a writer by society.

But the one thing about Bud she couldn't stand was his feeling about sex and creativity. Bud liked to write his novels in concentrated spurts. Once he began work on a book, he liked to work on it day and night until it was completed. This meant as much as six or eight months during which he hibernated in his office in their apartment. Janice understood and never complained about eating alone and going out alone. But the complete lack of a sex life with her husband during his writing bouts began to take its toll on her.

"Bud, I want to talk to you," she said one night as she caught him en route from his room to the bathroom.

"Not now, kid. I'm right in the middle of a crucial scene where José, the hero, comes face to face with his future. Does he go on as a cock-fight entrepreneur or marry Carlotta, the town prostitute?"

"I don't care about cock fights and Carlotta, Bud. I care about us."

"Us? Oh, you and me. It'll have to wait, kid."

"It can't wait any longer, Bud. I'm a normal, healthy, woman and I need sex as much as the next woman."

Bud threw up his hands, fell to the floor and started doing push-ups.

"Bud, come on," Janice pleaded. "You haven't touched me in three months. I'm climbing the wall."

"Oh, baby," he said, getting up and coming to her. He put his hands on her shoulders and patted them. "Just as soon as I put this new baby to bed, we'll go away and spend two months in bed, just the two of us."

"Just the two of us. That's very thoughtful, Bud. I expected a crowd of writers to join us. Look, I'm not interested in going to bed with my husband in the future. I want to go to bed with him now." Janice reached down and caressed Bud through his pants. He recoiled as though she had rammed her knee into his crotch.

"For God's sake, Janice. Have you lost your mind?"

"No, I haven't lost my mind. But I have lost my husband." With that statement, Janice became very aggressive. She tore at Bud's clothes, stripping off her own at the same time. Its only effect was to send him running for cover behind a couch.

"Don't you understand?" he screamed at her. "There is only so much creative juice in one man's body. It has to be pumped into the book. It can't be wasted on a woman!"

Janice and Bud got a divorce a year later. She talks freely of their life together, often mentioning how good it was when he wasn't working on a book. "He was a wonderful lover," she says. "But cramming your sex life into one or two months of the year just didn't satisfy me."

Fortunately, all creative people aren't concerned with preserving their creative juices. We've known many writers, artists and musicians and can only testify that they make wonderful, sensitive lovers, even while working on a book or a painting or a composition. Creative people seem just as productive and artistic out of bed as in it.

Long walks, cold showers and other strenuous physical exercise reduces the sex drive.

Oh, yeah. If you've ever dated a boy who's just returned from military basic training, you know what a joke this is.

Women do not have sex dreams.

Maybe not as often as men, but we do have them. Some of our most passionate affairs have occurred at three in the morning following a late supper of Chinese food.

Interest in sexual activity decreases with age.

There is no biological truth in this statement. Men in their seventies are perfectly capable of maintaining an erection, and there's no reason why Grandma shouldn't enjoy it. There is a retired airline captain living in Miami who, rumor has it, is one of the great lovers of our day. He's now seventy-four years old and, according to a few Miami-based stews, makes many younger men appear impotent by comparison. Every stewardess has had her share of passes made by older men, and it's obvious they could have carried through with their intentions if the opportunity presented itself.

Intercourse results in only a single orgasm.

True for the male, poor thing. But we women can have as many as five or six orgasms in rapid succession.

Sexual activity cannot be sustained too long.

Once again, it's the ladies who have the edge over the men. A man, as we've said, may ejaculate two or three times a night. But apparently, a woman can go on forever. They had to stop a recent experiment after the subject had achieved fifty consecutive orgasms. Either they ran out of male volunteers or everyone got too tired or hungry to go on. However, the lady was still more or less willing. Official records describe her as "tired but happy." Results like this lend further credence to the theory that women are the more highly sexed of the species. Don Juan, it seems, was a piker. Or maybe the ladies were ripping him off and he never suspected it.

If a man is impotent, he can never hope to have sex.

Untrue, but he needs help to cure his condition. It's not widely understood, but there are two separate kinds of impotence that plague some men—primary impotence and secondary impotence. Primary impotence is a situation where a male has never been able to achieve or maintain an erection long enough to complete the sex act. Secondary impotence is when he was once able to perform sexually, but is now incapable of it. Within recent years, a great deal of work has been done on these two problems and there is hope. A qualified doctor can give a man excellent advice.

All a "frigid" woman needs is a little force from a man.

Raping a so-called frigid woman is not going to force her into enjoying sex. The seat of her trouble might very well be psychological, but it also has some real physical symptoms. Two common female ailments are vaginismus and dyspareunia. Vaginismus is a condition where the muscles surrounding the vagina contract, sometimes so severely that the opening appears to be closed. This makes penetration difficult, if it can be done at all. Dyspareunia is a condition where sexual intercourse is invariably painful. Both of these can usually be corrected by proper medical advice.

Nothing can be done about premature ejaculation.

False. One of the most universal sexual failures is the inability of the man to hold back his climax. Often the woman has barely had time to be properly aroused before he has reached orgasm and is satisfied. The reasons for premature ejaculation are legion, but techniques have been developed that result in ultimate control. Consult a physician.

Some women can never achieve orgasm.

It's true that some women *have never* achieved orgasm. But that doesn't mean they never will. We've actually known a few strange creatures who are proud of this, but we suspect that most women would be happier if they could reach climax. Again, this is a medical problem, and if you're willing to be perfectly frank with your doctor, he can probably steer you to some help.

What is sexual deviance and how can it be recognized?

We're glad you asked. It's the subject of the next chapter.

CHAPTER VII

"Do I know the difference between what's normal and what isn't? Sure. Normal is what I like to do."
—A REMARK OVERHEARD AT A PARTY

"An Orgy Is Two Couples in Bed with a Goat."

Nobody has ever succeeded in establishing the exact point at which normal sexual behavior crosses over into deviancy. We have a friend who is fantastically turned on by making love in the woods. She concedes it's okay in the bedroom, too. But nothing, she says, beats the great outdoors.

"I can't describe the sensation of lying absolutely naked on a carpet of soft pine needles, watching the stars overhead. And if there's a full moon, I absolutely go out of my skull." Is that sick or abnormal? We doubt it.

Do you think only dirty old men get hooked on pornography? Women are aroused by stag films, too. We've heard of some couples reading erotica to each other to heighten their pleasure in intercourse. In fact, this is a practice highly recommended by some ancient Oriental marriage manuals.

Another couple found they were both stimulated by music. The only trouble was that he liked Bach while she dug the Beatles. Their solution? They got two sets of earphones and plugged into different tape decks. That way, each marched to the sound of a different drum. Sometimes, they got their wires crossed.

Each of these little rituals is designed, in its own way, to stimulate sexual performance and response, to increase desire or excitement. Each, in other words, is an aphrodisiac. In its most specific sense, an aphrodisiac refers to drugs, food or stimulating potions, but the wider meaning can include anything that makes the sex drive stronger.

People have sought the perfect aphrodisiac ever since Biblical times. In particular, certain foods have been mentioned as increasing sexual appetite and potency. Even today, many people are convinced that sharing a dozen oysters will send a couple to bed instantly. Our Victorian great-grandfathers thought highly of the virtues of the testicles of bulls, which they solemnly ate raw. However, they were referred to in those days as "prairie oysters."

A very popular aphrodisiac in China is powdered rhinoceros horn. Chinese gentlemen believe that if they eat enough of the stuff, their penises will grow to a size and strength comparable to the object from which the powder was taken. You may think that's funny, but it's no laughing matter for the rhinos. They're in danger of becoming an extinct species precisely because of the peculiar quality their horns are supposed to have.

Human gullibility being what it is, the list of foods that has been represented as sure-fire aphrodisiacs is enormous. In fact, just about everything we eat has been touted, at one time or another, as a foolproof way of turning a reluctant virgin into a raging sex maniac.

Human ingenuity being what it is, some fairly exotic concoctions have been advertised as effective ways of doing the same thing. They include such dainties as milk in which the testicles of a goat have been boiled, cow urine and crocodile semen.

Do any of these substances really work? Well, if people once thought they did some good, then we suppose so. Certainly, they never did anyone too much harm. There are, however, a few things that definitely have the properties of an aphrodisiac. Alcohol is one of them. Taken in small quantities, alcohol and wine remove inhibitions, relax fears and ease anxieties. But in just slightly greater quantities, they act as a depressant and sedative. They interfere with sensation, coordination and enjoyment of the sex act.

Another true aphrodisiac is testosterone, which is the male sex hormone. This chemical acts on the entire body of both men and women to cause powerful sexual desire. However, it can also have undesirable and often dangerous side effects. It should be used only by qualified physicians.

The folklore surrounding Spanish fly is vast and bawdy—with just enough truth to make it dangerous. Spanish fly, correctly known as cantharis or nux vomica, also has another name. That name is strychnine, a deadly poison. Minute doses are sexual stimulants. But a grain too much can be lethal.

The most widely heralded aphrodisiac of our culture today is marijuana. Many people swear by it. They say it enhances sexual activity, decreases inhibitions and sharpens desire. But, interestingly enough, they claim it only works when you smoke it with someone to whom you're already attracted. As one acquaintance put it, "When two people are already grooving, then the combination of pot and the feeling they have for each other makes sex stronger, sweeter, more subtle, than it's ever been before."

Some pot people say that each detail of the sexual experience occurs in a kind of slow motion. Each sensation is isolated and heightened. There is no feeling of pressure, no sense of time. A touch, a stroke, or an embrace are all felt with increased sensitivity.

Despite this, there is general agreement among users that pot does not turn people into galloping sex maniacs. Nor does it rob the user of self-control. All this sounds just dandy to us—except for two things. Pot is illegal, and its long-term medical effects have not yet been properly evaluated. In any case, it has always seemed to us that sex is the ultimate turn-on, and we've never felt the need to light up in order to get high.

Of course, we admit that a long-standing sexual relationship can become routine—unless both partners introduce a few novel variations now and then. When these are successful, they, too, are aphrodisiacs. But don't get too impulsive.

One young housewife we heard of decided she was tired of having her husband come home every night, apathetic and listless. So one day she decided she'd give it her all, and put a little of that old sparkle back in his eyes. Late that afternoon, she sank luxuriously into a warm, fragrant bath. Then she towelled herself vigorously and sat down before her dressing table to make up. At six thirty she was ready, and it wasn't a moment too soon. She heard her husband's key in the door, and ran to it before he could get it open. Wearing a broad smile and absolutely nothing else, she whipped back the door, flung her arms wide, and welcomed him with an enthusiastic, "Hello, darling!"

It was a pretty tableau. She stood there, entirely nude, still as a statue. Her husband was frozen into equal immobility, his key dangling lifelessly from his hand. Behind her husband stood a third party. This was a middle-aged gentleman carrying a briefcase. The only sign of emotion he betrayed was a flush of embarrassment rising slowly over his face. Her husband had brought his boss home for dinner, but had forgotten to tell his wife. The three of them stood there, suspended through what seemed an eternity.

All right, what would you have done? Would you have run shrieking out of the room? Would you have murmured, "Excuse me while I go slip into something more comfortable." Would you have slammed the door in their faces and retired into your room, vowing never to come out again?

Actually, what she did was this. She dropped her arms, smiled at the stranger in her most friendly fashion, and held out her hand. "Hello," she said. "I'm Brenda. I guess Tom didn't tell you we're nudists."

Her husband stood there, making funny noises like a fish just out of the water as she linked her arm through the boss's arm and led him inside. "Let me mix you a drink," she said, playing the gracious hostess role to the hilt, "while Tom takes off his clothes." Behind her, she could hear Tom going through his gargling routine, still apparently incapable of coherent speech. But she didn't look at him because her eyes were riveted on Tom's boss, who was doing a most unusual thing. He had taken off his jacket and was sitting on their sofa, wriggling out of his shoes, chuckling at Tom and Brenda.

"I never once suspected it, Tom. I admire a man who can keep his private life to himself. But, then, perhaps I'm partial. You see, my wife and I have been nudists for years." He stood up and zipped down his fly. "Why don't we all relax and get comfortable." His trousers fell in a heap at his feet and, in a moment, he was beaming at Tom and Brenda, completely naked.

"Well, Tom," he asked, "aren't you going to join us?"

Brenda said later that Tom looked as if he had been

hit on the head with a safe. He had that dazed expression of a man who had no idea where he was. But slowly, very slowly, his hand reached up to untie the knot of his tie. It was, she said, an unforgettable evening.

She also said that being naked before a strange man, and seeing him in the same state, did not turn her on particularly. And apparently Tom's boss felt the same way. He didn't, for example, go around all night long with an erection. They simply sat there and chatted, exactly as they would have if they had been clothed. All except for Tom, who never did manage to snap out of it entirely.

There are, however, others—and quite a few of them we understand—who *are* turned on by a roomful of bare buttocks. These are the so-called swingers who find private sex a bore, and are eager to try it *in* a crowd—and *with* a crowd. These people are convinced they are engaging in the most liberated kind of sex. The sex of the future they call it. Actually, though, group sex is as old as the hills. Almost all civilizations have known and practiced it in one form or another.

In an abstract way, we think we understand why people engage in it, but it has no appeal to either of us. If we had to guess, we'd say that the big attraction of group sex is that it provides variety without doing any great harm to the personal relationship of consenting couples. On the other hand, because of the absence of any deep emotional relationships, we think it's an unrewarding form of human behavior. But there are thousands who disagree with us. It's particularly popular in the larger cities of this country and Europe, where it is usually limited to the college-educated, economically secure middle-class, and to the younger generation experimenting with new forms of communal living.

A swinging session consists of every conceivable form of sexual entertainment—in twos, threes, fours, fives, and with members of the same sex. Both single and married people swing.

One stewardess we know who is a devoted swinger told us she considers group sex to be the most exciting and stimulating experience she's ever known. "We sit around naked after we've made love and just groove on being there. All the hostility is back on the floor, or in bed. I love it."

Another stewardess, this one from Lufthansa, considers group sex to be almost spiritual. She told us she feels rich after a group lovemaking session. "There is something liberating and meaningful to have twenty people's bodies touching each other at the same time," she said one night over coffee. "There is total peace within."

It may strike you, as it has us, that these lofty justifications for doing what no other animal on earth does might really be a cop-out, a weak and false excuse for immoral behavior. Maybe not. The fact that tomcats, with their reputation for total promiscuity, give each ladyfriend their undivided attention during lovemaking, doesn't really prove anything. We don't make the group-sex scene, but to each his own. There is nothing wrong with it if all the people involved approve.

We have another stew buddy from Delta Airlines who doesn't give spiritual justifications for her enjoyment of group sex. "What I love about it," she says, "is all the mouth-genital stimulation. A guy will go down on you very freely and quickly at an orgy." None of this "mystical experience" for her. At least she was honest about why she liked it.

Whether or not we like it, or whether or not *you* like it, swinging is definitely part of the current scene. Swingers even have their own formal organization, known as The Sexual Freedom League, and their own monthly magazine, which carries some pretty unusual classified advertising. An ad might read:

CHICAGO—YOUNG COUPLE. HE, 26, HEIGHT 5-11, WEIGHT 170, ATTRACTIVE; SHE, 25, 36-23-36, STUNNING. DESIRE TO MEET COUPLES AGES 21-30 FOR WEEKENDS. SEND PHOTO WITH FRANK LETTER.

People who place ads like this are not looking to start up a bridge foursome.

Sometimes, whole neighborhoods swing. Neighbors will visit a new family on the block under the usual pretense of offering a helping hand. What they're really doing is feeling out the newcomers as to their sexual appetites. Certain cue words and phrases are introduced into the conversation. If the newcomers react in the right way, a more specific approach is made. This neighborhood situation can be hell on a new family that doesn't swing, preferring their sex in the privacy of their own bedroom. They have a tough time trying to figure out why those warm and friendly folks who visited them when they first moved in don't come to call anymore.

We know a captain who lives in a "swing neighborhood." He's mentioned on a couple of occasions that new families soon become aware of the unique makeup and sexual practices of their new neighborhood and move out, usually within the year. "It's actually good for a neighborhood to swing," he says. "Once swingers settle into such a neighborhood, they never move. The neighborhood remains pretty stable. Everybody's having too good a time to ever consider leaving."

One theory holds that swinging is as popular as it is because so many people have an urge to exhibit themselves. Exhibitionism, when carried to extremes, can really be a sick business. Every big city has its share of pathetic men who find a kind of perverted pleasure in displaying their penises in public places. Sometimes the dislay is enough. Sometimes it is accompanied by masturbation.

The exhibitionist is said to be the most childish and passive of deviants. Often he spends his day in a subway station or in the park waiting for some woman—any woman will do—to take a look at him. It's one of the nuisances of living in a city. If you decide to move to one, you might as well steel yourself. It's almost bound to happen to you. But don't be unduly alarmed. The sickie who unzips himself is not likely to try to attack you.

There are also women exhibitionists, but ironically, most of them get paid for their work. The stripteasers, the topless waitresses, even your beauty queens, play a variation on the exhibitionist's game. And interestingly enough, despite their often excellent equipment, their reputation for mature, male-female sex is pretty poor. We read somewhere recently of a study of strippers which was conducted by a sociologist and his wife. Among the information they uncovered was the fact that strippers generally find more satisfaction in a homosexual relationship than they do in a normal one.

There we go again, letting our prejudices show. Yes, we admit that we can't help thinking that homosexual behavior, in either men or women, is abnormal behavior. However, we *do* qualify that statement by adding that we consider it abnormal behavior for *us*. For some, homosexuality is a way of life and, in recent years, society has become more tolerant of this behavior, but under the condition that it involves only consenting mature individuals capable of making up their own minds, and that it does not present a clear danger or infringe upon the rights and privacy of others.

The so-called straight world distrusts and fears homosexuals. Such an extreme reaction isn't really necessary. They're usually not dangerous. Most of them are simply in search of their own kind of fulfillment. Many women find male homosexuals good company. First of all, they are generally clever, witty individuals and, best of all, a woman doesn't feel the man is trying to make out with her. She can relax and be herself.

How can you tell if a man is a homosexual? The stereotype is a limp-wristed faggot who minces when he walks. Like most stereotypes, this one is shallow and often misleading. Margo, a girl we once knew in New York, floated into our apartment one evening with the announcement that she had finally met Mr. Right.

"His name is Rod," she said ecstatically. "He's six-foot-three, and built like a Greek god. He's got widely spaced eyes and nice, even teeth. . . ."

"I like 'em with nice, even eyes and widely spaced teeth myself," Trudy observed.

"Come on, don't spoil it for the girl," I said. But nothing we could have said would have spoiled it for Margo. Rod was a prince, a knight in shining armor. Along with his physique and good looks, he also had brains. And best of all, he treated Margo like a *woman*.

"How's that?" Trudy wanted to know.

"Not just as a sex object, but as a person," Margo explained. "He's kind, considerate and gentle. He likes *talking* to me."

"Oh," Trudy said, unhelpfully.

Two weeks later, Margo visited us again. This time she came in through the front door wearing a look of dismay. "Rod is a homosexual," she wailed.

"What?" we both cried.

"A homosexual," Margo repeated bitterly. "He likes men."

"I thought you said he likes you, too," I said.

"Oh he does," Margo admitted. "He told me he likes the companionship I offer him, but that he could never be attracted to me sexually."

"How do you know?" I insisted.

"Because two nights ago I invited him up to my place for dinner. And I tried to seduce him. He was horrified. I will never trust handsome men again."

"I told you guys with widely spaced teeth were best," Trudy said.

Margo had fallen into the trap of believing the almost universal stereotype. Actually, less than 10 percent of male homosexuals look or act gay. Even a transvestite does not necessarily look effeminate.

A transvestite is a man who wears women's clothes. Sometimes, he'll have a whole wardrobe of delicate, women's clothes which he puts on to feel sexually stimulated. This is usually done in privacy, although occasionally in public.

Ernie, a resident at a city hospital, told us about one case he had run across when he was on duty in the emergency room one night.

"A truck had hit a taxi," he said, "and the passenger was hurt. The ambulance brought him in unconscious. He was wearing an ordinary business suit, nothing special. We wanted to get at him fast, and didn't want to take the chance of moving him in case any bones were broken, so I told one of the nurses to cut his clothes off. I went in to scrub up, and when I got back, there were three nurses standing around the patient, who wasn't in a hospital gown yet. I asked them what the hell they thought they were doing. They turned and looked at me with the funniest expressions on their faces. One of them stepped aside, and simply pointed. Underneath his suit, this guy had on a dress, a slip, and, would you believe, panty hose?"

Because of their preoccupation with things like underwear, which they must be wearing before they can be sexually stimulated, transvestites' behavior borders on fetishism.

A fetish is a strong sexual attachment to a particular object. A fetishist may be passionately aroused by an article of clothing, a brassiere, for example. He may even prefer a brassiere to the female breast. Other favorites are panties, garter belts, stockings, girdles, bikinis. There are shoe fetishists, glove fetishists, handkerchief fetishists and flower fetishists.

At this point, you're probably wondering, "Why are those two nuts telling me all this? We're not going to get mixed up with any weirdos like that. And if by accident we do, we'll let them have our old sneakers to fondle while we get the hell out." Right on, sisters, BUT—you won't be able to avoid them unless you know their habits. They do not go around wearing big signs on their backs that say, "Deviant." At first meeting, they look and act like the boy next door. What's that you say? The boy next door just got busted for sodomy? Oh, well.

You probably don't realize how common these offbeat fixations are. We'll give you just one example from the German neurologist Krafft-Ebing, who made it his business to collect the case histories of these little beauties. And you'd be surprised at how many he managed to find.

It seems there was this character Krafft-Ebing called "Z" who had a thing about ladies' handkerchiefs. He had, you see, been masturbating in them ever since he was twelve. Now, this kid was a model boy in every way. He even sang in the church choir. But he couldn't break himself of the habit. It got so bad that he couldn't even *see* a handkerchief without having an orgasm. Not any old handkerchief would do, you understand. It had to be a lady's handkerchief, and it had to have either black and white borders or violet stripes running through it.

He managed to keep his hobby a secret, grew up, and married a young girl who probably thought she was lucky to snare such an attractive, promising man. She probably changed her mind on her wedding night. Or maybe her Mama had never told her what to expect and she thought it was perfectly normal. In any event, Z carefully wrapped a handkerchief around his penis before making love to her. It was, he explained, the only way he could get or maintain an erection.

So if your guy ever tells you the *only* way he can make it with you is if you let him smear you with cream cheese, you know you've probably got a fetishist on your hands. And you'd be well advised to get out, because, while most fetishists don't necessarily inflict any physical or mental humiliation on their partners, they can come close to other deviations that can be dangerous.

We're not talking here about people who like to experiment with sex. If you and your guy are having a perfectly satisfactory, sexual relationship, and he impulsively suggests that you take a shower together, and he'll soap your back if you soap his, and then maybe you two can see what will happen, that's not sexual deviancy. As a matter of fact, it sounds like fun. However, if you meet a man you're attracted to, and if he wants you to indulge in terribly painful or degrading acts, or if he wants to perform only one act to the exclusion of all others, he is a sickie.

If you're ever faced with a situation like that, there's probably no need to holler for the cops. Most people who suffer from perversions—and it *is* a form of illness—do not force their tastes on others. This sort of person prefers to play with those who enjoy playing with him. He'll probably pack up his case of whips and move on in search of a more willing partner.

Now that we've introduced you to the cozy habits of exhibitionists, perverts, fetishists and sadomasochistic behavior, you probably figure that's about as far into the subject of strange sex as you want to go. We wish the world were such that it's as far as you *need* to go. But there's an even darker side of sex that women— all women—should know about, and we intend to talk about it in Chapter XI. The New Morality does not bring any guarantee of unrelieved joy and freedom.

But to enjoy it properly, to have a chance to find out where you fit in this crazy, mixed-up world of ours, you should at least be aware of some of the ways people try to find happiness in it. If you read only *Little Women* or *Little Men,* you wouldn't have a very clear picture of what life was like in the days of Louisa May Alcott. And if you're about to strike off on your own, you can't afford anything less than clarity.

About the activities we've discussed in this chapter, and whether or not they're true perversions or harmless preferences, perhaps the clearest advice was the comment made by Trudy to our friend Jeannie back in Chapter V. Remember what she said? She said, "An unnatural sex act is one that threatens mental or physical harm." We've thought it over, and we've both decided we can't come up with a better definition than that.

CHAPTER VIII

Successful living depends on knowing what not to do. He who realizes when to say 'no' and can say it pleasantly and without embarrassment has won half the battle.
—DAVID SEABURY

"I'm New in Town... Don't Touch."

More bad advice has been scattered around on the question of how to meet, attract and hold a man than almost anything we can think of. Perhaps not bad, but certainly limited. That's because the one who's offering the advice is telling you how *she* met, attracted and held her men. She'll start out by saying, "The first thing I did when I became vice president of the advertising agency...." Well, *you're* not the vice president of an advertising agency. You're the hard-pressed secretary of a junior partner in a law firm, and her experience certainly isn't yours. To make matters worse, in our opinion, too many of these would-be den mothers talk about "catching" a man, as if he were some sort of unpredictable animal, with you out on safari tracking him down. They lard their books with instructions on how to build elaborate traps and lures, how to bait your hook so men will be fighting for a chance to snap it up. They keep you so busy playing Sheena, Queen of the Jungle, that you don't have any time to be your natural self. And that's disastrous, because if you "catch" a man—ugh, how we hate that phrase—while you're playing a role, disillusionment is bound to set in. It won't take him very long to discover that your enthusiasm for mountain climbing is just a fake, designed to get him interested in you. Of course, if you're *genuinely* interested in mountain climbing, that's a different matter.

So, what we've tried to do in this chapter is two things. First, we've stressed the importance of behaving naturally, and, second, we've assembled a composite that shows you how a lot of different girls with different personalities and interests have found their men. Somewhere, there should be a formula that's right for you. We admit that we've suggested a ruse or two, but they're pretty harmless and, besides, it never hurts to give nature a gentle push now and then.

Before you go galloping off in all directions, have you ever given any serious thought to the kind of man that might be best for your needs? We have. Sitting around one rainy night in London, four of us stews with nothing better to do decided to see how many types of men we could list. We immediately found that it isn't as easy as it sounds because there's usually more to any man than the category he falls into, and, as one girl pointed out, just when you think you've got him typed, he moves into another classification. Anyway, here is our list.

Grade A, clean-cut, run-of-the-mill, available bachelor: He's nice looking in a Neil Armstrong way, predictable, relatively normal and, most often, impressively dull. He has great energy and is driven by ambition to succeed in business. When you marry him, you become a tool in his drive up the corporate ladder, with hostess duties for his business associates occupying much of your time. Your house will be nice, your car a large station wagon and you will have 2.3 children. But don't think you'll ever occupy the center of his attention. His career will take over on the first morning of your honeymoon. You'll move every four or five years as his company advances him in the corporate ranks. Your 2.3 children will have runny noses, measles, whooping cough and an occasional touch of snobbery as their father accumulates corporate letters after his name. You will spend more and more of your time trying to fulfill yourself and to escape your 2.3 children, your house, your station wagon and your now paunchy and even duller spouse. But don't knock it too much. It is steady.

The "single-till-I-die" bachelor: Not a common breed, but there are enough of them around to warrant a category all their own. Many of this type really don't mean it and will marry someone someday. Some will remain true to their pledge, if only to avoid paying off the 2-million dollars in bets they made while in college. Bachelors of this ilk make pretty good lovers, but don't have much else to offer a single girl. And if you want to retain his services as a lover, don't make the mistake of bringing up marriage—EVER. He'll run faster than a New York City cop who has just been spotted taking graft from a prostitute.

The "I'd-get-married-if-I-could-find-the-right-woman" bachelor: This species would like to marry but lives in mortal fear of ending up with a scheming, conniving female. What he's looking for is someone to be standing at the door with his drink, pipe and slippers each evening when he comes home from a hard day at the toy factory. This type of bachelor is sweet, a little pitiful and very hard to get rid of once you've done duty at his door. Enjoy him, but don't encourage him to hang around as a convenience.

The "I-get-a-headache-if-I-don't-get-laid" bachelor: This is the lover, the romancer, the bachelor who views every woman as a challenge. He *must* get you to bed with him. He might even *need* to make you fall in love with him. Of course, he'll dump you then because you are no longer an item to be conquered. Even if you know all these things about him, you do find him attractive, and damn it, what's a girl to do? Well, all we can say is enjoy being added to his trophy shelf and chalk it up to the learning curve of life.

The "wine-improves-with-age" bachelor: Like older men? There's good reason to. Older men are more mature, have more experience and often have more money than anyone else you know. Interested? You should be, provided he isn't so old that he has a reservation at the Sunset Years Retirement Home and perks up at the mention of sex only when it refers to the French ladies he knew during World War I. If your relationship with Daddy was normal, you might make a go of it with your new daddy. If there was something hidden and deeper, see a reputable shrink and stick to the younger generation.

The "I-was-with-her-to-the-end" bachelor: Widowers are the hardest bachelors to find. If his marriage was a good one and he checks out as being relatively normal, he'll be snapped up so fast you'll think the breed is extinct. Men who saw a marriage through, present an extremely attractive image to a single girl. Don't hesitate if you find one of these creatures because, like good buys in houses, they don't last long.

The "glad-to-be-rid-of-her" bachelor: Divorced men often understand women and are kind and considerate to them. But more often than not, they're bitter about marriage and women. This now-single man is still emotionally and financially tangled up with his former family. You must be prepared to share that former family with him if you decide to become involved. And once you do make that decision, don't back down on it. There's no more detestable woman than the one who agrees to share the guy with his former family and then begins to bitch about it.

The "as-soon-as-it's-final" bachelor: Don't get messed up with one of these almost-divorced fellows unless you want to spend evening after evening sharing his problems. And believe us, he'll have them. He's suffering, and he wants a handholder and someone to make him a meatloaf now and then. Don't hitch your wagon to this star unless you like playing nurse to a bruised and battered child in his forties.

The younger man: Well, here's to you, Mrs. Robinson.

The homosexual: You might think the problem would never arise, but many homosexuals go both ways. He can make love to you on Tuesday and hanker after a nubile young boy on Thursday. This can be a mess.

The married man: All right, let's settle back and talk about this one. Why is it a problem? Numbers, mainly. Most of the men you'll meet are married. So the law of averages will tell you that sooner or later you'll probably run across one that gives you a chemical reaction. What do you do about it? We know what you'll do about it. You'll make a perfect ass of yourself and louse up your life for a short period of time. Even so, you should know the facts.

The facts in his favor are these: He may really love you and remain devoted for years. He may love you much more passionately than he loves his wife. He will appreciate everything you do, and he is frequently marvelous in bed and careful not to get you pregnant.

The facts against him are these: He almost never gets a divorce, but if he does, it's usually an ugly messy thing, with you cast in the role of a home-wrecker. He's never around on weekends, holidays or the time you really need him. You can't take him home to mother. He can't take you home to mother. The very nature of your relationship has got to make a liar out of him, and he'll resent that and probably blame you. You may fall permanently in love with him and be badly, badly hurt. While you're waiting around for him to call, you're missing out on other more eligible men.

What if he says he's single, but you suspect he's not? How can you tell if a man is married? Check his ring finger. Is there a circle of pale skin where the ring might have been before he took it off to slip in his pocket?

Ask him for his address. If he admits to suburbia or is evasive about it, chances are he's married.

Examine his car. If he drives a station wagon, he's probably guilty. Are there crayons in the glove compartment or lollipop wrappers on the floor? Definitely guilty.

Smear lipstick on his shirt. Apologize so he'll notice the stain and watch to see how worried he is.

Talk about pets and children. If he's married, it's hard to keep from slipping up.

Ask to meet his friends. Listen carefully to his excuse if he says no.

We had a friend who was seeing a lot of a guy she was convinced was married.

"I just know he is," Gloria would say to us, drumming her fingers impatiently, "but I can't prove it."

"How do you know?" I'd ask her.

"I can tell," she'd insist. "There's a certain feeling about a married man."

Well, Gloria tried all the regulation tests and they all turned out negative, but she still wasn't satisfied. She telephoned his home during the day and once, when a woman answered, she thought she had him nailed. It turned out to be his mother. She even went down to the Hall of Records to see if a marriage license had ever been issued to anyone with his name. It hadn't, but that didn't faze Gloria.

"He could have gotten married in another city," she insisted.

"Maybe he really is single," Trudy suggested wearily.

"Never," Gloria said firmly. "I'm never wrong."

She continued to pry, refusing to abandon her conviction that he was cheating on his wife. It became an obsession with her, a mania. "And I don't even like the guy *that* much," she complained.

Finally, Gloria decided to force a confrontation. She told him she was madly in love with him, but that if he didn't marry her, she'd have to break off the relationship.

Gloria came into our apartment in a state of shock. "What have I done?" she mumbled. "My God, what have I done?"

We sat her down and decided she needed a drink more than she did coffee. After mixing her a stiff one, we asked her what had happened.

"I played the scene perfectly," she began. "I really had him convinced that I'd leave him if he didn't marry me."

"So what did he say?" we both asked.

Gloria looked at us miserably. "He said okay. We're engaged. I was wrong all the time. He never *was* married."

The perfect, absolutely right guy for you: This is the twelfth and final category. He's a bachelor with prospects who wants more from life than just security. He turns you on like crazy. He likes the things you like, dislikes the things you hate. He shares your idea of a perfect life. He's there when you need him. You know all about that, you say? But where is he? Keep looking. You'll find him. Have you ever thought of astrology? We know a girl who believes in it 100 percent. The first time she meets a guy, she asks him what sign he is. If it's compatible with hers, and she likes him, on goes the green light. We asked her for her astrological sex chart, and she gave it to us. We pass it on to you.

ARIES (March 21–April 20)

No	The best	Maybe—proceed with caution
Capricorn Aquarius Pisces Taurus Cancer Libra Scorpio	Leo Sagittarius	Aries Gemini Virgo

TAURUS (April 21–May 21)

No	The best	Maybe—proceed with caution
Aquarius Pisces Aries Taurus Gemini Libra Scorpio	Capricorn Virgo	Cancer Leo Sagittarius

GEMINI (May 20–June 21)

No	The best	Maybe—proceed with caution
Capricorn Aquarius Pisces Taurus Gemini Cancer Virgo	Aries Leo Libra	Scorpio Sagittarius

CANCER (June 22–July 23)

No	The best	Maybe—proceed with caution
Aries Gemini Cancer Virgo Libra	Pisces Scorpio	Capricorn Aquarius Taurus Leo Sagittarius

LEO (July 24–August 23)

No	The best	Maybe—proceed with caution
Capricorn Aquarius Pisces Taurus Leo Scorpio	Aries Sagittarius	Gemini Cancer Libra Virgo

VIRGO (August 24–September 23)

No	The best	Maybe—proceed with caution
Aquarius Pisces Aries Leo Libra Scorpio	Capricorn Taurus Virgo	Gemini Cancer Sagittarius

LIBRA (September 24–October 23)

No	The best	Maybe—proceed with caution
Capricorn Pisces Aries Cancer Libra	Aquarius Gemini Sagittarius	Taurus Leo Virgo Scorpio

SCORPIO (October 24–November 22)

No	The best	Maybe—proceed with caution
Aquarius Aries Taurus Leo Virgo Libra Scorpio	Pisces Cancer	Capricorn Gemini Sagittarius

SAGITTARIUS (November 23–December 21)

No	The best	Maybe—proceed with caution
Capricorn Pisces Gemini	Aries Libra	Aquarius Taurus Cancer Virgo Libra Scorpio Sagittarius

CAPRICORN (December 21–January 20)

No	The best	Maybe—proceed with caution
Capricorn Aquarius Gemini Libra	Taurus Virgo	Pisces Aries Cancer Leo Scorpio Sagittarius

AQUARIUS (January 21–February 19)

No	The best	Maybe—proceed with caution
Capricorn Aquarius Pisces Aries Taurus Virgo Scorpio	Gemini Leo Libra	Cancer Sagittarius

PISCES (February 20–March 20)

No	The best	Maybe—proceed with caution
Aries Taurus Gemini Virgo Libra Sagittarius	Cancer Scorpio	Capricorn Aquarius Pisces Leo

An observation about our friend's chart—it's okay as far as it goes, but if you're a Libra, you're never going to find your Aquarius soulmate unless he's around. It does you absolutely no good at all if he happens to be in Denver and you're in Delaware. And even if he is around, how do you two make contact? Where, precisely, do you stand the best chance to meet men?

A Geography Lesson

Some parts of the United States have a real shortage of eligible men, while others have a bumper crop. You want to meet interesting types in publishing? Then don't go to Fond du Lac, Wisconsin. The places with the shortest supply of eligible males are Washington, D.C., Massachusetts, New York, Alabama and Pennsylvania. The only states with an excess of males over females are Alaska, Hawaii, Nevada, Wyoming, North Dakota, Montana, Idaho, South Dakota and New Mexico.

On the Job

Some jobs have a higher romance potential than others. Elementary-school teaching used to be dismissed as a dead end. Things aren't as bad today, but the ratio is still much too high—and not in favor of women. Romance has seldom been known to flower within the office typing pool. In fact, any job where you're one of an army of female clerical workers is going to be a bust. We modestly recommend instead that you try flying. Stewardesses have very little trouble meeting men. If you're scared of heights, get some training and become the personal secretary of an executive in a male-dominated industry. Some girls we've met think nursing is a hard-to-beat profession. You meet so many cute young doctors that way, all of whom will turn out to be cute, rich doctors in a few years. If that's your reason for putting on a white uniform, listen to our friend Celia.

"Nursing is a wonderful and rewarding way of life, but if you're in it to meet men—well, you can forget all about that. Let's say you *do* find a nice-looking guy. He's about twenty-six, competent and hardworking. Perfect marriageable material, right? Not on your bedpan, he isn't. The chances are he's an intern with, maybe, three more years of training to go before he starts to earn a decent living. And let me tell you, he's working his tail off. When he's not, he's hitting his books. Okay, so he asks you for a date, you lucky girl. At last you're going to play a role in his life. You know what that role is? To him, you're a safety valve to release all the pressures that have been building up inside him. Look, a big date with an intern is a fast ham sandwich in the cafeteria, and then up to his place for a slam, bang, thank you, ma'am, and back to business. Why I've heard of interns taking nurses to their place and practically *ordering* them to take their dress off. 'Let's get those buttons unhooked, Nurse, I don't have much time.' Romance? There's more romance on a Detroit assembly line."

Where You Live

You've got an apartment in a building filled with screaming kids and tired fathers? We *told* you to check for tricycles in the halls, but you didn't listen. Okay, you'll move. This time, pick a building that attracts bachelors. Then, if you're lonely, you can ride the elevator until you meet someone.

Visit the laundry room in the basement on what you figure is the bachelor's equivalent of blue Monday. If someone interesting lives on your floor, carry your garbage to the incinerator by the spoonful. If all else fails, borrow some Scotch tape. Or borrow some Scotch. You might just have a party there and then. In many large cities, Los Angeles for one, some apartment buildings have been designed specifically to cater to singles. The emphasis in these places is on fun. They're often built around swimming pools or facing beaches. Frequent parties are the rule, and an open door at cocktail time is an open invitation. The atmosphere is one of an enormous co-ed dorm.

Let Me Fix You Up

Matchmakers have the best of intentions, but for some reason they usually think up the unlikeliest pairings. How do you avoid three hours of total boredom when your friend Selma asks you over to her house to meet a nice veterinarian who'd be just right for you? Suggest you all go out to a movie instead of sitting around. That way, the evening won't be a total loss.

Blind Dates

They can be super. But why don't you make it for lunch or cocktails? If it's not working out, you can say you have to get back to the office, or plead another engagement.

Sports

Yes, indeed. You're relaxed, he's relaxed. You're both out there because you think it's fun. "No, no," comes a voice. "Put more weight on your downhill ski, and bring your shoulders around."

"Like this?" you reply innocently.

"That's it. You're getting it."

And a beautiful friendship has begun.

We took a poll among our fellow stews and discovered that nearly eight out of ten had met gorgeous men through their interest in one sport or another. But not all athletic activities rank equally high in the romance department. Here's the way we rate them.

Swimming: All you need is a towel and a good book. One girl on a big beach towel alone is very sexy. If your figure is good, wear a little bikini and a big hat. If it's not good, why isn't it? Go back to Chapter III. Do not pass Go. Do not collect $200.

Skiing: If you can't ski but want to, take lessons. The instructors are nearly always single and handsome. But don't get a reputation as a ski bunny. These are the girls who never venture out on the slopes, but lounge around the fire all evening dressed in expensive ski outfits. These all-too-obvious manhunters are the objects of ridicule and fun.

Ice skating: If you've put together an interesting skating costume and fill it nicely, you won't make it twice around the rink before you'll find a partner with whom to skate.

Sailing: Harder to manage. But if you do have a friend with a boat, ask him to teach you how to sail. Do it even if you're convinced he'll never develop into a romantic interest. Later on, you'll find that a girl who knows her way around a boat is a prize skippers fight over.

Tennis: Take along a girl friend, wear a smashing tennis dress and find the courts where interesting men play. Be ready for mixed doubles before the afternoon is out.

Cycling and jogging: Great for city parks.

Horseback riding: Expensive and often inconvenient to arrange in a metropolitan area. Unless you love horses, it's not worth it.

Golf, bowling and roller skating: Ditto. The birdie golfers are interested in is not you.

The racetrack: Fine, if you've got a thing for bookies.

Football, boxing, hockey and wrestling: Tennis, anyone?

Hunting and fishing: Okay, if you've got a thing for ducks. On the other hand, one friend spends warm Sundays aboard a charter fishing boat. She's met lots of interesting guys that way, and her freezer's always full. Only trouble is, she doesn't like fish.

Sky diving: Are you really *that* desperate?

Whatever sport you choose, remember this. Participate in it. That doesn't mean you have to excel. It just means you have to be involved. A girl who takes part in a sport just to show off her figure and lure men is considered silly and not worth meeting.

Singles' Bars

They're cropping up in big cities all over the country. You ought to sample the scene once or twice. Otherwise, you won't believe what goes on. It's wall-to-wall people with elbows in your face, and an air of frantic desperation everywhere. Guys are convinced that the girls they meet at singles' bars will provide them with instant sex. Several years ago they were great fun and more relaxed, but now they resemble a flesh market a little too much to suit us.

Singles' Clubs

You've seen the ads:

SINGLES 21-35. MEET ELIGIBLE MEN AND WOMEN. WEEKLY PARTIES. LIVELY, FUN ATMOSPHERE! GUARANTEED INTRODUCTIONS. MUSIC. REFRESHMENTS SERVED. COMPLETE EVENING COSTS ONLY $5. CALL BU 8-9876.

One night, on an impulse, Trudy and I decided to attend one of these "lively, fun" parties to see what they were like. When we called the appropriate number, we were instructed to go to a place we recognized as a second- or third-rate nightclub. You know the kind—vinyl banquettes striped to resemble tiger skins, while overhead, dim red and blue lights play through a thicket of plastic palm fronds. The whole place was permeated by an odor made up of stale cigar smoke, last night's booze and air conditioning.

What a depressing scene! Fifty or sixty figures moved despondently through the gloom; a knot of them collected at the table where the so-called refreshments were being served. These consisted of wilting potato chips, damp pretzels and cracked plates covered with the most tired-looking canapes either one of us had ever seen. No one touched the hors d'oeuvres, and I suspect they were saved and put back out for the next week's party.

The music was supplied by a cracked Beatles' record, and blared with ear-splitting loudness over the amplifying system. Five or six couples danced dispiritedly to this music, neither touching nor looking at each other. We had, we decided, stumbled upon a convention of morticians.

After standing hesitantly near the entrance of the club for several moments, we were approached by something that looked like a battleship—a tightly corseted female with a great pile of henna hair done up in an elaborate topknot. She had a bosom that would have made Betty Big Boobs weep with envy. This apparition bore down on us as we stood there, transfixed, unable to move.

"Hi there," she boomed with a forced heartiness. "My name is May. Who are you?"

After we told her, she gave us both a vast, conspiratorial wink. "Well, Rachel and Trudy, do I have something for you! Just wait until you meet them." Seizing us by the arms, she propelled us across the room to a pair of men seated at a table. "Hey, boys," she cried. "I want you to meet Rachel and Trudy. Girls, meet Sidney and Wallace." After this gracious introduction, she gave us a little push that practically sent us sprawling into the table. The next moment, she was gone. She had discharged her duty, and we were on our own.

The one called Sidney at least had the grace to stand up. Offering us chairs, he suggested some punch.

Wallace continued to sit without saying a word, preferring instead to chew his lip and look deep into Trudy's eyes, a practice he evidently considered to be irresistible. The uncomfortable silence was relieved by Sidney's return with punch. Trudy mechanically took it up, swallowed a taste and immediately put it back on the table.

"What's that?" she demanded.

"Punch," Sidney said brightly.

"What do you do with it?" Trudy wanted to know.

This confused Sidney. He frowned. He looked at her with concern. "Why . . . what do you mean? You drink it."

"Oh," Trudy said. "I thought maybe you gargled with it."

By this time, Wallace, who still hadn't said a word, was going through a perfect frenzy of lip chewing. He was obviously working himself up to something. Whatever it was, Trudy decided she wanted no part of it. She pushed back her chair and stood.

"It was grand meeting you boys, but Rachel and I have got to be running now."

Sidney looked disappointed. "But you've just arrived," he protested. "I thought maybe we could have a dance."

Trudy looked at him sweetly. "Oh, I wish I could. I really do. But I never dance."

"Never?"

Trudy shook her head. "Ever since I caught my disease," she whispered darkly.

"Oh," said Sidney. This even got to Wallace, who paused in mid-chew to contemplate Trudy with alarm.

Trudy favored them both with a sunny smile, and swept me out of the club in short order. We decided later that the only people who profit from Singles' Clubs are those who run them.

Computer Dating

In return for a fee, ranging from $5 to $500, a computer dating service gives you a long form to fill out about yourself and guarantees that you will receive the names, addresses and phone numbers of a number of "matched" mates. We have no idea if they work. We can only pass along a story we heard about a young girl who moved to a new city after a particularly unpleasant divorce. Feeling lonely, and not sure about how to best meet men, she registered with a computer dating service to the tune of $100. About two weeks later, she got a list of three names and addresses, with a notice telling her to expect a phone call from any one of them. One of the names on the list was her ex-husband. By chance, he had moved to the same city.

But this story has a happy ending. He called her up, and they were both so amused by the coincidence that they suddenly found themselves talking civilly to each other again. They agreed to meet, and two months later, agreed to remarry.

If you're simply not up to the activities or devices we've suggested, don't despair. You can still meet men in the most unexpected places. One girl we know met her guy when she rounded a corner in a supermarket and crashed her wagon into his. Another needed some change at a laundromat. The man at the next machine was not only accommodating, it turned out he was young and unattached. So give yourself a little time. You'll make contact eventually.

But when you do, make sure he notices you. This means looking your best at all times. It does *not* mean you have to have your hair done and be wearing a Pucci jumpsuit whenever you take out the garbage. Just be neat, simple and distinctively you.

Oh, and another thing. Be approachable. If he looks at you, return his gaze with a direct look. No grinning, winking or squirming. No pretending you don't notice. If he speaks to you, *pay attention. Listen.* People don't listen any more. A friend of ours proved it to us by going around at a party and acknowledging each "How are you?" by calmly answering, "I'm dying." What sort of a reaction do you think he got? In every case, he was met with a smile and a hearty, "Hey, that's swell, fella. Glad to hear it," or "That's good," or "Wonderful."

The art of good conversation depends more on listening than it does on talking. If a guy decides he can really talk to you, it's the first giant step to a deeper relationship. Interestingly enough, right here is where a lot of girls panic. They've met a man, and a couple of nights later he calls for a date. Now they worry. They've got him interested. But how do they keep him that way. "Oh, rats," they moan. "What if he doesn't think I'm sexy enough?"

What does "being sexy" mean anyway? There are no set rules on how to possess this mysterious quality. What is sexy to one man won't be sexy to another. Actually, sexy is a state of mind. If you look like you would enjoy sex, you will probably be thought of as sexy. Sexy is interest in what the man is saying, interest in the world around you and interest in the whole business of men and women getting together.

We talked with a few dozen flight crew members (captains, first officers and engineers) and asked them to tell us what they thought constituted *sexy*. We give you their answers.

". . . shiny hair. And if a girl has lots of thick shiny hair cascading down her back, that really turns me on and over. Of course, it always has to be clean, super clean. . . ."

". . . naturally, a good body. And I really dig girls who don't wear underwear."

"... I love the way a girl smells. A gal who smells great...."

"... any time I can look down a broad's dress, she's sexy to me. Of course, it helps if she's got something down there to look at."

"... it probably sounds weird, but I dig a girl who can sit still. I can't stand girls who fidget and don't listen to what you say."

"... I like healthy girls. If a girl looks like she's going to burst out of her skin with health, I think she's sexy. I don't go for the pale, indoor types...."

"... a girl's voice means a lot to me. Low warm voices really get to me, especially if she's inviting me to her apartment."

"... I guess I just have a thing about no makeup. Show me a woman who looks as good without makeup as with and I'll show you a sexy woman...."

"... there is nothing more sexy than a girl asleep. I don't mean on a park bench. But whenever I can look over in my bed and see a sleeping female, I react."

"... I hate loud girls. Give me a smart, quiet girl anytime. That's sexy to me."

"... I think sexy girls are always a little bit mysterious...."

"... I enjoy straightforward girls. Frank, candid, straightforward girls who are available are a real turn on...."

"... any girl who likes men is sexy."

"... any girl who looks like she might like to go to bed with me and really have fun is sexy."

Things can be sexy, too. Having a sexy apartment, for example, is a turn-on. Does that mean satin sheets, fur bedspreads, mirrors on the ceiling and you wearing black lingerie? Not at all. A sexy apartment is an interesting apartment. Comfortable furniture and lots of pillows are sexy. A luxurious rug or a few high-pile area rugs is sexy. A good sound system and an interesting collection of records are sexy. Thick, fluffy towels are sexy. Men despise what were once called face towels. An orderly apartment is sexy—well, it isn't really, but a very messy apartment is unsexy. Soft lighting is sexy. A big bed is sexy.

A well-stocked bar is sexy. Ideally, you should have a bottle of Scotch, a bottle of bourbon, a bottle of gin, a bottle of vodka, a bottle of dry vermouth, a bottle of brandy, a bottle of sherry, a few different cordials and several bottles of wine. This calls for a substantial outlay of money, we recognize that, but it will last a long time and probably will be supplemented by gifts from friends. You also should have a good supply of various kinds of glasses (no jelly glasses, please), a bottle opener, a long mixing spoon, a mixing pitcher and strainer for cocktails, an ice bucket, a jigger for measuring and a corkscrew.

Good smells are sexy. The aroma of perfume in the living room combined with something great bubbling on the stove is an unbeatable combination. Many men consider the kitchen the heart of any home—even a single girl's home. It's hard to describe what's so sexy about a well-loved, well-equipped, often-used kitchen except to say that food and sex are closely related.

Keep your kitchen bright, clean, uncluttered. Have some handsome, substantial pots and skillets, a big wooden salad bowl, a good coffee-maker, an interesting cookbook or two and some nice dishes and silverware. Have some sharp knives, a well-filled spice rack and a few gadgets, such as a vegetable peeler, garlic press, nutcracker and a strainer. Avoid having your kitchen look sad and neglected or cold and sterile like an operating room.

Having plenty of food on hand is sexy. Nothing depresses a man more than a refrigerator empty except for a loaf of stale bread and a bottle of cocktail onions. Nothing impresses him more than your ability to whip up an interesting snack or dinner with little apparent effort. The key here is to plan ahead. Food planning, like wardrobe planning, means buying things that go together in a meaningful, successful way.

Knowing how to cook and serve with style is sexy. Here's a ten-step checklist for a faultless but simple dinner for two.

1. Clean your apartment the night before.
2. Wear something special, but not too fussy. Your favorite shirt and pants will do. Look your best.
3. Plan your menu ahead of time. Make a list of everything you'll need. Be sure you don't have to run to the store at the last minute. "Oh Rudolph, do you mind running down to the store for me. I forgot the kohlrabi." Yes, he does mind, but he'll go. He may never come back, but he'll go.
4. Prepare a plate of hors d'oeuvres. Don't make it too involved and don't make too many. Raw vegetables around a cheese dip is one idea. A dish of fresh, chilled shrimp and hot sauce is another.
5. Cook everything possible ahead of time, so that it will all seem perfect and effortless. Make sure your menu does not exceed your abilities. Steak, baked potato, salad, hot rolls and dessert (your own or from the bakery) is deservedly a favorite, and he will not think any the less of you for preparing it, especially if you add an extra touch such as a Béarnaise sauce for the steak.
6. Give him his favorite drink or cocktail before dinner. Serve wine with the meal.
7. Put a stack of records on the record player. Program them carefully.
8. Serve a memorable dessert and plenty of rich, hot coffee.

9. For God's sake, leave the dishes in the sink.
10. Take the telephone off the hook.

Many girls never learn the secret of entertaining successfully. That's because, to them, a party means a sit-down dinner for six. But it needn't be. Why not be more adventuresome? Consider a picnic, or a traveling meal where a group is invited for cocktails to one person's home, the first course in another, and so on, through dessert.

One New York single we know was the hostess of a memorable Saturday party last May. She invited twelve friends to join her on a ferry ride to the Statue of Liberty. Cocktails were served at her place beforehand. On the ferry ride over, she served homemade cheese sticks and cold shrimp out of a basket. Coming back, she produced hot lobster bisque from a thermos, cold spiced chicken which she had sectioned into bite-size pieces and fresh tomato wedges. Dessert and coffee were waiting back at her apartment.

Still another variation is a wintertime cheese- or meat-fondue party. A half-dozen people huddled around a bubbling fondue pot makes for a very cozy evening. When the warmer weather comes, a sliced turkey and Caesar salad can be accompanied by gin and a selection of juices and mixers. A Sunday brunch of Bloody Marys, creamy, scrambled eggs, hot rolls with butter and hot coffee is not only delicious, it's economical as well.

As long as the food is good, hot and ample, it need not be costly. Hamburgers served with imagination and style are more fun than filet mignon without. Again, the key is planning and self-confidence. Just don't be too ambitious. You may have always wanted to try roast suckling pig, but it'll never fit in the tiny oven of your kitchenette.

One final word of advice. Don't serve a recipe you

haven't tried before. There's been many a hostess who has brought the casserole of curdled beef stroganoff to the table and considered suicide.

Having met him, attracted him and fed him, now comes the question of whether or not to bed him. You really have only two choices. It's either yes or no. For some reason, both seem to present problems for some girls. They don't know how to say no tactfully, and they can't say yes gracefully. First, let's take up the matter of saying no.

Believe it or not, in most cases it won't even come up. If you've decided no, he'll probably feel it. However, if he's not up on his non-verbal sensitivity, make sure you avoid compromising situations. Don't go away with him for a weekend, no matter how platonic he claims to feel. Don't accept invitations to visit his apartment. Don't sit too close to him, and don't tell him your troubles. Don't dance in the dark. Keep the overhead lighting on. Don't allow him to spend much time or money on you, and don't accept costly or intimate gifts.

If he still hasn't gotten the message, you'll have to be a little firmer. Turn away a kiss by remaining composed and very cool. Don't scream, "How dare you!" Don't laugh at him. Slapping him in the face is rather extreme punishment for expressing a perfectly natural desire. One girl we know uses a rather novel turndown. When a man she doesn't particularly care for begins to get amorous, she looks concerned and says, "Please be careful. You'll unhook my wooden leg."

What if you don't know. You may be interested in him, but want more time to think about it. In that case, you can say any one of the hundred variations of "not now," or "not yet." But don't lie. Don't let yourself get involved in a lengthy discussion and *never* let a man talk you into it.

If the answer is yes, then feel "yes" and look "yes."

Try to walk the admittedly fine line between being coy and being aggressive. Be spontaneous and ready to go whenever he is. If he calls you early on Sunday to say, "It's too beautiful to stay in the city. Let's drive out to the shore for a lobster lunch," don't assume he's called four other girls before he called you. Take him at his word.

Take advantage of chance meetings. You've met him before and you're interested. Now you're standing next to him in a crowded elevator. It's 6 P.M. on a weekday and you've nothing to do. Wait for him to make the first move. If it's not forthcoming, you take the initiative. Invent something fast and ask him to join you. Say you're on the way to Brentano's to pick out a book for your father's birthday. Invite him to come along and help. If he accepts, one thing will probably lead to another.

However, unless you're positive you want to end up in bed with him, don't take him directly home. See what develops after you've bought your book. If it's sharing a spaghetti supper and a half-bottle of Chianti, then you can invite him up for the traditional nightcap without committing yourself. Of course, if you do commit yourself, then you will have embarked upon AN AFFAIR.

Having an affair, learning how to enjoy it and knowing when to end it is a terribly complex business as you will see if you will kindly read the following pages.

CHAPTER IX

"Women get married . . . broads get laid . . . ladies have affairs. . . ."
—A FLIGHT OFFICER FLYING FOR A MAJOR AIRLINE WHO SHOULD KNOW BETTER

"This Is the Nicest Affair I've Ever Had."

An affair is a free-lance relationship designed to meet the current needs of both partners. Ideally, it should be flexible and not binding. At the same time, each of you should understand the other's present feelings and expectations. Or look at it this way. An affair should be a short-term contract which comes up for renewal often enough for both partners to alter it if they so desire. The greater the understanding, the more honest and healthier the affair.

The only trouble is that many people don't understand their own motivations for having an affair. They think to themselves, "I like the guy. Maybe I'm even in love with him. So let's have an affair and see how it turns out." By "having an affair," they generally mean sleeping with a man. But important as this is, that's only part of it. A woman has an affair because she has certain needs she wants fulfilled, and she believes a particular man can fulfill them. And these needs should not be vague or undefined. Quite often, this isn't easy. It's hard to be totally objective with yourself, especially when your deepest feelings are involved. Perhaps looking at a few typical affairs will be of some help.

Nancy and David

Nancy is a biochemist at an eastern university. She is over thirty, and strikingly beautiful. She is also very independent and content with the kind of life she has built for herself. She is at ease with her intellectual friends, and is just slightly disdainful of anybody who works with his hands. Then one rainy night, she met David. Her car had gotten a flat and she was trying to wrestle off the old tire as best she could, spitting mad and soaked to the skin, when suddenly he appeared and offered to help. As she watched him work she knew he was a man used to hard, physical exertion. Probably a construction worker, she thought. When he finished, he stood and looked down at her with smiling grey eyes. There was an instant chemical reaction, and both of them knew it.

"Thank you," she said holding out her hand and introducing herself. "I thought the age of chivalry was dead."

"Not quite," he replied. "My name is David Lloyd. And I don't think I've ever seen a wetter, madder female." They both laughed. "You know," he said. "I'd like to buy you a beer, but I don't think they'd let us into any bar."

"No, I don't think they would," Nancy agreed. She looked him straight in the eye. "Why don't you come up to my place? It's not far. I can fix us something to drink and we can both dry off."

"Done," he said. "You lead and I'll follow."

As Nancy showed him the way in her car, she thought to herself there would be more to the evening than a few drinks. But it was a development she was prepared for and mature enough to handle.

David, it turned out, was a salvage diver who regularly journeyed all over the world in pursuit of his profession. He was full of wonderfully amusing and colorful stories, and was great company. Before the first hour was up, there was an unspoken agreement that he would spend the night. Their sex was exciting and satisfying.

Early the next morning, after a breakfast of eggs and coffee, David and Nancy kissed warmly and parted. He subsequently went on to a job in Dakar, and she returned to her lab and the amino acids project that was currently absorbing her. They would occasionally think of one another, but they would never again meet.

Theirs was the perfect one-nighter or short-term affair. It left both partners with good feelings, but no unrealized demands. Many people are entirely incapable of this kind of liaison. They are too guilt-ridden, possessive or greedy. On the other hand, those who go in for one-nighters to the exclusion of any other sort of contact are probably fearful of emotional as well as physical intimacy.

Amy and Phillip

Amy and Phillip are both librarians. You know what people say about librarians. But it's not true, at least not in their case. They first met while standing next to one another at the registration desk in the Washington hotel where their regional librarian's convention was being held. Both had come from small cities and both were alone. Phillip offered to hold Amy's briefcase while she filled out her registration form, which is the grown-up variation of the let-me-carry-your-books routine and very effective. They introduced themselves and spoke briefly. The next morning, they found themselves in the same workshop. The next evening, they found themselves in the same bed.

Both were a little surprised at how uninhibited they felt and how rapidly their affair had progressed. What they didn't know was that being put down in a strange city will do this to almost everyone.

The minute most people step aboard a plane, they're ready for new experiences and eager for new adventures. The stewardess sets the mood. She greets you with a sweet smile and a pillow for your head. You want a drink? A Scotch on the rocks materializes magically. You're hungry? A steak and apple pie appear at your elbow. After an hour of this treatment, you're convinced that the world really is your oyster, and that anything you want will be yours, including sex.

Each convention has many Amys and Phillips. Most of the time their relationships last until the farewell breakfast. Sometimes, it "takes" and becomes something more permanent. Or sometimes, it means exchanging Christmas cards with the message, "Hope to see you in Atlanta at next year's convention."

Miriam and Harold

Here we are on the French Riviera near Cannes. And look, over there in that snappy red sports car, isn't that Grace Kelly and Cary Grant? No, it's Miriam and Harold, playing Grace Kelly and Cary Grant.

Harold is a shoe buyer from Cincinnati. Miriam is an executive secretary at a large insurance company in Hartford. Throughout the long, drizzly winter months, both dreamed of an exotic vacation in far-off places. Both scrimped and saved, spending their evenings with booklets of travel literature, trying to decide where to go. Both chose the south of France, and both spent many hours weaving elegant fantasies about the adventures they would encounter once they were there.

Both dreams had one feature in common. Neither Miriam nor Harold saw himself alone as each casually riffled the stacks of chips lying on the gaming table of the casino.

Miriam's dream centered around a stranger who would mysteriously enter her life the day she arrived and would, just as mysteriously, fade away the day she boarded the plane to return to Hartford. Harold saw himself in the company of a stunning Swedish starlet who had fallen unaccountably in love with him, and who was partial to nude, moonlight swimming in isolated coves. They would share this brief moment together, and their parting would be hard, yet bittersweet. Later, she would become an international star and perhaps one day their paths would cross again, and they would recapture briefly the ecstasy they had once shared. Harold had quite an imagination. As you can see, although neither one of them knew of the existence of the other, they needed each other to make their private dreams come true.

They met on the beach at Cannes. Harold suggested a drink, and asked if he could take her picture. Miriam hitched up her bikini and posed for him. The drink turned into lunch, and later they swam together in the blue Mediterranean. The next day, Harold rented a car and, driving faster than he ever had in his life, took her up into the mountains. There, they found a turn-off with a breathtaking view where they opened the picnic hamper packed by the hotel chef. The afternoon was perfect, and ended with Miriam in Harold's arms. They spent two golden, sun-and-sex-filled weeks together, and finally parted, vowing to write and see each other again. Of course, they never did. They knew that if they met in the familiar surroundings of home, Harold would be what he was, a shoe buyer from Cincinnati, and Miriam, a secretary from Hartford. Gone forever would be the dream the two of them would always cherish, the dream of being Cary Grant and Grace Kelly on the French Riviera.

Carla and Dan

Dan is a vice president of a large paper firm headquartered in New York City. His greying temples, perfectly cut suits and tortoise-shell glasses mark him as an important man. He knows his way around good restaurants and good hotels. Several times a year, the business in his handsome attaché case brings him to Los Angeles.

Each time he comes, his first telephone call is to a girl in an apartment on the beach. She expects his call, for he has written to say he is coming. He checks into a hotel, and then hails a taxi which he takes to her place. Together, he and the girl have a three-day honeymoon, interrupted now and then by business appointments. Dan calls home every night to see how his wife and the kids are doing. This is a precaution to prevent her from telephoning his hotel unexpectedly.

Carla, his girl, is a computer programmer. She is quiet, relaxed, intelligent. She met Dan a few years ago when his firm was first installing some electronic data processing devices in the Los Angeles office. He was impressed by her efficiency, and by her good looks. One night, after they had both worked late, he invited her to dinner. That night, they slept together. Carla knows Dan is married, but that doesn't matter to her. She accepts the relationship for what it is because it meets a certain kind of need. For Dan, it is a pleasant, safe diversion. Neither demands too much from the other. One day, undoubtedly, Carla will get married and their transcontinental affair will come to a halt. Dan understands this and, when the time comes, he should accept it philosophically.

Barbara and Paul

Barbara is a secretary at a large auto-leasing company. She works for Paul, who is a regional maintenance manager. She also sleeps with him on those evenings when he can arrange to be absent from his home and family in suburbia.

Barbara has a small, orderly apartment facing a park, just a few minutes walk from her office. She is extremely feminine, enjoys cooking, housekeeping and sewing. She loves being Paul's secretary, but is less enthusiastic about being his sometime-mistress.

He, in turn, appreciates her efficiency and care. He welcomes the peace of her small apartment, contrasting it with his noisy, turmoil-filled household where he often finds an army of small children creating chaos while his wife looks on, tired and defeated.

It would seem that theirs is an ideal arrangement. But it's not, because Barbara wants more than just casual sex. Paul needs the comfort of somebody who will take care of him and give him her undivided attention. Barbara gives this to him, but he has little to offer in return.

Paul has explained to Barbara that his family is more of a responsibility than a joy, but that he takes his responsibility seriously enough to prevent him from establishing anything more permanent with her.

She has said she understands. She has told herself that expecting more from Paul is unrealistic and immature. But that doesn't keep her from wanting it. This creates periods of uncomfortable silence between them. Sometimes, as she sits quietly mending, Paul senses she is on the verge of making some demand, and this worries him. Another worry is the hint he heard last week at lunch that a promotion to national headquarters might be in the works for him.

Of course, he might arrange to have Barbara transferred with him, but how would that look to everyone? And his wife wasn't exactly stupid. If the transfer came through, he would have to leave Barbara behind. Perhaps the fair thing to do would be to end the relationship. That would set Barbara free to find another man. Yet he didn't want to give her up. And what would such a move do to their working relationship. It would make it exceedingly uncomfortable to say the least.

The affair between Barbara and Paul is essentially unsatisfactory to both. But then they fell into a common trap. Office romances are never without their difficulties. As Eric Berne once remarked, bosses should never get involved with their secretaries because it's easier to find a good mistress than it is to find a good secretary. And, as he said, the opposite is also true. It's easier to find a good lover than a good boss.

Linda and Joe and Charlie and Mike and Ed and Ralph and...

Linda works as a teller in a New Orleans bank. She has short, curly brown hair, blue-violet eyes and a sensational body. Many afternoons, shortly after she comes home from work, her telephone rings. A voice asks, "Free, tonight?" If Linda is, a date is set for dinner.

She meets the caller at a little restaurant in the French Quarter. His name is Joe and he's a sportswriter for a national wire service. He's a little older than she is, fairly attractive but somewhat overweight. He likes good food, good liquor—and Linda. After a few drinks and a long, leisurely dinner, they go back to her apartment. They talk, have another drink and make love. Both of them enjoy it.

When Linda wakes up the next morning, she sees Joe, a towel around his middle, coming out of the shower. "Don't get up," he says. "It's early yet." He dresses, kisses her and leaves. When Linda gets up, she finds an envelope on her dresser with a $50 bill in it. With the money is a note that says, "See you in a few weeks."

Linda is a semi-pro. She isn't "in the life," a term which means someone who earns a living solely from prostitution. She doesn't even consider herself a hooker. "I'm just part-time," she explains. "And the truth is, I'm just more honest about it than those who accept expensive presents but think they're doing it for love. Besides, I don't do it with just anybody. I've got to like him and enjoy his company." Linda enjoys the company of a lot of men.

You'd be surprised at how many Lindas there are in the world. Recently, some ingrate ratted on a group of suburban housewives who had actually organized themselves into a ring. They were available in the mornings and early afternoons at a local motel. But they went off duty after three in the afternoon so they could be at home when their children arrived back from school.

"We do it for pin money," one woman was quoted as saying. "It sure beats dusting and ironing any day."

Kim and Ben

Ben has a highly developed sense of the romantic, and enough money to indulge his whim. He met Kim one spring night at a friend's party. She was wearing a flowing chiffon dress and flowers in her hair. "Let's drive up to Vermont tonight," he said by way of greeting. "I know this great little inn way up in the mountains."

"Let's talk first," she said. They talked. And early the next morning, just as the sun was coming up, they arrived at the inn in the Vermont hills.

"Where shall we go next weekend?" he asked her that night.

"Let's fly to San Francisco," she suggested.

Ben gave a sigh of contentment. He had finally met somebody who shared his tastes.

In the weeks that followed, they camped on the shores of Long Island Sound, flew to Nantucket to sail, hiked the Appalachian Trail and then drove to Canada to spend a vacation together.

Ben and Kim are one of a growing number of couples who take part in traveling affairs. We don't know whether traveling is the excuse for sex, or if sex is the excuse for traveling. In either case, these people, with plenty of time and money, seem to enjoy sex in different settings. One of the things they have in common is a tireless wanderlust. Glamour is a necessary ingredient to their relationship.

Usually, these couples never stay in one place long enough to focus on each other. As a result, they seldom manage to see their partners as individuals, and the affair is generally a shallow one that will eventually peter out.

Ursula and Marvin

Marvin is a dress manufacturer. Several years ago, when expanding his company to include a young, chic and expensive junior line of sportswear, he hired a young, chic and expensive junior designer named Ursula. Marvin soon discovered that, in addition to being a good designer, Ursula was clever about promotion, advertising and publicity. Even more, she had a flair for creating pace-setting fashions.

Watching the profits grow, Marvin began to pay more attention to Ursula. He took to asking her advice, and began including her in business lunches and conferences. One night, after a late dinner with some out-of-town buyers, Marvin took Ursula home. There were some business matters still to be settled, so she invited him in.

Several weeks later, he took her to London to help him work out some overseas distribution arrangements. A few months later, at her suggestion, they took a trip to Mexico to look at some local fabrics they thought they might import. Several months after that, Marvin made her a vice president.

Within a few short years, they had established a nationwide network of fashionable boutiques and Ursula and Marvin were partners. During this entire time, they had good sex together and good fun but, most of all, they had good business.

The principal difference between this affair and the dreary relationship between Barbara and Paul was that Ursula and Marvin were equals, each of whom had professional and personal qualities to contribute to the other. It was no accident that their affair flourished because it did not depend solely on sex. In their case, they had many mutual interests, and sex was merely pleasant icing on their cake.

Leslie and Larry

Leslie is a painter. Larry is a painter. Both have studios in Philadelphia where they lead separate, busy, relatively happy lives. Someone offered Leslie the rental of a barn in Bucks County for the summer, but the cost was more than she could afford. Still, the idea was too good to pass up, so she asked Larry if he wanted to go halves with her. Before he agreed, he asked her a few questions.

What would their living arrangements be like?

Would they share everything, including a bed?

Even if they were together, would they lead separate social lives?

Would each respect the other's privacy so they could both get some work done?

Gee, it never occurred to Leslie to settle these matters in advance, but she said she'd think about it. A few days later she came back to Larry. About separate social lives, why didn't they both cut away from everybody they knew and get some work done. As for privacy, how about each one of them setting aside certain hours of the day when the other one could not intrude. She didn't know about sleeping together. Why didn't they just move in and see what happened? It was only for a couple of months. Larry said okay.

By the middle of June, they were fully installed. Before July was a week gone, they were playing married. He painted, she painted. Both got great suntans all over. On Labor Day, they divided up the linseed oil and rags, and went back to their separate pads.

They continued to see each other and considered the possibility of another summer together, this time in an old grist mill in Connecticut. It never once crossed their minds to live together in the city. Theirs is strictly a summertime romance, made possible by a joint escape from routine.

You've heard of summer affairs. They blossom like the flowers each June. If both partners understand what they're doing, it can be a beautiful experience.

Ellen and Will

This is an example of an affair headed for trouble. Ellen works as a media buyer for an advertising agency in St. Louis. She's got those fresh-out-of-the-shower good looks and is clever, especially at math.

Will is an accountant with a wife and family in suburbia. He had a crew cut for years until the day he realized that only he and Marine drill sergeants still had crew cuts. The day he decided to acquire sideburns and some Bob Dylan records was the day he also acquired Ellen.

Under the pretext of taking an advanced course at a local university, Will is free every Tuesday and Thursday evening. He and Ellen have dinner together, then go back to her apartment.

Being a practical girl, Ellen realizes that she and Will will never have more than a few evenings a week together, and she accepts that. Two evenings with Will and five to live her own life is a formula she can follow. But Will can't.

He has a tendency to question her closely about her activities on Monday, Wednesday and Friday evenings, and to positively grill her about her whereabouts on weekend nights. He often calls her at about eleven o'clock just to say he's mad about her. Ellen suspects his calls are more than an opportunity to whisper sweet nothings in her ear. She suspects they're something of a bed check. Sometimes she doesn't answer the telephone.

Will has explained to Ellen that there's no real affection between him and his wife, that they're just staying together because of the children, and that he'll leave her the day the youngest goes off to college. He has suggested that Ellen not date other men. She has suggested that that might be slightly unfair. Just last week, he suggested he might like to have a key to her apartment. She suggested she didn't think much of the idea.

Ellen still more or less enjoys her Tuesdays and Thursdays with Will, and she used to enjoy his constant telephoning. Now she's wondering what he'll say when she tells him she's planning a trip to South America this summer. When they first began seeing each other, they agreed that she was a free agent. Ellen keeps reminding Will of that conversation, but she's convinced he regards her as his own personal piece of property, to be kept in the deep freeze and warmed up on Tuesday and Thursday nights.

Louise and Bart

Bart is a lawyer. Louise is a receptionist at a very elegant beauty establishment. Bart lived with his mother until she died a few years ago. Louise was married at 17 and divorced at 26. She had no children. Both of them are in their forties and have worked out an arrangement that is mutually satisfactory. They have agreed to go steady.

Bart and Louise met in the waiting room of a dentist's office almost ten years ago. They began dating occasionally, sharing a dinner, a movie, a drink at Louise's apartment. They discovered they both loved music. They considered living together, but Bart felt uncomfortable about leaving his mother alone. The subject of marriage simply never came up.

Bart's law practice keeps him busy several evenings a week. He continues to keep the same apartment he shared with his mother. He and Louise see each other several times a week. They have sex either at his place or at hers. They almost never spend the entire night together. An exception was a week-long vacation in Bermuda last year.

Their relationship is excellent in every way because it suits their current needs. They talk about their situation quite frankly and admit they are too accustomed to independent living to make good permanent partners. Both say they love each other. Perhaps, someday, they'll marry. Who knows? But it isn't a burning issue with them now.

Libby and Billy

Libby, a handsome lady in her early forties, lives in a suburban Colonial just outside Nashville. Her children are in school and seldom at home in the winter. They spend their summers in camp. Her husband is out of town on business almost as much as he is at home.

Libby's tragedy is that she needs to feel she is wanted. But even that is denied her since her family has made it clear they are all self-sufficient and require very little of her.

Last summer, Libby and her husband decided they wanted wood paneling and bookshelves installed in their family room. Libby's husband was too busy to do it, and suggested they hire the eldest son of the family next door who was home from college and looking for work.

Billy is young, handsome, muscular, and works with his shirt off. It was clear to Libby that he was also extremely shy and needed to gain self-confidence. She decided that, if she could do nothing for her family, at least she could bring some happiness and assurance to Billy. One morning, when Billy reported for work, he was met by Libby wearing only a light robe.

When the summer ended, Bill returned to college and Libby knew she would see him only on occasional vacations. But she didn't mind. She had accomplished what she had set out to do. However, the experience gave her a new lease on life. There must be hundreds of uncertain, insecure Billys she could help.

Just last week, she found one. A young, local electrician was hired to install lighting on the outdoor patio. It was possible, she told him, that the bedroom also might have to be rewired.

Adrienne and Andrew

On a narrow, tree-lined street in Georgetown, the houses are charming, tiny, authentic Colonials. The rents are astronomical. Two houses in from the corner lives Andrew, a successful TV network commentator. Directly next door, in the third house from the corner, lives Adrienne, the fashion coordinator for one of Washington's largest department stores.

Adrienne has a pocket-size swimming pool behind

her house, and Andrew's great pride is his garden. Last year, they had the fence between the two removed. Andrew and Adrienne share everything except the same front door. She shops, cooks, often helps him entertain. He manages her finances, reminds her to pay her automobile insurance and helps keep her checkbook balanced.

They have been loving neighbors for the past five years. From time to time, Andrew, the more practical of the pair, considers how much time and money they could save if they were to share the same quarters. But he recognizes that neither of them are strictly monogamous. Each has had affairs with others during their time together and, so far, it has not altered their relationship. It was one of the basic rules they established a few months after Adrienne rang Andrew's doorbell to ask for help in starting her car which had stalled in the middle of their narrow street. Unlike the situation between Ellen and Will, it was an understanding that both of them continued to honor.

Both have been married before, and neither has children. Both enjoy the flexibility of their present relationship and neither feels alone. Companionship and good sex without ties form the basis of their relationship. Both Andrew and Adrienne say they are happy with things just as they are.

Doris and Fred

Neither Fred nor Doris is happily married. Fred and his wife quarrel constantly. Doris and her husband ignore one another. One evening, at a neighborhood party, Doris approached Fred and asked if he would consider taking on the chairmanship of the PTA. "We really need a man like you," she said warmly. They agreed to meet for lunch to discuss it, and so the next day, Doris, who was feeling curiously excited, took the 10:28 into the city. After a long, enjoyable lunch,

Fred was still undecided. A few evenings later, they met again to talk about it. Doris' husband was working late.

As they talked, Doris realized she was feeling things she hadn't felt for a long time. The talk veered away from the PTA and into more personal matters. Fred reached out for her. They kissed. He suggested they go upstairs. Doris said no. Tomorrow, she said. At a motel.

They began to meet regularly at various motels on the outskirts of the city. Occasionally, when Doris' husband is out of town, Fred crosses the patch of grass that separates their two houses. Once, they even managed a weekend together.

Neither Fred's wife nor Doris' husband suspects, or so they think. They talk about divorce and remarriage. Doris is convinced it's a good idea. Fred isn't so sure. It would make for very complicated financial arrangements, and it would be hard on the children. Maybe they'd be better off staying as they are. After all, aren't things better now than before they had one another?

Sandy and Rob

They live in a respectable middle-class apartment building on Long Island. Each morning as they kiss each other goodbye and leave for their jobs, they appear as unremarkable as any other young suburban couple. But the name on their mailbox is Callahan-Ferrara. Not some odd hyphenated combination, but two separate last names, the first clue that this pair lives together without benefit of a formal marriage ceremony.

Sandy is a nurse, blonde, snub-nosed, her long hair twisted up and pinned beneath her starched white cap. No one could appear less like what was once called a painted lady. Yet past generations, and even not-so-distant generations—such as her own parents—accuse her of "living in sin."

Rob is a teacher. His hair is slightly longer than most, but his suit and tie are conventional. Their apartment is neat, colorful, but quite casual. There are no matched sets of china or silverware, booty from the engagement and wedding parties that other couples have had.

They met in college, dated for awhile, then parted. Last year, they met again when their jobs brought them to the same Long Island town. They dated once more, and agreed to live together.

Both are committed to the idea of remaining unmarried. And neither makes any attempt to hide their unmarried state. "Both of our families know," Sandy says, "and both think it's scandalous. They're so uptight about something we think is perfectly natural."

Sandy's mother even made the effort of journeying from her home in Harrisburg, Pennsylvania to reason with her daughter. They had quite a scene in Mrs. Ferrara's hotel room. Mrs. Ferrara indignantly refused an invitation to stay with Sandy and Rob.

"But why *can't* you get married?" Mrs. Ferrara implored. "Other people do."

"Is marriage really that important to you, Mother?" Sandy wanted to know.

"Of course it is," Mrs. Ferrara replied. "It's terribly important."

"But *why?*" Sandy asked. "Can't two people just love each other and live together?"

"No," her mother said firmly. "You just don't understand, Sandy. I should think you'd want to get married out of a sense of self-respect."

It was Sandy's turn to look confused. "I don't know what you mean."

"Don't you have any feeling of shame?" Mrs. Ferrara asked. "What do you suppose the butcher thinks of you when you come in to pick up an order of meat? You don't take the trouble to hide the fact that you're not married. So he knows exactly what you are."

"Mother!" Sandy said in a shocked voice. "Honestly, you don't make any sense at all. First of all, you tell me that marriage is the most important step a woman can take. And then you tell me I should get married in order to spare the feelings of my neighborhood butcher. If that's not the lousiest reason for getting married I ever heard of, I don't know what is. You say you respect the institution of marriage. Well, I think I respect it more than you do."

Mrs. Ferrara returned to Harrisburg, feeling lonely, frustrated and cut off from her daughter. But deep in her heart, a few doubts stirred. Maybe Sandy *was* right when she said that her relationship with Rob was more important to her than the good opinion of the world, and that right now their relationship was better than it would be if they were bound to each other legally. She just didn't know.

"Things are perfect—for now," Rob says. "We share everything, including an old Volvo. We also share the work. She cleans. I clean. Actually, I'm a better cook than she is."

"We've talked about having children together," Sandys says, "and how we'd feel about not being married then. We haven't decided."

"Who knows where we'll be a year from now?" Rob points out. "If we split, we split. We don't worry too much about it."

What about the problems of breaking up a shared home if they decide to separate? "It'll be rough," Rob concedes. "But would it be any easier if we were married? Anyway, it will have been worth it. We've had more in the last eighteen months of living together than we would have had if we'd been living apart and just dating."

By the thousands, young people across the country

are coming to the same conclusion. To them, the old dating game, where a girl's success was measured by the number of fellows she could attract, is artificial and shallow.

"I just hate it," one girl said recently. "Under the old rules, you were encouraged to see as many boys as possible. It was considered perfectly okay if you let them kiss you goodnight. And there was this smug tolerance of couples necking heavily in the back seat of a car. Maybe you were being a little bit naughty, but letting a boy put his hand in your pants wasn't *that* bad. But God help you, if you *went all the way!*"

Another complained bitterly that the dating game virtually guaranteed tension and repression. "Also," she said, "it was almost impossible to develop a real or a meaningful relationship with a boy. You were both so hung up on the sex thing that you never thought about anything else. This way, sex is just one activity among many that we do together."

Does this casual attitude toward the sexual relationship encourage promiscuity? The dean of a prominent eastern women's college thought not.

"Sex has always played a role on campus," she said. "But because no one wanted to talk about it, and no one wanted to notice it, it was a problem. In the years that I've been here, I must have talked to hundreds of girls about their emotional crises. Nearly all of them had to do with their relationships with men. Now, however, we don't see that kind of problem too often. And from what I've gathered, the girls don't 'sleep around.' They're very mature about it. In fact," she added dryly, "we've found they're being more careful about whom they sleep with than their mothers were."

One thing that both students and educators agree on is that a truly satisfying sex life usually results in improved academic performance.

"Oh, wow!" says Alex, a junior at a large midwestern

university, "does it ever! Where I come from, the old folks sure had this double-standard thing going for them. You know the crap. It's okay for boys, but nice girls don't. Well, all I knew were nice girls, so what was I supposed to do? My folks had drummed it into me that I should never take advantage of a nice girl, that I'd be considered an absolute rat if I did. So I ended up thinking about sex all the time and beating my meat every night. My first year here it was even worse. It got so bad, I was in danger of flunking out. Then I met Gerry. We really got into each other. I discovered she was as hung up as I was, so we both decided to say to hell with it. Next thing you know, we're living together off campus, and is that ever a beautiful scene! Here we thought we were doing something secret and special, and we found out there are hundreds of couples into the same bag. We've made lots of great friends. We both study hard, and my grades have gone way up. Hell, isn't that why my folks sent me to college in the first place?"

In a way, the young people on campuses are the lucky ones. They live in a climate that is permissive and tolerant of sexual behavior. They are youthful enough to enter into affairs with each other without having to consider marriage. No one expects an undergraduate to take on the additional responsibility of a wife or a husband.

Try as she might, a single girl working and living in a city cannot completely escape the pressures on her to get married. But she also cherishes her independence. In attempting to balance these two opposing forces, many girls settle on having an affair.

As we've said, this can work out successfully if you understand fully why you are embarking on this new course. At the same time, you should ask yourself a few searching questions.

What does he expect from you? If it's only good

times and good sex, are you capable of giving that with no strings attached? How much will you suffer if those are his terms?

If he's single and determined to avoid marriage, can you honestly accept that? No fooling?

If his is a lukewarm or worn-out marriage, and he's ready to adore you passionately for three hours a week and then exit, can you accept that?

Are you using this affair mostly to achieve security, glamour, a sense of personal worth, and a relief from boredom? Unfortunately, lots and lots of affairs have these motivations as their basis. But they are as poor a foundation for building an affair as they are for building a marriage. Expect trouble.

Do you fully understand the difference between an affair and a marriage? Marriage is supposed to be a lifetime insurance policy which prevents one partner from taking advantage of the other. It really doesn't work out that way, but it does afford certain kinds of protection. Marriages are harder to terminate than affairs.

On the other hand, many marriages are dishonest. It may be an inflexible contract, but nothing can force one partner to continue to like, love or even be humane to the other.

An affair need not be dishonest. Yet too many of them are because people find it difficult to be honest with either themselves or with others. How easy it is to say, "Of course I still love you," even though you suspect you love him less than before. Oh sure, your motives may be the best. You don't want to hurt him. It's not *that* bad. You're still comfortable together. So what if he doesn't spark the same kind of dazzling electricity you once felt. You can live with it.

We're sorry to have to tell you this, but these are the first signs of trouble. You cannot afford to ignore them. If you let things slide, you're bound to end up in a painful scene. But take comfort in this. No relationship ever runs its course without periods of self-doubt. When these rocky times hit, what should you do? Is there anyone or anything that can be of help?

A trusted friend might. It can be either a man or a woman. Sometimes a man is better. He can cast a masculine perspective on the situation. Don't, however, unburden yourself to a man you suspect wants to be more than a friend. A girl friend can help enormously just by listening. But don't ask her to call him for a heart-to-heart talk. It's not fair to her and, besides, it won't work.

What else can help? Your mother? Maybe. Your father? Never. A punching bag? A week in bed with the pillow over your head? A trip to New Zealand? They might take your mind off things for a time, but the best source of help is *him*.

A little honest anger often clears the air. There's been a great deal written lately about creative fighting, and it does have its merits.

Cindy and Art had been living together for nearly a year. As far as either of us could tell, it was a happy, mutually satisfactory relationship. Then, little by little, it began to turn sour. We first suspected it one evening when Cindy telephoned asking if she could drop in. We thought she meant with Art, but when she arrived, she was alone.

"He's working late," was her reply to our question about where he was. "He's always finding some excuse to keep from coming home," she added. Cindy seemed listless that night, without her usual bounce and energy. She found it difficult to concentrate and would lose the thread of a conversation. Finally she admitted she was worried.

"I don't know," she said in a despair-filled tone, "maybe I've changed, maybe he's changed, but it's no fun anymore. Even making love has fallen into a routine."

"Have you talked about it with him?" Trudy wanted to know.

"We don't talk about anything anymore," Cindy replied bitterly. "You'd think we were old Ma and Pa, married forty years and just sitting in our rocking chairs."

I was shocked. "But that doesn't sound like Art," I protested. "I've never known him to be still for more than a minute."

"Oh, we talk all right," Cindy explained. "But we don't say anything to each other. It's, 'Well, how did things go at the office today?'" she mimicked. "And, 'Would you mind if I had the first bath?'"

"Well, at least you're not fighting," I said, trying to be cheerful.

Cindy made a face. "You can say that again. He's the politest bastard I've ever met. He's so polite, sometimes I could just scream."

"Does he irritate you?" Trudy asked.

"Incessantly," Cindy declared. "And in a thousand ways."

"Like what?" Trudy persisted.

"Like he never, *never* puts the top back on the toothpaste tube," Cindy cried out. "And that means that when I get to it, it has usually dried out. Or the toothpaste has run part-way out of the tube and made a mess on the sink."

Trudy shook her head gravely. "Oh, that's serious, Cindy. That really is."

"Now you're making fun of me," Cindy said angrily. "You might think it's a little thing, but when it happens day after day after day, it gets on your nerves, I can tell you."

"Don't tell me," Trudy replied. "Tell him. Have you ever told him the habit annoys you?"

"No," Cindy admitted. "I haven't."

"Then you don't have any right to bitch," Trudy declared firmly. "Look, one of the reasons that Rachel and I get on is because we tell each other if one of us does something that annoys the other. We work it out."

"All sweetness and light, I suppose," Cindy said sarcastically.

"No, not all sweetness and light," Trudy shot back. "We fight like hell sometimes. But by God, the air is cleared afterwards."

Cindy thought that over. "Hmm," she said at last. "I wonder why Art's never criticized a thing I've ever done?"

"Oh, you're probably perfect, Cindy," Trudy answered. "Not a single flaw that bugs him."

"That's impossible," Cindy said flatly.

"You know what?" Trudy said after a pause. "I agree with you."

Cindy seemed excited about her new discovery. "You know, I've never thought of it before, but in nearly a year of being together, Art and I have never had a serious disagreement. We've never had anything like a fight. He's never told me anything I do that he doesn't like. And, come to think of it, I've never said a word to him. I've never said anything about the toothpaste. I've never said a thing about him always leaving his shoes in the middle of the floor so I fall all over them when I go to the bathroom in the middle of the night. I haven't told him how I hate that hair tonic he's wearing." She stood up suddenly, her eyes flashing with anger. "Thank you," she said to us. "Thank you. You've made something very clear to me. That I've been a dope to take what he's been dishing out." She started to move to the door.

"Are you leaving already?" Trudy asked.

Cindy nodded. "Yes," she said. "I want to be home to greet that son of a bitch when he gets there."

The next evening, shortly after six, our doorbell rang. It was Cindy, back again, but this time full of sparkle and vitality.

"I've only got a moment," she said. "I'm on my way home from work, but I just had to see you first. After all, you were the ones who put me straight."

Cindy's story came out in a rush. When Art had let himself into the apartment the previous night, Cindy was, as she had promised, ready for him. From what she said, we gathered they'd had quite a row. But what surprised Cindy was the way Art struck back. He rattled off a list of her faults and told her they had been driving him up the wall for months. She demanded to know why he hadn't spoken up before. He wanted to know the same thing himself. Suddenly, at the height of their argument, both broke out laughing simultaneously.

"And then you were able to sit down and discuss your differences rationally," Trudy said.

"Well, no," Cindy replied. "Not then. First we had to make up." An ecstatic smile flooded her face. "And oh, it hasn't been like that for months. Later, in bed, we talked things over. I've never felt closer to Art. It's a whole new life for us both." She glanced at her watch. "I've got to run. I promised Art I'd be ready at seven. We're going out to celebrate."

She paused at the door and looked back at us. "You know what I like best about having fights?" she asked. We shook our heads. "Making up," she said. "Art and I plan to have lots more fights—just so we can make up afterwards." The next instant she had closed the door and was gone.

The story of Art and Cindy had a happy ending. But sometimes, the differences are so fundamental they simply can't be patched up. Some affairs are going to end with pain for somebody. If that happens to you, and you're the one who's hurt, maybe your only consolation is that a broken affair is less destructive than a broken marriage. In any event, if your beautiful romance gets busted up, accept the fact that you're in for a bad time. What can we tell you that will help you get over him? Nothing, we're afraid. But we can tell you a few things *not* to do. It really isn't a good idea to:

Threaten to kill yourself.

Threaten to kill him.

Move away. (Unless, of course, you've been living together. In that case, moving is a pretty sound idea.)

Quit your job and join a religious order.

Write him a series of long letters saying it was all your fault and promising to change.

Hang around his front door.

Keep his picture on your dresser and cry every time you pass it.

Take to your bed for a month. (A week is the absolute maximum.)

Eat six gallons of chocolate ice cream at one sitting.

Marry the first guy who smiles at you.

Run up a $600 bill at Bergdorf Goodman.

Tell the full story, without omitting a single detail, to everyone you meet, including your grandmother.

Shoot up.

Smile and say it doesn't matter, you're glad it's over.

On the other hand, it IS a good idea to:

Breathe deep.

Do yoga.

Go for long walks (but not in his neighborhood).

Talk to a few selected friends.

Admit you're mad, hurt and feeling emotionally unstable.

After a week of feeling mad, hurt and emotionally unstable, find a new project, interest, class or friend. Get involved, and trust your old ally, time.

Things will get better. Believe us. We know. It's happened to both of us. You'll recover. We did. There will be someone else. We guarantee it.

Besides, it could be worse. You could be pregnant.

CHAPTER X

My father was the keeper of the Eddystone Light
And he slept with a mermaid one fine night.
From this union there came three,
A porpoise and a porgie, and the other was me.
—A SEA CHANTEY

Self-defense: The Pill and Karate

The mermaid could have used some of the advice you'll find in this chapter. With a little care, she could have frolicked with the lighthouse keeper on many a fine night without a worry in the world. Perhaps no one told her. In those days, the subject was never mentioned. Today, however, a girl needs all the information she can get about keeping up her defenses, both against men whom she wants no part of, as well as the man to whom she has willingly opened her arms. Of the two, the man who claims her love and shares her bed can unwittingly do her the more harm. She can bear his child at a time that neither one of them wants to assume the responsibilities of parenthood. It is a prospect most women dread above all others, and one that has kept many of them from experiencing the warmth and excitement of an intimate relationship with a man.

There is ample justification for this widespread fear. Even in this day of the Pill, some 300,000 unwanted babies are born each year to unmarried women. What is the reason for this appalling statistic? Ignorance, pure and simple. Despite the ready availability of masses of information, too many women are still ignorant of the practices and devices that can prevent pregnancy. In this area, too, a little knowledge is a dangerous thing. Birth-control experts report that a surprisingly high percentage of the female population uses methods that are ineffective and that are, in some cases, potentially harmful. Desipte the risk, these women persist in subjecting their bodies to unnecessary peril because they are too timid to get reliable information. Here, then, is the information you need to stay un-pregnant while single.

One of the oldest birth-control devices is the chastity belt. It was purportedly much favored by knights in the Middle Ages, who strapped a metal plate over milady's crotch and locked her into it with a key which he carried off to the crusades. There were two things about this device that were awkward. If the knight happened to bite the dust in battle, the key was lost forever. However, even if he survived, crusades had a habit of dragging on for years and years. A lady could be locked up tight for a long time. But, somehow, we doubt they really were. We have the suspicion that, with a little feminine ingenuity and the help of an enterprising blacksmith, most of the ladies managed to free themselves before their knight got into the next county. Still, while they were on, chastity belts were 100 percent effective against conception.

In all probability, the most ancient form of birth control is one that is mentioned in the Bible—with-

LAY IT ON THE LINE 199

drawal. This method calls for the man to quickly withdraw his penis from the vagina a fraction of a second before ejaculation. The man then has his actual climax outside the woman, and his semen does not enter her. Fine, in theory. But, as we have said, a drop of semen nearly always forms on the head of a man's penis well before orgasm. And since this drop can contain as many as 50,000 sperm, the method is hardly foolproof. In addition, the method goes against the grain of every natural instinct. A man instinctively wants to thrust forward during orgasm. If he practices withdrawal, he must learn to control himself, precisely at the moment when he has the least control. It is true that withdrawal is better than nothing, and some couples use it regularly. They are, however, living dangerously and on borrowed time. Withdrawal as a method of birth control is not recommended for either relaxation or safety.

Another time-honored practice is the so-called rhythm method. This calls for a couple to avoid intercourse during the woman's period of ovulation. Theoretically, it's a flawless method of birth control because pregnancy cannot occur unless the woman is ovulating. So, no sex during ovulation, no babies. The problem, however—and it's a major one—is to figure out the exact day when the egg is released from the ovary. Too many women make the fatal mistake of counting the days *after* menstruation to come up with an accurate idea of when ovulation will occur. But it's almost never that regular.

And besides, ovulation generally occurs fourteen days *before* the first day of the next menstrual period. The trick is to predict when the next period will begin, something which very few women can do with complete accuracy. To lengthen the odds even further, ovulation can occur on any day of the menstrual cycle, even during menstruation itself. Because of these reasons, rhythm is considered a very unreliable method of birth control.

A third method, widely used for many years, is the douche. The trouble here is that, immediately after intercourse, the woman must rush to the bathroom and wash out her vagina with a solution designed to inactivate sperm. Using a douche bag, which is a small rubber sac connected to a long plastic tube, the woman fits the nozzle of the tube into her vagina and, by squeezing the rubber bag, pumps in a solution.

What sort of a solution? The fashion changes with the times. Many products are sold over the counter at the corner drugstore, and one is probably just as effective as any other. Before she discovered the Pill, Betty Big Boobs had her own favorite formula—Coca Cola.

"If ah happened to forget mah diaphragm," she told us once, "ah'd always use Coke. Ah'd put a bottle on the bedside table, and take a little nip now and then. Later, ah'd use what was left as a douche. It worked every time. Ah tell you, they know what they're sayin' when they tell you that Coke is the pause that refreshes."

Does it really work? We were skeptical when Betty first touted its virtues, but there is a scientific basis for her confidence. Warm Coca Cola contains carbonic acid which kills sperm cells. To be fully effective, the Coke should fizz up into the vagina and into every crease of the vaginal lining. Even so, Coke, or any other douche for that matter, is not really recommended. No solution presently known can wash out every sperm that enters the vagina during intercourse. What about a douche made of a household disinfectant? No! No! You'll destroy the lining of your vagina.

More reliable are vaginal suppositories. These are little cylinders made of wax and are available without prescription in the drugstore. They are designed to be placed in the vagina immediately before intercourse. The idea is that the body temperature will melt the wax and release sperm-killing chemicals. What often happens, though, is that the wax doesn't melt. Even if it does, some sperm may get through.

Better still are jellies, cream or vaginal foam. These are also readily obtainable at drugstores. The jelly, cream or foam is squeezed into an applicator and, just before intercourse, the applicator is inserted deep into the vagina where the material is deposited by pressing a plunger. A chemical in these products inactivates sperm. Of the three, foam is most often recommended, and is considered about 90 percent effective. Sometimes, though, the foam produces unwanted side effects, such as irritation or a burning sensation in both the man and woman.

Another variation is to use vaginal foaming tablets. Again your neighborhood druggist is the source. The tablet is moistened with saliva or water and placed deep into the vagina *at least five minutes before intercourse*. The foam produced covers the mouth of the uterus and prevents the sperm from entering. A new tablet must be used at least five minutes before each intercourse. Also, you must take care they are properly moistened. Douching after intercourse is not recommended, because this will wash away the protective seal.

A similar method is the use of a sponge and foam. A sperm-destroying liquid or powder is sold in drugstores along with a soft, plastic sponge. The sponge is dipped into water, squeezed out, combined with the liquid or powder and worked into a lather. Inserted deep in the vagina, the sponge will effectively destroy sperm for several hours. A second sponge is usually provided in the kit in case intercourse is repeated. Do not douche.

Obviously, all the methods we've mentioned so far have serious disadvantages. None of them are guaranteed 100 percent safe. But even more awkward, their use makes impulse sex a virtual impossibility. Just when the romantic moment comes, you have to excuse yourself and do something as tedious as lathering a sponge. That's no fun. That's why the overwhelming majority of women we know use either a diaphragm, the coil or the Pill.

Until recently, the diaphragm was the method of birth control favored by most women. Resembling a tiny beanie, it is a thick rubber dome stretched over a rubber-covered ring. After covering it with contraceptive jelly, it is bent, slipped into the vagina, and into place covering the cervical opening. Considered about 90 percent effective, a diaphragm must be fitted by a doctor and refitted at intervals. You *cannot* use one that belongs to your sister, your best friend or even your own if it is more than a few years old. Aside from its relative reliability, the diaphragm's chief advantage is that it can be inserted long before intercourse. This means no interruption during lovemaking. On the other hand, it can be improperly inserted, it can be shaken loose during intercourse or tiny pinholes can develop in the membrane. You can guard against this last eventuality by checking your diaphragm frequently. Pour a little water in the cup. If there's any leakage, the diaphragm is worthless.

The coil, or IUD (Inter-Uterine Device), is another very popular birth-control method. This is a polyethelene plastic coil which is inserted into the uterus by a doctor in a simple two-minute process. It remains in the uterus and by some method yet unknown prevents pregnancy about 90 percent of the time. Its principal attraction lies in the fact that, once the coil is in place, you need not remove it for months. You are, in short, always ready for fairly safe sex. In some women, however, the coil causes vaginal bleeding, abdominal cramps and pelvic discomfort. Other women expell it spontaneously and are often unaware of the fact.

Then there is the Pill. Developed only recently, this is an oral contraceptive consisting of a combination of estrogen and progesterone which alters the body's hormone balance and prevents ovulation. If taken according to directions, the Pill offers virtually 100 percent protection.

However, if even a single day's dosage is omitted, effectiveness drops sharply. If one dose is forgotten, it should be taken as soon as it is remembered, even if that means taking two in one day. If more than one dosage is omitted, the tablets should be continued, but another contraceptive should be used for the remainder of the current menstrual cycle.

The most common side effects of the Pill include mid-monthly bleeding, the possibility of some weight gain, headaches, nausea, breast tenderness and bloating, and perhaps most serious, possible blood clotting in veins and lungs. Despite these objections, most physicians are enthusiastic about the Pill and prescribe it for their normal patients.

The most drastic birth-control method of all is an operation in which the woman's fallopian tubes are cut and tied, which prevents the egg and sperm from ever reaching each other. All other female functions continue without change. It's known as tubal ligation, and is fast, painless and without many complications. However, it is a fairly expensive procedure and almost impossible to reverse. A young woman should think very seriously before she submits to it. Once done, she'll never have babies.

If you're wondering why it is that birth control should be practiced only by women and think it's a little unfair, then you might try to persuade your man to use a condom. Also known as a rubber, this is a thin sheath that fits over the penis and collects the sperm after ejaculation.

Most men, and quite a few women, too, dislike condoms, primarily because they require an abrupt break right in the middle of foreplay. A condom must be put on after a man has achieved erection. This can be frustrating and annoying to both partners. In addition, many men report that their sexual pleasure is considerably reduced because condoms dull sensation.

Along with these drawbacks, there is a chance for breakage during intercourse, and condoms have been known to slip off after climax. Doctors suggest that adequate lubrication and careful withdrawal after ejaculation can help to prevent many of these accidents. The lubrication, however, should not be petroleum jelly which dissolves rubber. Water-soluble surgical jelly should be used instead.

The condom is considered fairly safe and is the only contraceptive that can have a playful touch. All the others are drearily utilitarian, but a condom can be colored, fringed or feathered. Condoms even come with eyes, nose and a smiling mouth painted on them.

Men, as well as women, can undergo minor surgery to achieve an absolutely foolproof form of birth control. Known as a vasectomy, it involves the sealing of a section of tube that prevents living sperm from entering the semen. Everything else, including ejaculation, proceeds as before. The operation can be done in a doctor's office in a few minutes and is just about 100 percent effective. In contrast with tubal ligation, it is possible to reverse the procedure in about 40 percent of the cases, if the man decides he wants to be fertile again.

A word of caution in the event your man agrees to a vasectomy. A man continues to ejaculate live sperm for about six weeks after the operation. Often the doctor who performs the procedure suggests a sperm test after a month or two to be sure the male is totally sperm-free.

As you can see, there is no single ideal form of contraception. Each method has its advantages and its drawbacks. However, under development at the present time is a new contraceptive that would require one injection per month to be used by both men and women. Also under investigation is a "morning after" pill which would be taken by the woman some time after intercourse to prevent the fertilized egg from being implanted on the walls of the uterus. This one, however, is far from being perfected.

Until either or both of these devices come on the market commercially, you're going to have to pick one of the alternatives we've mentioned if you want sex without the fear of pregnancy. However, let's just say that, despite all the precautions you took, IT happens. You're pregnant.

First of all, how do you know? The first clue, of course, is a missed menstrual period. In addition, you may have all the typical early pregnancy symptoms—dizziness, nausea, vomiting, weariness. Or you may have none of these. You may simply be a few days late. Nothing to worry about. But underneath, there's a nagging doubt. What if that night with Herbie. . . ?

In a case like this, a calendar in which you've been keeping a record of your menstrual periods will help tell you if you're late and just how late. What's that, you're nearly three weeks late?

Well, don't panic, and don't bury your head. The sooner you find out whether or not you're pregnant, the greater number of options you have. In some cases, if you think you may have become pregnant and see your doctor the next day, he might easily be able to counteract the conception. By accident, of course. During the course of your examination. It all depends how understanding your gynecologist is. However, if he merely confirms your fears, here are your alternatives.

1. Have the baby and give it up for adoption.
2. Have the baby and raise it alone.
3. Talk HIM (or someone) into marrying you.
4. Have an abortion.

None is very attractive. The first two choices are difficult ones to make for obvious reasons. The third is a lousy one on which to base a marriage, and the fourth is illegal in most states. Yes, you may as well face it, you're in an awkward position. What should you do first?

See the man who fathered your baby. Don't be an hysterical female. Don't accuse him and say it's all his fault. You made love *together,* remember? It's your responsibility as much as it is his. Most men, when faced with the consequences of their sexual behavior, will react well. They'll provide warmth, understanding and support. Together, you and he should be able to talk about your dilemma frankly and openly. Together, you should be able to reach some conclusion about what to do.

We're not about to advise you what to do. That's up to you and your guy. But we will give you the facts so you can make the decision based on knowledge, and not on fear or misinformation.

There's little we can tell you if you decide to have the baby and give it up for adoption. There are any number of responsible adoption agencies in every large and medium-sized city in the country. If this route is for you, contact one of them as soon as possible. Inquire about their practices. Find out as much as you can about the types of homes to which they send their children. Some agencies have so many rules and are ensnarled in so much red tape that childless couples who are eager to adopt become discouraged. Don't hesitate to find out as much as you can about the agency that may assume the responsibility for your child. You and your unborn child are entitled to full cooperation. If the agency ignores your request or otherwise tries to put you down, our advice is to go to another one.

If you decide to have your baby and raise it alone, you'll have to be perfectly frank with the world that you're an unwed mother. Don't try to hide the fact. It will make it just so much tougher for you, and you're going to need all the help you can get. Explain what's happened to your doctor, and reach an early understanding with him. Find out exactly what he's going to charge to deliver your baby. Find out from him what hospital he's associated with, and find out what they charge for a normal delivery. Make sure you have enough money. Once these details are settled, sit down and review your overall financial situation. For the first few years of his life, your baby will need someone to watch over him constantly. Can you afford to do that? If you can't, who'll do it for you? Can you afford to hire someone? Don't fudge these questions just because you're carried away by the thought that you're going to have a baby to cuddle and love. Love is fine, but it's not enough.

Should you marry the guy? Only if you love him and he loves you. Don't marry him because of the baby. That's a surefire formula for unhappiness—for everybody involved. However, if you do decide on marriage, our congratulations, and we'll leave you two alone to decorate the bassinet with pink and blue ribbons.

Should you have an abortion? We don't know, but here are the facts.

Abortion is either downright illegal or performed only under very specific circumstances, such as to save the mother's life, in every state of the Union except for New York. That doesn't mean you can't get an abortion in, say, the State of Oregon. You can, but it's illegal. It means you have to make contact with a doctor who is willing to break the law for a fee, and this can range anywhere from $250 to $1,000 in cash, no checks accepted.

The names of those willing to perform illegal abortions are usually easy to come by. They are circulated freely among young singles and particularly among young women. The process of making contact with these people can be tricky. You can't simply call up a number and say, "Doctor, I'd like an appointment for an abortion." His line might be tapped. Along with his name, you'll be given a procedure to follow, which will probably include a password. This spy stuff may sound ridiculous and childish, but don't forget, you're engaged in an illegal act, and the abortionist could end up with a stiff prison sentence.

At present, the single exception to national abortion laws can be found in New York state. In New York, any woman in the early stages of pregnancy who wants one can have an abortion. Just call any doctor. If he won't do it himself, he'll refer you to one who will or to a clinic. The cost ranges from nothing for certain patients who qualify under Medicare to an average of $300 to $400 for private patients. Some clinics are performing early abortions for about $150.

If you decide to have an abortion, *do not wait too long*. The ideal time for an abortion, that is to say, when it is least dangerous to the woman, comes during the sixth week of pregnancy. The outside limit of safety is three months. If you wait longer than that, it may be too late.

Under proper medical supervision, an abortion is not particularly dangerous or painful. Three methods are used. In cases of very early pregnancy, suction is employed to draw the embryo out of the uterus. In cases of late pregnancy, a salt solution is injected into the uterus which triggers a spontaneous abortion anywhere from twelve to forty-eight hours later. This procedure requires constant medical attention, even though it is quite safe. Because the patient is under medical care for an extended period of time, salting out, as it is called, is the most expensive form of abortion.

The most common form of abortion is dilation and curettage, or a D and C, as it is generally called. This is such a routine procedure that one gynecologist we know refers to it lightheartedly as a "dusting and cleaning." It involves dilating the vagina to permit an instrument to be introduced into the uterus. This instrument is then used to scrape the walls of the uterus in order to dislodge the embryo from its attachment.

One final word of warning. If you find yourself pregnant, *do not try to abort yourself*. We say this for two reasons: It won't work, and you can do irreparable harm to yourself. We've all heard the old wives' tales about ways to get rid of an unwanted baby. But unfortunately, they're just that—old wives' tales. Remedies from the local pharmacy purported to bring on menstruation are usually totally worthless. Hot baths or lifting heavy objects in an effort to spontaneously abort don't work.

We've heard of cases where women have tried to abort themselves with a coat hanger, a knitting needle or a piece of rubber tubing. The chances of infection here are astronomical. So is the chance of perforating the uterine wall, the bladder or the rectum. Also, because the body resists the introduction of a foreign object, it can bring on a state of shock and even cardiac arrest.

Similar dangers exist when douching during early pregnancy. During pregnancy, the veins that supply the uterine lining are dilated and close to the surface. If air is injected into the uterus under pressure, it may enter the veins and cause a possibly fatal air bubble in the circulatory system.

Avoid drugs. Despite what your high school locker mate might tell you, such drugs as aloe, quinine, ergot and tansy will not terminate pregnancy. Such things as arsenic, lead and mercury might work, but they can also kill you. And there are other substances that will only deform the unborn baby, not kill it.

Quite a few state legislatures are considering bills that relax current rigid codes. Within a few years, safe, inexpensive abortions may be available throughout this country. Until then, New York is the only really safe place to have an abortion, because only in New York can you have it performed under the proper medical supervision. No other solution is worth the risk.

Prompt, professional medical attention is also the only answer for another problem that "nice" people aren't supposed to discuss—venereal disease. But venereal disease is a serious illness and far more widespread than anyone would like to admit.

Here's a synopsis of the VD picture.

Syphillis

Contrary to popular opinon, you don't get syphillis or gonorrhea from a toilet seat. These diseases are always transmitted by sexual contact. The first sign of syphillis is a small painless sore at the site of the infection about two weeks after exposure. These sores can appear on the genitals, on the fingertip, the breast or on the lips. The primary symptom will suddenly disappear within a few weeks. Many of the men and women who are infected never develop this primary symptom at all.

Two or three months later, secondary symptoms appear. It can be a mild skin rash, inflamed patches inside the mouth or on the sexual organs. They can be small flat warts around the vagina or anus. These symptoms, too, may disappear for a period ranging from four months to twenty years, and no new symptoms may occur. Then, the final and most serious phase of the disease occurs, when the nervous system, the heart, the bones and other portions of the body may be very seriously damaged.

Ever since 1910, it has been possible to cure syphillis, but thousands of people have avoided treatment because of the general social attitude toward the disease. However, once treatment is sought, the rest is easy. A series of penicillin injections will cure the disease, provided permanent damage has not developed because of neglect.

Gonorrhea

Anywhere from two days to two weeks after contact, a man afflicted with gonorrhea notices that urination produces a burning sensation and is accompanied by a white discharge. This inflammation lasts for awhile, then disappears. If untreated, the infection begins to build up scar tissue in the urethra and eventually seals it off so the man cannot urinate.

In a woman, the obvious signs of infection are rare. It works deep in the reproductive organs, causing serious damage and eventually sterility. For this reason, some prostitutes welcome it. However, it can also cause arthritis of the joints. In newborn infants of infected mothers, it can cause permanent blindness.

The treatment for gonorrhea is the same as for syphillis.

Syphillis and gonorrhea are not the only venereal diseases. Three other forms of VD are *chancroid, granuloma inguinale* and *Lymphogranuloma venereum* (LGV). Chancroid is caused by bacteria that causes pus-filled blisters in the genital area. They become painful ulcers over the whole pubic area. Once diagnosed, chancroid can be cured with sulfa drugs.

Granuloma inguinale is also caused by bacteria. Little bumps form on the genitals, become raw and ooze. Early symptoms are painless and appear harmless. This form of VD must be caught early and treated by antibiotics. In advanced cases of untreated granuloma inguinale, death can occur.

Finally, there is LGV. This is probably the most diabolic of all venereal diseases because there is no treatment or cure. Early signs are small bumps on the sexual organs which are usually followed by an egg-sized lump in the groin. The infection spreads from the lymph glands in the groin to those around the anus. The anus may close, making defecation impossible unless the anus is continually dilated. Other swollen lymph glands may break through the skin at various points and ooze pus. Fortunately, cases of LGV are quite rare.

"So what?" you say. You don't need this information because you don't sleep with dirty people who have these kinds of diseases? Maybe so, but you never know when you're liable to be raped these days, and rapists don't carry health certificates in their pockets. If, by chance, you do happen to be raped, consult a physician immediately. There is a chance that the man who attacked you is a carrier. Speaking of rapes, every woman should have a knowledge of self-defense. Like first aid and lifesaving, self-defense may mean the difference between an unpleasant experience and a personal tragedy. By self-defense, we don't mean the dazzling judo theatrics of Batgirl, which are all worked out beforehand with a stunt man. We mean the rudiments of self-protection, a little more than just the fast knee-to-the-groin instinct most girls have. This by the way, is not recommended for two reasons. It puts you within grabbing range, and most men instinctively protect their groin.

Many women, in situations where they are threatened

or attacked, become willing victims, so ineffective as to be almost an accomplice to the crime. They become paralyzed with fright or plead pitifully for mercy. Both responses assure the assailant of your helplessness, and encourage him to go ahead with whatever he had in mind.

A spirited show of defense, even if you're not trained, has a chance of being successful. Lois is barely five foot two and weighs 105 pounds soaking wet. One night, several years ago, she was on her way from the subway to her apartment after having gone to a concert at Carnegie Hall. As usual at that time of the evening, the main thoroughfares were busy. Not exactly crowded, but there was some traffic and there was at least one pedestrian on every block she could see. But the side street where she lived was deserted. The only sound she could hear was her heels tapping smartly on the sidewalk. Then she heard another noise. It was a shuffling gait of somebody behind her. Without breaking stride, she crossed over to the other side of the street. The shuffler in back of her did the same. It was then she knew she was in for trouble. She knew there was no use in running, and she instinctively knew that if she tried to let herself in the front door of her apartment building, whoever it was would force his way in after her. In fact, the chances were that this is what he was waiting for. She decided to face him down.

Dashing into the middle of the street, she whirled and saw a man stop and stare at her in a startled fashion. He was well over six feet tall.

"All right, you stop right there," she commanded.

To her surprise he did as he was told.

"Now I want to see you walk back down to the other end of this street," she said in the firmest voice she could muster.

"What are you talking about, lady," the man began. But Lois cut him off.

"I don't want to argue with you. I don't even want to talk to you. You start marching. And if you're not on your way by the time I count to three, I'm going to scream this block down."

"Lady, I didn't...."

"One."

"Gee, lady, you've got it...."

"Two."

"All right, all right."

He spun on his heels and marched off. Lois waited until he was at the end of the street before she dashed to her front door. Letting herself in quickly, she made her way to her apartment, and sank gratefully into her sofa. Not until then did her knees start to tremble.

Lois' experience perfectly illustrates the point that an attacker is more reluctant to face an angry and resolute girl than a submissive, panicky female.

The principal thing to remember is to use your common sense. Install a sturdy lock in your front door. A policeman once told us that a man equipped with nothing more complicated than a thin sheet of plastic can open 90 percent of all the locks in New York City. He merely inserts the plastic in the crack between the door and the jamb, pushes the plastic against the inclined face of the lock, and in a moment the door is open. When we heard that, we went to our local hardware store and asked the owner to advise us on what to buy. He recommended a lock, and sent a man over to install it—all for less than $25. We consider it one of the best investments we ever made.

Of course, the most burglar-proof lock in the world isn't going to do you much good if you open your door whenever somebody knocks. Make sure you know who's on the other side. If he says he's from the phone company, ask him for his office number. If he's legitimate, he won't mind. If he says he's the parcel-post man, ask him to slip his identification under the door.

An open window is an open invitation to trouble. Keep them locked, especially at night, If it's too hot, buy a window air conditioner. Sure, they're expensive, but they're worth it—both for comfort and safety.

Unfortunately, even when you're cozily in your own place, surrounded by maximum security, you can still get harassed. You can get singled out by your friendly, neighborhood obscene telephone caller who has decided to give you his undivided attention this week. These weirdos usually do their stuff in two different ways. The first kind talks dirty and makes obscene suggestions. The second kind doesn't say a word. He just breathes heavily into the phone. Both enjoy calling up repeatedly in the middle of the night.

What can you do about this all-too-common pest? First of all, you can get an unlisted number from the telephone company. If that's a drag, ask the company not to list your name in the directory as "Mary Smith." That's a dead giveaway that you're a single girl living alone, and just what the obscene caller is looking for. Have them list you instead as "M. Smith." That way, he can't be sure. If he gets to you anyway, and keeps annoying you, the phone company may be able to help. Within the last few years, phone companies working together with the police have developed a number of ways to track down these nuisances. Failing that, you can do what a friend of ours did. After having been annoyed for two nights by an obscene caller, she bought herself a police whistle. Next time he rang up, she blew it as loud as she could right into the receiver. It probably tore the guy's ear right off. End of obscene phone calls.

A police whistle, by the way, can be a girl's best friend. An acquaintance of ours never gets on an elevator without first taking one out of her purse. One night it paid off. She was alone in the elevator—it was an automatic one—and the door was closing.

But before it could shut all the way, a mean-looking customer flung open the outside door and made a grab for her. Our friend gave it everything she had. The man's eyes bugged out. "Jesus Christ!" he muttered as he beat a hasty retreat.

Girls alone in cars are also considered fair game, so be sensible. Make sure your doors and windows are shut and locked. That young girl down the road looking for a ride might be a lone hitchhiker and perfectly innocent. On the other hand, there might be a guy hiding behind that sign ready to pounce the minute you pull over and open the door for her. Don't take the chance.

If you pass a car on the side of the road with its hood up, don't stop. Drive until you hit the next service station and tell the attendant about it. What do you know about fixing a carburetor anyway?

Nine times out of ten, if you're assaulted, the motive will be robbery. If your assailant makes it clear that he wants only your cash and valuables, hand them over without an argument. Police officials advise against trying any heroics. The street mugger is usually young, often armed with a knife, and almost as scared as you are. A false move from you can cause him to lash out. Even a precious family heirloom isn't worth the disfiguration of a knife scar.

But what if the attacker wants you and not your money? Is there any way to fight him off? If you're really serious about learning self-defense, enroll in a judo class. We're told that if she knows how, a woman can easily deck a man twice her own weight. But once you've acquired the skill and are the proud owner of a black belt, be careful how you use it.

Patty had been taking judo lessons for three years. She enjoyed it for the exercise it provided and for a new feeling of self-confidence it gave her. Naturally when you enjoy something, you end up being pretty good at it, and Patty was good at judo. However, she had never had the chance to practice her art outside the gym until one afternoon on a lonely stretch of beach on Fire Island. She had just emerged from a path in the woods that led to the beach when she heard a movement behind her. She turned to find two hundred pounds of muscle bearing down on her.

Letting go with a scream of rage that is supposed to get your own system worked up while it paralyzes your opponent with fright, Patty lashed out with her foot, slamming into his knee with her heel.

"Ow!" yelled the guy.

"Aieeeee!" shrieked Patty, settling down to work.

She grabbed him by the wrist, yanked him forward, and with the side of her palm, cracked him sharply against the neck.

"Ugh," grunted the guy.

"Whawhooooo!" yowled Patty, driving her hand as hard as she could into his solar plexus.

"Poof," whispered the guy as he slowly collapsed and lay gasping on the sand. Patty held up her attack.

"Okay," she demanded. "What's the idea?"

The guy made a few fish-like sounds as he tried to regain his breath. "I . . . I . . ."

"Come on, quit stalling," Patty ordered, "or I'll really work you over. What do you want?"

There was terror in his eyes, but the guy managed to pull himself up into a kneeling position. Patty was wondering whether or not to break his nose, when she heard him say, "Here."

She looked down and he was holding out a comb, her comb.

"Here," he repeated. "I just wanted to give you your comb. You dropped it back there on the path."

"He was," Patty said with a regretful sigh when she told us about it later, "a gorgeous hunk of man. The most eligible guy I met all weekend. But for the next two days, everytime he'd see me, he'd kind of edge away."

"Well, do you blame him?" we asked.

Patty shook her head sadly. "No," she said at last. "I guess I can't."

Patty had achieved the ultimate in self-defense.

CHAPTER XI

"This model we insist will bring you many hours of pleasure or we will disappointed be, but you never."
—FROM A CATALOGUE OF SEXUAL STIMULANTS OFFERED BY A JAPANESE MAIL-ORDER HOUSE

"If I Masturbate, Will I Become an Asexual, Incestuous Lesbian?"

You're young, healthy and vibrantly alive. The world is interesting, challenging, fun. Good, open sex really turns you on. Doesn't everybody feel the same way? Unfortunately not. You're one of the lucky ones. While you rejoice under the sun, exulting in your new freedom, there are others who live shadowy, unfulfilled lives on the edge of darkness. These uneasy, unhappy women we call emotional or sexual cripples. They have one thing in common. They all lack the ability to reach out and make lasting, human contacts. Many of them try to fill their emptiness in strange ways. Some of them are just confused.

Carole is the kind of girl who looks dazzling in hip-huggers and a T-shirt. Her heavy blonde hair falls halfway down her back. Her smile is wide and direct, her complexion flawless. She has the lithe body and energy of an athlete. Yet a certain sadness emerges, a curious puzzlement, as though her life has been in some ways a disappointment.

In intimate conversation with a good friend, the reason finally emerges. At twenty-three, Carole is still a virgin.

"I've never admitted it to anybody before," she says. "It's too awful. Everywhere I go people are talking about what great sex they've had with this guy and what a fantastic weekend with that guy. Everyone I know is going to feel-ins and orgies. And I'm still as pure as the leading laundry product."

How did it happen, this rarity in the world of turned-on sex? "I'm sort of shy with men," Carole explains. "I've met only a few that I've really liked. If they're too pushy or direct, it scares me. And of the ones who aren't, no one's ever asked me."

She pauses, remembering something. "No, that's not true," she says. "One did. I met him skiing at Aspen. We spent a few days on the slopes together. He seemed marvelous. On the third day, I fell down and he picked me up. We talked for awhile, standing as close together as our skiis would allow. He was rooming alone up at the Lodge. He asked me if I'd have dinner with him. I knew he meant more than dinner. I said yes. It felt great knowing that I finally was going to get rid of this curse I've been carrying with me like a stone around my neck. Ever since I was eighteen, I've waited. When I got to be twenty, it seemed like a joke. Now, at twenty-three, it's a curse.

"Anyway, I liked him, and I was going to sleep with

him. I was pretty turned on, but there still were a few hours of good skiing left. I worked my way up to the top of the slope. I felt as if I could fly. I started down, skiing better than I'd ever skiied before." Carole buried her head in her hands. "Then, I fell. I broke my leg. It was a multiple fracture. I was in a cast for months.

"Ever since then, it's been like I've been fated to end up a dried-out, old virgin. I've met other men since, but none I liked well enough to help me with my problem. I don't know what I'm going to do!

"It's come to the point now that I think I'd go to bed with any man who asks me. Sometimes, when I pass a good-looking man on the street, I think about walking up to him and saying, 'Sir, would you mind coming home with me to relieve me of my virginity.'

"I know I could go to one of those single places for a weekend and just announce my availability. But I keep waiting, hoping it'll happen in a better way." Carole is near tears. "I'm probably the only accidental virgin left in the world."

Carole only thinks she's a rarity. There are thousands just like her, attractive enough to have any man they want, but unable to endure the idea of having a physical relationship with him. They tell themselves that's what they really want, but deep down underneath, they'll find some excuse to postpone it. Some psychologists would even go so far as to say that Carole's crack-up at Aspen was no "accident." Her subconscious, over which she has no control, rebelled against her conscious decision. In the end, it proved powerful enough to force the fall that kept Carole out of her friend's bed.

Jeanne suffers from no such conflict between her conscious and subconscious. She, too, is a virgin, but aggressively proud of it. "Ah'm savin' it up for mah husband," she announces. "It's an old family tradition. Ah don't care one fig what anybody says. Anybody wants what ah have to give is gonna have to trade a l'il old gold band for the privilege. Fair is fair!"

How does Jeanne manage her own sexual tensions? She necks, she pets. But she doesn't go "all the way." Jeanne is a person who cannot deal with the New Morality. She is afraid of the freedom it brings. She isn't sure she'd be able to handle it, and so she tries to convince herself and everybody else that her caution is a virtue.

Cynthia is also a virgin, but for different reasons. "I've never been able to figure out what all the fuss is about," she says. "It started when we were in high school, with all the girls panting and sweating to make it with the football captain or the head of the honor society. There was always a lot of grabbing and pawing in dark corners or in cars at the drive-in. I tried it, but I just couldn't get interested. I still can't."

Cynthia likes her apartment. She loves her job. She enjoys talking to men and working with them. "But I hate it when they start breathing all over me," she says. Cynthia seems puzzled for a moment. "There must be something to the whole thing," she says at last. "But I guess it's just not for me."

Cynthia's problem is that she's one of a statistically small group known as "low sex potentials" or sometimes "asexuals." She is not a lesbian. She simply has no interest in sex, whether it be with men or with women.

Mandy's situation is somewhat different. "I'll say it straight out," she declares defiantly. "I like girls. I always have. When I was fourteen, I had this fantastic crush on my father's secretary. She used to spend a lot of time at our house—Daddy worked at home a great deal of the time—and when my parents went out, she'd stay overnight and keep me company.

"She taught me that it was perfectly all right for a girl to love another girl, that men don't even have to enter the picture. She and I stayed together until I was seventeen and went off to college. I didn't really want to go, but it would've looked peculiar to my parents if I didn't. But it was all right in the end," she smiled. "My roommate was more my age anyway. And we didn't have to worry all the time about being discovered. We just locked the door."

Mandys are to be found everywhere. One prominent sex researcher reported that 28 percent of the women he interviewed had had at least one homosexual arousal or orgasm. Estimates vary, but there are certainly several million practicing female homosexuals in the United States today.

Eloise's situation, too, is out of the ordinary. "I have this very wonderful Daddy," she says. "When I was ten, my parents were divorced. It was all Mummy's fault, of course. She sent me away to a boarding school so I wouldn't interfere with her social life. I never really got to know Daddy until he took me on a long vacation with him the year I turned fifteen." She smiles. "He taught me everything I know. That summer was marvelous. I guess some people'd call it kind of sick. But both Daddy and I are happy. And that's what counts. The only thing I regret is that we can't have a baby. Oh, I suppose we could, but I guess it wouldn't be fair to the baby."

The variations run the whole gamut, from the accidental virgin to the asexual girl, from the homosexual to the incestuous. In each case there is some emotional flaw that prevents the individual from experiencing or enjoying natural sex.

Finally, there's Frederika. "I take care of my own needs," she says. "You've heard the old saying—a honeymoon in the hand? Well, I've tried it with men and found it a drag. And I've tried it with women, and didn't like that much better. Why wait around until somebody else feels like doing what you feel like doing? I guess you'd say I'm pretty much self-sufficient."

Frederika has been so emotionally crippled that she cannot successfully relate with either men *or* women. She has drawn in entirely upon herself. She can find pleasure only through masturbation.

"I could write a book about the dozens of interesting ways to masturbate," Frederika says. "I've researched the subject thoroughly and tried them all. Most everyone starts out by using their plain old hand," she says. "Some rub the entire pubic area with the heel of their hand. Some use pressure on and off. Some explore the area inside the lips of the vagina around the labia and uterus and finally concentrate on rubbing one side of the clitoral shaft until orgasm. You can have one orgasm after another and you needn't stop until you're tired.

"There are lots of variations to explore," Frederika continues enthusiastically. "You can try stroking the clitoris with one finger and the vagina with another. If you're really persistent, you can reach orgasm 95 percent of the time. However," she adds, "if you still have trouble reaching a climax, then the thing to try is a vibrator. It's guaranteed, 100 percent."

Frederika is talking about an inexpensive little machine you can buy in any drugstore. You know the kind. You strap it on the back of your hand, plug it into the wall switch, and the electric motor sends rapid vibrations through your hand and fingertips. They're meant to relax stiff muscles, and that's what most people use them for. But as Frederika has discovered, they can have a far more interesting application. Some women masturbate with these vibrators and achieve literally dozens of orgasms.

Another type of vibrator is reported to be even more effective. This one consists of a small motor set into a plastic case. The motor moves a steel shaft, activating a set of rubber tips. These tips are supposed to drum gently against knotted muscles to loosen them but again, more imaginative uses have been found for this instrument.

A third kind of vibrator, also widely available in drugstores, is a plastic shaft shaped remarkably like a penis. Inside the shaft a motor causes the entire device to vibrate rapidly.

Before you dismiss the use of vibrators as totally sick, consider this. Some sex researchers claim that vibrators are very useful for women who have never achieved an arousal by means of manual stimulation. Once a woman has begun to experience orgasm by using a vibrator, it is often easier for her to duplicate the sensation by means of other stimulation.

These researchers point out that women have artificially stimulated themselves for years. They report that many women use streams of water directed at their clitoris to achieve orgasm. Water from a bidet, a whirlpool bath, a showerhead or even the garden hose can produce fascinating sensations.

So can other vibrations as varied as horseback riding or plastering your body against any kind of vibrating machinery, such as a washing machine, an energetic refrigerator or a motorcycle. There is an account, written by a woman who worked in the sweatshops of New York City's garment center in the early part of the century, which claims that many of the operators were highly aroused by their treadle-type sewing machines. It was, she says, the only thing that made life bearable for the women who were forced to labor under such intolerable conditions.

Psychologists tell us that it is very common for women to want to put something into their vagina. The list is endless, but soft penis-like objects such as bananas, cucumbers and carrots are favorites. These penis substitutes are known as dildoes. Historically, dildoes have been constructed of gold, silver, ivory, sealing wax, rubber, and now, of course, plastic. Today's model, advertised and sold through the mails, is offered in a choice of lengths from five to nine inches. You can even choose the diameter you prefer, up to two inches. The cost ranges from about $15 to $60 for the super deluxe model. We've never seen a deluxe model, so we can only speculate why the top of the line is worth $60. Maybe it has automatic transmission, white-wall tires and carpeting.

The center for the trade in these sexual stimulants is Japan and, indeed, the Japanese seem to have spent much time and ingenuity in inventing devices designed to enhance certain kinds of sexual pleasures. They are credited with what is, without a doubt, the ultimate in masturbatory equipment. It is called the ben-wa or more vulgarly, the Japanese tickle. This device consists of two hollow balls about the size of pigeon eggs, usually made of brass. One ball is empty while the other is partially filled with mercury. The woman inserts them inside her vagina and then seats herself in a rocking chair or she reclines in a hammock. The slightest body movement causes the mercury-filled ball to roll and the resulting vibration is considered exquisitely titillating. Praise of this device from satisfied users is almost lyrical. Apparently, Oriental women would amuse themselves with hours of sexual pleasure by using their beloved ben-wa.

Once more, never having seen or tried a ben-wa, we can only pass along this information as hearsay. But one thing we do know: A ben-wa is perfectly harmless, unlike some other devices women have tried. Hairpins, pencils and even closed safety pins are among the objects women have inscrtcd in their vaginas.

We've listed a wide, perhaps weird, variety of masturbatory devices and techniques. But that shouldn't detract from the fact that masturbation, within reason, is a happy, healthy, normal act that increases a woman's sense of well-being and helps develop her sensuality. It is only when she foregoes heterosexual activity entirely, concentrating exclusively on masturbation, that she becomes emotionally handicapped.

Back in the 1920s, a pioneering English gynecologist named Helena Wright, disturbed by the sexual paralysis of her patients, taught them to masturbate to reawaken themselves. After instructing them in the art of clitoral stimulation, Dr. Wright suggested that her patients begin to involve the vagina so that it, too, "might come alive."

Unfortunately, we have no evidence that indicates how successful Dr. Wright was in her attempts. But at least she was trying to turn a whole generation on to the delights of heterosexual love. There are some women who never have this experience at all. These are the female homosexuals, or lesbians as they are called. While there is a tendency today for homosexuals of both sexes to be franker in publicly stating their sexual preferences, there are still no absolutely reliable figures on their number in the United States. One statistic, however, has emerged. The number of active lesbians seems to be about half that of male homosexuals.

One researcher suggests that this difference is due to the fact that women are taught from birth to be greater conformists to the social norm than men. It follows that if they are less adventuresome in all their activities, they are more conventional in sexual matters as well. Also, they are fewer in number partly because of the career element. Since it is men who do the hiring and the firing in the world, they can afford to be more daring, even in sexual matters.

Many lesbians believe that all people are born bisexual and that whatever happens in their life experience dictates the direction they will take. "If people were more free, less uptight, less prejudiced," one lesbian says, "they could and would respond to either sex." Generally, lesbians do not prefer women because they can't have good orgasmic sex with a man, but because they get along with, understand and fall in love with women more easily.

And "falling in love" is exactly the correct expression to use in describing many lesbian relationships. A lesbian attachment can be affectionately warm and lasting, with the partners living together for many years.

It is as erroneous to believe that lesbianism is always the pairing of a masculine-looking woman, popularly known as a "butch" or a "dyke," and a frail, feminine-looking girl as it is to believe that all male homosexuals are limp-wristed. The female homosexual who can be termed a "bull dyke" is very much in the minority. If you visit any big-city bar that caters to lesbians, you'll see a room filled with girls dancing, holding hands, talking with other girls. Most appear feminine and quite attractive.

Many heterosexual girls wonder what physical form lesbian love takes. It really isn't much different from what men and women do together during the foreplay portion of lovemaking. Lesbians kiss, caress each other's bodies and build toward a climax together. To reach orgasm, they must resort to masturbation. This is accomplished with the hands or the mouth and tongue, better known as mutual cunnilingus. Lesbians consider themselves experts at this oral-genital technique and claim to be able to prolong sexual pleasure for hours through skillful use of the mouth and tongue.

Some lesbians prefer what is known as tribadism. This, too, involves masturbation, but it is accomplished by pressing the pubic areas together and rubbing. As the movement becomes more hectic and the rhythm faster, the friction on the clitoris brings on an orgasm.

Some lesbians like to use a dildoe. One of the women straps on a sponge-rubber or plastic penis and uses it with her partner as a male would use his natural penis. There is also a Japanese device known as a "harigata," or double dildoe, which has two heads. Both women are able to enjoy its penetration simultaneously.

Of course, there is always group sex for lesbians. As with male-female group sex, the all-female groups employ hands and mouths to bring pleasure to others in the group. It's interesting to note that many women, otherwise heterosexual, will enjoy homosexual activity when in a group-sex situation. Men in those situations are known to feel intense sexual pleasure watching women making love.

Many prostitutes are suspected of being lesbians. There is a theory that these women feel such inner disgust for their paying male customers that they simply cannot feel sexually outgoing toward men. Another theory is that prostitutes are so humiliated by their customers that they feel secure only in the intimate company of other females.

We find no substantiation for this last theory in what we've read or been able to learn from talking with a few prostitutes. We've never heard of a prostitute who truly felt humiliated by her profession. It was a business, a job she did and the only enjoyment she got out of it was financial.

Men are far more romantic about prostitution than women are. It is the men who have written the books and stories that perpetuate the myth of the hard hooker with a heart of gold. Prostitutes, themselves, simply have no time for such sentimentality.

A generation or so ago, girls were initiated into the life when they fell upon hard times in the city. The one who recruited them was usually an ex-prostitute, who had saved her money, and now ran a house. Again, it is the men who are responsible for the romantic fables about essentially decent madams, or madams who were great company. But these ladies were shrewd, tough businesswomen who ran a tight ship and expected both their customers and their girls to behave. It was cash on the line as far as these cookies were concerned and if a man spent more than a quarter of an hour with one of her girls, he'd be charged overtime.

Today, the industry—and it is indeed an industry—has taken on a far freer form. There are many different kinds of prostitutes and those who dance in attendance around them.

At the very top of the heap are the chic, expensive, $100-a-trick call girls who are answerable to no one. These are, in effect, independent operators whose business depends on the word-of-mouth of satisfied clients. Their ranks are usually made up of models or ex-actresses who never made it on the stage. They're often stunning, always well turned-out and give their customers individual attention. One of these girls can service as many as four or five clients a night. This fast turnover is entirely due to a man's sexual limitation.

A way of life where a girl can make several thousand dollars a week sounds like a pretty good deal. Unfortunately, however, a high-priced call girl's productive years are notoriously short. The number of men who can afford her is usually small, and there's always new talent appearing on the scene. Usually, she has no more than two or three good years. After that, it's all downhill. If she's been careful and saved her money, perhaps she can go into a more legitimate line of work. But, of course, the kind of person who is attracted to this profession is generally not a careful manager.

If she hopes to keep a roof over her head, she must now turn to a pimp who will take on the responsibility of finding her clients. When a girl puts herself into the hands of a pimp, she has lost all her freedom. He dresses her, feeds her and houses her. He gives her some spending money. In exchange, he expects her to do exactly what he tells her to do. She has no control over her customers. No matter what or who the pimp produces, she must oblige him. If she challenges his authority in any way, he may beat her and kick her out.

This puts her one notch down in the hierarchy of hustling, for she is now out on the street. She becomes what is known as a B-girl, working bars and cocktail lounges. If she has any looks left, she'll ply her trade in the more expensive places. But as she loses her figure, and lines begin to appear in her face, she'll be reduced to frequenting seedier spots. Eventually, she won't be welcome anywhere, and then she will literally be on the street, once again in the clutches of a pimp.

Street whores generally have no independence whatsoever. Even though they do their own soliciting from dark doorways, they are kept in line by a pimp who controls their lives. If they try to object, the pimp straightens them out. He may subject them to such a merciless beating that they plead with him to stop and agree to any terms he demands.

The pimp pretends he is the father confessor and protector of his stable of girls. He is actually nothing of the kind. He expects all of his girls to report in at the end of the night and put their earnings on the table. If he decides it's not enough and that they've been lazy, another beating ensues. Whatever money they bring in, he takes the lion's share. He could not care less if they live or die.

And so we end our gallery of sexual cripples with the prostitute, a person who experiences degradation from an act that should bring exultation. As we said at the beginning of this chapter, these women, and the others we've described, live on the edges of darkness. Mercifully, their numbers are relatively few. Their tragedy is that they are incapable of ever feeling the warmth and excitement of a deep and strength-giving relationship. Through inertia, bitterness and because of deep-seated psychological problems, they have allowed a wall to build up around them through which very little human love can enter. They are unable to taste the freedom of the New Morality because they have never acknowledged any morality whatsoever.

CHAPTER XII

"I don't know whether to get married or go back to school next year and face my problems."
—COLLEGE GIRL WRITING TO A FRIEND

"Marry You? All I Wanted To Do Was Go to Bed With You."

It's bound to happen. Someone, someday, is going to ask you to share the rest of your life with him. He wants you to be more than his girl friend. He wants you to be his wife, the mother of his children. Which will it be, yes or no?

A million thoughts zip around in your head. Dreams, hopes, worries and fear chase each other in a dizzying confusion inside what you used to think was a reasonably well-ordered brain. How do you sort out your feelings? How do you decide?

First of all, don't allow yourself to be seduced by the dream you've cherished since childhood. The dream of a white dress and veil, candles and flowers, the teary smiles of those closest to you, the aisle, the altar and HIM. Along with that one, there's probably the dream of a perfect little place where the two of you will share the plans, the joys, the quiet laughter, the soft touch of a hand, the long peaceful evenings, the warmth of bodies joined, the comfort of a problem you can talk over with someone, the wonder of complete understanding and total caring.

We're not saying these dreams never work out in real life. They can. What we *are* saying is that all too often they are cruelly shattered. Look at the married couples you know, their problems, their frustrations, anger and bitterness. Is that what marriage is all about, you wonder?

It could be a disaster, you think. Maybe it could.

But maybe it'll be different for us, you hope. Maybe. It all depends upon how you approach the whole idea of marriage. The wedded state is not automatically blissful, nor is it the hell some people tell you it is. It is what you and your husband make it. If it is based on realistic hopes and plans, it can be a sound marriage. If you insist upon fantasy, it will become a nightmare. Ask yourself first, do you really want to be married?

Fifty years ago, even twenty years ago, people would have thought there was something the matter with us for asking such a question. Of course you wanted to get married! Wasn't that the goal of every single girl? Marriage was seen as fulfillment and liberation.

But today, it's not as simple as that. The lure of a gold and white wedding, a sterling silver place setting for twelve and a house in a fashionable suburb is not the end-all for today's liberated girl. That's because she sees marriage more realistically than her sister did a quarter of a century ago. Sure, there's still the wedding cake, the rice and shoes, but she knows that, after the reception guests have gone home, she'll be faced with such mundane chores as a sinkful of dirty dishes and a washing-machine load of dirty diapers. And she wonders if that's a fair trade.

Furthermore, she knows that the odds, while not exactly stacked against a good marriage, are still not overwhelmingly in favor of it. She's perfectly aware that one marriage out of every four ends in divorce. She also knows that, of those marriages that do not end in divorce, more than one third are considered dismal failures by the people involved.

She's been told that if she's fantastically lucky, she'll marry a man who'll devote himself to carving out a successful career. But she's read the stories of the wives of high-powered, high-pressured businessmen who have described how dull the life of the lady of the manor can be. She's aware of how difficult and often unrewarding it can be to be wife, mother, housekeeper, chauffeur, nurse, loyal standby, errand girl and cook.

Is she to give up the freedom she has found in the New Morality to spend her days making beds, folding laundry, and unplugging stuffed drains, or even, in a more financially privileged household, presiding over a ladies' luncheon and supervising the housekeeper?

Yes, of course, she *knows* that marriage is not one long honeymoon, or a lifelong sunny, situation comedy. But does life hold nothing more than the difficult early years of marriage, the frantically busy middle years, the sad and empty later years? Is that the road map she will follow for the rest of her days?

Consider the story of Carla and Randy. They met, they fell in love, they decided to get married. Both were intelligent, sensible individuals. Neither of them expected perfection. Sure there'd be those days. They even joked about it together. They assured each other that they knew exactly what it was they were getting into. The wedding and the honeymoon were all Carla could want. The first years were great, too. They found an apartment, and had great fun fixing it up. Randy went off to work each morning, and Carla spent the day bargain-hunting, planning her menus, thinking of ways to surprise and please her husband. The night that Carla told Randy she was expecting a baby was perhaps the happiest night of their lives, equalled only by the night they brought their daughter home from the hospital.

Taking care of little Susan absorbed much of Carla's time. But it was time she counted as pleasure. Even after Peter arrived, Carla would have described her life as varied and happy. Then, when Susan reached the age of three and Peter was a little more than a year old, a change began to set in. Randy's hours, for one thing, were longer. When he came home he would often be distracted or tired, or both. Several evenings a week, he brought his briefcase with him, and would shut out his family as he concentrated on his work. Almost imperceptibly, Carla fell into a routine that altered very little from day to day.

This consisted of cleaning up the breakfast dishes, tidying up the house and dressing the children for their outing in the park. Twice a week, she cut the park mornings short in order to do a fairly big shop. This was always a chore, because she had to lug both the kids and the basket of food around the store. Then it was home, lunch, a nap for Susan and Peter, and washing and ironing for her. Another hour or so with the sandbox set in the afternoon and it was time to put the kids in their bath, and think about dinner. She fed Susan and Peter first and was usually just washing them up when Randy arrived. The next hour was her busiest as she tried to do a number of things all at once. It was reviewing the day with Randy as she juggled with the drink he had poured her. They had long since given up the delightful custom of sharing a leisurely drink before dinner. At the same time, she supervised the getting-ready-for-bed routine, and in between she got a second meal together. Afterwards, it was dishes, of course, and by that time it was after nine o'clock and she was exhausted.

After about six months of this pattern, she realized it was getting to her. She caught herself being cross with the kids and even a little short with Randy. She decided she'd better pull herself together and talk over her problem with her husband.

"I don't see your problem," was Randy's comment when she had unburdened herself.

"But I'm not *using* myself," Carla explained. "I'm turning into a vegetable."

"Now, look, dear," Randy said. "You're not doing anything that a million other women aren't doing."

"Perhaps not," Carla said bitterly. "But have you asked them how they feel about it? Everybody I know feels the same way."

"Then you and everybody you know are being a bunch of pretty unrealistic females," Randy said. "I mean, that's the way it is. Right?"

"But does it have to be?" Carla practically wailed.

Randy put down the paper angrily. "For heaven's sake, Carla, what does that have to do with it? It's the way it *is*. I thought you were a grown-up woman, not some adolescent girl hugging an impossible dream of a perfect marriage. You're old enough to know what life is all about. I've got my job to do and you've got yours. So let's stop bitching about it, shall we?"

The notion there is a division of roles according to sex is laughingly dismissed by Lisa and Stewart, proud parents of William, 5, and Johnathan, 3. "Oh sure," Lisa admits, "I'm the one who has the babies, and Stewart brings home more money than I do. But the first distinction is biological, so I don't think we'll ever do much about that. The second?" She shrugs. "Who knows, maybe some day that will change."

How did they achieve this partnership? "We talked

it over before we were married," Stewart says. "I told Lisa that I didn't want to be married to a housewife. I wanted my wife to be an interesting, vital, intelligent human being who was proud of herself as a person."

"And," Lisa adds, "the only way that could happen was for me to continue my work." Lisa teaches reading skills to retarded children. It's a vocation that demands special training and much patience. But the rewards, at least for Lisa, make it all worthwhile.

"The first few years of marriage," Lisa says, "presented no particular problems. Stewart worked, and I worked. When we came home, we had time for each other. In order to get chores over with, we shared them. I know a lot of women don't agree with me, but I never thought Stewart was less of a man just because he happened to fold some laundry. It just meant I wouldn't have to do it, and we could have more time together afterwards."

What happened when the babies started to come? "Well," Stewart says, "we played it the way we felt it. For the first year of William's life, Lisa didn't want to work. She wanted to stay home and take care of him. So that's the way we did it. For over a year, we did the traditional role bit."

"Then," Lisa says, picking up the story, "I began to get restless. So we talked about it and agreed I could go back to work. The only hitch was finding someone to take care of the baby. Finally we got somebody," she adds ruefully, "and it cost the earth. But we figured it would still be worth it. After that, I went out looking for a job. I found one, and we all settled down to a new routine. Then guess what happened? I got pregnant again."

"So," Stewart says, "she quit for the second time and had Johnathan. As far as I'm concerned, that's it. No more babies."

Lisa nods her vigorous agreement. "I'm with a new

school, working hard every day and back at home by three thirty, with enough energy to really pay some attention to the boys. It's not the old routine of 'Go away and play, Mummy's tired now.' I get involved with them, and we have a marvelous time. On the whole, I'd say we have a marvelous life."

"We are not," Stewart concludes, "a partnership where husband is breadwinner and wife is homemaker. We are two people who find we can communicate beautifully with each other because we've got exciting interesting things to say. As far as I'm concerned, there's no other way to live."

What is the difference between these two marriages? The difference is that Lisa and Stewart reached an understanding long before their wedding day. They talked over what kind of life they wanted to build together. Carla and Randy allowed themselves to drift into marriage. Despite the fact that they prided themselves on their realistic attitudes, they were totally unprepared for what befell them later. In all probability, Carla never once asked herself why she wanted to get married in the first place.

There are many reasons why women marry and most of them are bad ones. Here are a few of the more rotten reasons women have for marriage.

FINANCIAL SECURITY

Oh, of course, you're not marrying him for his money. After all, he's not a millionaire. But he does have a good job and prospects. You'll never have to worry about starving. And, best of all, it's a one-way ticket out of the secretarial pool, which you've endured so long only because you had to have a roof over your head. If you marry him, you can relax.

Lady, if you're thinking about marriage in those

terms, you're really headed for trouble. Talk about role-playing and type-casting. You've set him up as Daddy Warbucks. His job is to go out and bring in the bread while you spend it. The trouble with this arrangement is that there's never enough bread. No matter how much money he earns, you'll find ways to get rid of it. After a while, you've got a relationship that's bound to go sour. Pretty soon, he doesn't see a woman in his home. He sees a sponge that's soaking him dry. On top of that, you'll begin to hate yourself. You might not be able to stop it, but you'll despise yourself for being nothing more than a passive, greedy bitch whose only job in life is to go through your man's trouser pockets every night when he comes home from work.

Don't get married if your chief consideration is financial security.

SEX

Believe it or not, people still get married today in order to enjoy sex. Despite the changing times and the New Morality, they are unable to enter into a sexual relationship with a man unless he offers the security of marriage. The principal trouble with this reason for marriage, it seems to us, is that great sex never made a great marriage. It's true that a great marriage includes great sex, but that's not the same thing.

Okay, so for the first couple of months, you two have a sensational time in bed. You've found a beautiful release for all those sexual tensions that have been hanging you up for years. Then what happens? Do you share any other interests?

Another reason why getting married for the sake of sex is a lousy idea is that your passions will fade one day. What's that? Never? We're sorry, but in five years, sex will not be as important to either of you as it is today. That's not to say it will cease to play a role in your marriage. It's just that it will not have the overriding urgency it has during the first months of continued physical intimacy.

We're glad that the guy turns you on, but sexual electricity alone is not enough of a reason for marriage. Have an affair with him instead and get it out of your system.

CHILDREN

You've always wanted children. The idea of having a brace of babies to cuddle and mother turns you into a sentimental glop of Jello. A guy asks you to marry him. He's okay. He's nice, actually. But he's got one thing going for him that makes him irresistible. He can give you those babies you've always yearned for. So you marry him, and wait for biology to take over.

This is a perfectly dreadful reason to get married. First of all, it's unfair to the guy. All he is in your life is a dispenser of semen, and a force that sees to it your kids always have new sneakers when they need them.

Secondly, you're shortchanging yourself. Suppose you have all your kids by the time you're thirty. How long do you think they'll be under your roof? When the youngest is fifteen, he'll be little more than a boarder in your house. His life, his interests, his friends will all be outside your orbit. Within two years, he'll be gone for good, and you'll see him only during an occasional visit from college. At that point, and you're just over forty-five years old, you've got nearly a quarter of a century to look forward to with a man you hardly know, a man you married simply as a convenience.

What are you going to say to him? "Finish your

breakfast," or "Don't forget to wear your rubbers, I think it's going to rain?" He will not be amused.

BOREDOM

Life is a drag. The job is monotonous, and you think if you have to come home to your apartment one more time, you'll scream. Suddenly, this guy shows up, and he wants to marry you. Great. It's a change. Maybe he'll provide you with a few new kicks. You decide you're going to marry him.

Please don't. A husband is not a stand-up comic. His job is not to keep you amused. If you're bored with life as a single, you'll be just as bored married. And that'll be the end of one more marriage.

SELF-ESTEEM

One friend put it this way: "I decided to marry him because I was sure he could help me feel better about myself. He seemed so strong, and I was so . . . nothing! I told him that and he laughed and said we were a great pair. Later on, I found out why. He really needed me around just so he'd have someone he could feel superior to. When we argued, he always won, and I always felt like a stupid worm. It wasn't that he really meant to be cruel. He just needed a doormat, and he found one."

Even if he doesn't use you as a foil for his intelligence, wit, charm and handsome looks, he will never be able to give you a feeling of being a worthwhile person. That has to come from inside you. Yes, sometimes a great relationship can help, but it's impossible to tell from the outset what's going to be a great relationship and what isn't.

GLAMOUR

Diana was a fellow stew. We'd both known her and flown with her for many years. Diana used to complain that nothing much ever seemed to happen to her. Then, one magical, mystical day, when she was working First Class on a transcontinental flight, who was sitting in an aisle seat but Mr. Movie Star. You'd recognize the name if we told you. Anyway, Mr. Movie Star liked the way Diana served coffee or something, so he slipped her a note asking for a date. Did she accept? Are you out of your mind? Of course, she accepted.

They began seeing each other regularly, and, lo and behold, he proposed. And Diana, hardly able to believe her good fortune, said yes. They were married. They did *not,* however, live happily ever after. Listen to Diana tell it.

"At first, life had this unreal quality. We'd fly to Rome where he'd be in a picture, and I'd meet the international movie colony. You know, whenever Liz and Richard were in town, we'd have them over to the villa we rented, or they'd ask us to join them on their yacht. That sort of thing.

"Then in California, I got to be something of a celebrity myself. Fan magazines kept asking me for interviews. They wanted to know what it was like being married to a famous actor. There'd be these articles, 'My Life with Ralph J. Movie Star,' that kind of thing. Pretty soon I began to notice something. He only talked about himself, his career and about other people. We had been married for eight months and we had never once had a serious discussion about anything. It was always gossip. Whenever I tried to steer the conversation around to something a little more serious than who was sleeping with whom that month, and how much did I think he was getting for his next picture, he'd shut me up. 'Come on,' he'd say, 'get off that dreary stuff. Life's too short. Let's have some fun.'

"Well, I like fun as much as the next girl, but not as an exclusive diet. After a while, I saw that the people we were with were exactly like him. They were all plastic. So I began thinking to myself, 'What am I doing here?' and I had to admit to myself that I didn't know. I didn't really love him. He was, in fact, quite dull and, despite his reputation as a great lover, not so hot in bed. He didn't satisfy me sexually, emotionally or intellectually. Once I reached that conclusion, I could only do one thing. I asked him for a divorce. And was he ever a surprised man! He couldn't conceive of the idea of me not wanting *him,* the idol of millions. His ego was really crushed.

"Anyway, I got my divorce, and now I realize that what first excited me was the *idea* of marrying him. *He* personally didn't excite or interest me one bit. But it took me nearly a year to work that out for myself. Oh, well, live and learn."

LONELINESS

There's an old saying that goes, "If you can't live with yourself, you can't live with anyone." Sure, people get lonely, but that's still a pretty weak reason for getting married. One sturdy spinster aunt of Trudy's told us she couldn't see what all the fuss was about marriage. Much better, she said, was to get yourself a parrot. Her reason? "Parrots," she sniffed, "live longer than husbands, have brighter feathers and generally make more interesting conversation." We wouldn't go quite so far as that, but we applaud her for her independence and self-sufficiency.

All right, what then? If these are all lousy reasons for marrying, what's a good reason?

Unless marriage begins as a great companionship and grows into an even closer one, it will be either a partial or a total failure. Companionship, then, is the key. A successful marriage depends upon an initial sense of companionship before marriage, and a widening, deepening closeness based on shared experiences, shared interests and shared goals as time goes on. With a generous helping of good sex and good fun, the formula is complete.

That's the definition. It's easy to say. It's easy to understand the logic in it. But, like all simple definitions, it creates as many problems as it solves. How many of us, for example, can really define our goals, our purpose in life? How many of us know what we will be ten years from now?

Many people *never* define their life's purpose. And for those lucky ones who do, an understanding of their real goals develops slowly as they mature. This is the reason why the high school or college steadies, who seem so perfect for one another in their teens and early twenties, become, over the next thirty years, total strangers who just happen to share a home, children and a joint bank account.

What's the answer, then? Do we eliminate teen-age marriages? Statistics tell us they have the highest rate of failure. But would a prohibition of early marriage really be possible? Who's to say how long a person should wait before marrying?

In any case, if we all waited for our life's goals to become clear, most of us would remain single forever. And there's a further consideration. People need other people in close relationship to help them grow. Still, a common rate of growth and continuing compatibility over the duration of an entire marriage is a very rare occurrence.

Now you know why Cupid is pictured as he is: blindfolded, firing his arrows wildly and at random into the air. Many hundreds of years of bitter human experience are embodied in that foolish portrait.

Does this mean that marriage is largely a game of chance? Is there no way of making even reasonably sure that you and your mate will continue to share a rich and rewarding life? Must the penalty for failure to achieve emotional growth always be a broken home, bitterness and frightened and scarred children?

Within recent years, some observers have felt there *must* be a better way. It seems unreasonable to them that we have allowed a situation to develop where so much is riding on a single throw of the dice. We must, they say, accept the fact that people change and that their needs today are not necessarily their needs fifteen or twenty years from today.

However, they warn us that if we adopt such a new flexibility, we must rethink our position on the entire institution of marriage itself. We must be open to consider a completely different type of accommodation between individuals of opposite sexes. These people are not preaching free love. They are not as simplistic as that. They are preaching a revolutionary new approach to the male-female relationship and to the idea of the family unit where responsibilities are clearly spelled out, and where both parties owe each other affection and loyalty—up to a point.

Their approach depends upon public recognition that an individual's physical and emotional needs change dramatically over the years. Let us, they say, accept that fact, and not put artificial restrictions on human behavior that can cause unhappiness and even tragedy. For example, young people of high school age are obsessed by sex. For many, it is a great and forbidden mystery, yet the desire they feel is so powerful they sometimes do not function to full capacity. If you look at it without prejudice, we think you'll agree that teenage boys and girls are put in an intolerably difficult situation. They want sex desperately, but society tells them it's wrong. They're torn apart by their desire, which pulls them one way, and their conscience, which pulls them another. What do they do?

You know perfectly well what they do. They have sex anyway and are frequently burdened by a sense of personal guilt. Furthermore, the sex they have isn't usually that good. It's hurried and furtive, and distorted by fear that they will be caught red-handed. Psychologists tell us that this can cause serious emotional problems later on. Some people never achieve emotional maturity because of a disastrous early sexual experience.

What are the alternatives society offers these young people? It's either abstinence or marriage. Abstinence is recommended, but if the couple insists upon it, marriage is grudgingly allowed. But this, the reformers say, is madness. A boy of seventeen or eighteen is not emotionally prepared to take on the responsibility of a wife and, perhaps, a family. He needs more time to develop. He needs more time to continue his education. Why force him to marry?

"Sorry," says society. "That's the way it is." But why? Why must it be that way? Instead of presenting a couple with only two choices, neither of which is attractive, why can't society recognize that the sexual drive in young people is so strong that it must find an outlet? Let's assume that John and Mary are classmates at the local high school. They're both seventeen, and both have been dating for a couple of years. They've known each other for a long time but one day, quite by accident, they find themselves talking quietly together. He asks her for a date. She accepts. A number of dates later they both realize that this is different from anything they have experienced before. This is something special.

According to the rules of society as they are now set up, John and Mary would probably start "going steady." This would be recognized by their classmates. Other boys would stop asking Mary for dates, and John would be expected to stay away from other girls. John's and Mary's parents might not approve, but they wouldn't bring the law down on either one of them. They might say, "We think you're too young to be going steady," and there might be a family scene, but, in the end, they would accept the situation.

Now, back to John and Mary. What do they do about their newfound mutual attraction? They neck. They pet. Perhaps even to climax. They urgently want to make love to each other. If they don't, they're torn apart by frustration. If they do, they're riddled by anxiety.

The solution offered by those who would alter the institution of marriage is this. If society today recognizes that a teen-age couple can "go steady," let them also accept the fact that this special relationship could include sex. Not hypocritically, but openly. Mary's mother and father would have to learn to get used to the idea that she is sleeping with John. In fact, they should encourage her to do so, and be supportive and warm.

This does not mean that Mary now has free license to sleep with any boy to whom she takes a fancy. It would be clearly understood by Mary, by her parents and by society as a whole, that she and John are seriously trying to establish a relationship that is important to both of them. This does not include "cheating" by either party. It does not include irresponsible behavior. By giving its blessing to this kind of trial marriage, society is allowing John and Mary the freedom to discover emotional security without guilt or trauma. And it is not imposing the demand that they get married first.

"But what if it doesn't work out?" the critics ask.

What if they're really incompatible? What if they decide they want more freedom than their current arrangement gives them? Then the trial marriage is terminated. The relationship is dissolved. Isn't that simpler than a legal separation or a divorce?

"Oh, well," say the horrified critics, "what you're doing now is simply setting up a state of affairs where a boy and girl can say to the world on Monday that they have a special relation, and then cancel it on Thursday. It makes it easy for them to be promiscuous. All they have to do is make a public declaration that is not binding on either party. Theoretically, a girl could form a new relationship each week."

Perhaps. But what's to prevent her from doing that now? If a girl is going to sleep around, she'll find ways to do it. Furthermore, if this idea is going to work, it must be made very clear that these relationships cannot be entered into lightly or casually. In that way, responsibility will be encouraged, and the whole process of individual maturing hastened.

Do John and Mary live together? Not during this first stage, and for a very simple reason. They can't afford to maintain a separate home. Neither one of them has much income. However, as soon as John or Mary becomes more financially independent, then they would live together, *provided they want to continue the relationship*. If they both went off to the same college, for example, they should be able to share an off-campus apartment without society attaching any stigma to their arrangement. Both sets of parents would know they had set up housekeeping together and, instead of disapproving, would watch over the young couple with care and concern.

During this stage of their relationship, John and Mary would be discovering important truths about themselves as individuals, and about each other. Bouncing into bed with a boy a couple of times is one thing. Living with him, taking care of him, having him take care of you, is an entirely different matter. Both partners can't help growing and developing that sense of sharing that is so crucial to human happiness.

After college, John and Mary are presumably on their own. They are no longer financially dependent upon their parents. They are now ready to make career choices and to develop their own unique life-styles. If they continue to live together, they have made a further commitment to each other. They have also assumed full responsibility for where and how they live. This is truly marriage without the wedding ceremony.

"Well, why don't they get married, then?" you ask. Why should they? It is only custom and, in some states, the law. Both can be changed. And both *should* be changed if the change will bring about greater individual freedom and happiness.

"What about children?" you ask. "Where do they fit into all this?" By the time John and Mary have passed through these three stages of intimacy, they should have a much clearer idea of whether or not they are prepared to assume the additional responsibility of a family than most young couples. They had two years of free, open sexual activity in high school, they lived together for four years in college, and they've been sharing the same apartment in the city, let's say for three years. That's a total of nine years together. And now they're ready for children.

At this point, John and Mary make still another commitment to each other, and to the family they are about to produce. This commitment involves a mutual agreement to stay together until the last of their children achieves personal independence—in other words, until he's ready to go out on his own. Having behaved in a responsible manner in the past, they both realize the seriousness of this commitment, and both are prepared to abide by it. If more young couples reached a thoughtful understanding such as this, think of the number of broken homes that would be saved. We all know that the most serious casualties of divorce are children. Under this arrangement, they would be spared the emotional trauma of watching their parents drift apart.

Once their children are grown, John and Mary can decide to remain together for the rest of their lives. Or they can decide they prefer to live separately, each pursuing some newfound interest or profession. Again, this choice would be widely understood by society. Nobody, including their own children, would think the worse of them if they chose separate paths. Part of the bitterness that stems from divorce can be traced to feelings of guilt on the part of both husband and wife. No matter which one initiates divorce proceedings, both feel that they *ought* to stay married. Even though they can't bear the thought of living together, they have been taught that divorce is somehow wrong. But under the arrangement we've just described, it's perfectly okay for John and Mary to seek new lives, *provided they have discharged their parental responsibilities.*

Does all this sound like the reformers are dreaming? Could we as people ever accept these strange new moral values? There are some who say we must. Otherwise, we will continue to pay the penalty of anxiety, frustration and guilt. They point out that societies and even whole civilizations have operated quite successfully on moral assumptions that would be repugnant to us.

Among some South Seas tribes, young boys and girls are encouraged to engage in sexual experimentation. However, when a girl becomes betrothed, she's expected to abstain from such activity, reserving her body exclusively for her husband. Moslems find nothing unusual in the practice of having more than one wife. We, of course, would punish such behavior with a prison sentence.

And so, within the human race, custom can vary greatly. There is no one set of laws that governs all. We can, and should, be flexible in these matters. Above all, we should adapt our customs more realistically to our needs as human beings, and not try to impose a rigid standard of behavior in the name of something being "right" or "wrong."

Perhaps, then, this will be the "marriage" of the future. But none of this, you say, helps solve your immediate problem. A guy is asking you to marry him. He wants a forever marriage, with a good, old-fashioned ceremony. Besides, you're not so sure you want to be one of the pioneers in radicalizing the institution of marriage. How do you know whether to say yes or no?

This seems to us to be a two-part question. First, are you, as an individual, ready for marriage? Secondly, do the two of you have the potential for a good marriage? Remember, we defined a good marriage as one in which there was growing companionship, the possibility of common life goals and good sex. Let's look at the first question.

Are you ready?

1. Have you had a wide and varied experience with many different kinds of men? Janice and Eddie were what was once known as "childhood sweethearts." Janice had never even dated another boy. They were heavy steadies straight through high school. After graduation, Eddie got a job as an apprentice electrician. Later, when he had made journeyman and was earning good money, he and Janice got engaged. For more than eight years, Janice's mother urged her to see other boys. "How do you know Eddie is right for you?" she used to say. "You don't have anyone with whom to compare him."

Janice always brushed these arguments aside. "I know Eddie as well as it's possible to know any boy, and I know he's right for me."

They married, moved to a nearby city and, five years later, they separated. "Mom was right," Janice admitted. "It's not that Eddie was mean or rotten. Actually, he's a nice guy. But after I got to know some other husbands, I saw that Eddie was dull. I guess I just want more out of life than Eddie can give me. I wish I'd known that earlier."

2. **Have there been times when there were several men in your life at once rather than one "going steady" experience following closely on the heels of another?** There are times when playing the field has its advantages. It's true, you may not develop the kind of deep, lasting relationship you're looking for, but at least you get a chance to form warm friendships with a number of different men who have different personalities and varying outlooks on life. That's terribly helpful when it comes to choosing a man you're going to live with for the rest of your life.

3. **Have you, at any time in your life, been "on your own?"** When Roberta, or Bobbie as she was known, graduated from high school, she applied to four colleges and was accepted by three. Two of the schools that wanted her were out of town. One was more than a thousand miles away. The third was a university located in the city where she had lived all her life. Which one should she choose? After lengthy discussions with her family, Bobbie finally selected the school in her home town. This pleased her parents enormously because it meant that Bobbie wouldn't have to leave. She could commute to her classes and family life would continue exactly as if Bobbie were still in high school.

Four years later, Bobbie stood, smiling broadly in her cap and gown, as her Dad took her picture. Later, Bobbie returned to her familiar room at home, hung her diploma on the wall and started to look for work.

The job she found was pleasant and rewarding. She settled easily into a comfortable routine which almost exactly paralleled her father's. Each morning the two of them would leave for work. When they returned at night, Bobbie's mother had dinner waiting for them. Naturally Bobbie felt she should pay for her share now that she was earning money, so each week she turned over part of her paycheck to her mother. The rest went into her personal bank account.

This placid life continued until Bobbie was twenty-five. That was the year she met Tim. Tim, handsome and eager, swept Bobbie off her feet. On a beautiful Saturday afternoon, just three months short of her twenty-sixth birthday, Bobbie married Tim. She had barely turned twenty-eight when she was back at her parents' house, nursing the wounds of a broken marriage. It had all been so perfect at first, but then, abruptly, the dream had collapsed. What had happened?

Bobbie had never in her life been responsible for herself. She had never been forced to make decisions about what curtains to buy for her living room, what to eat for dinner that night. She had never drawn up a budget and attempted to live within its limits. For twenty-five years, everything had been done for her. As a result, when she took over the management of her own home, she was at a total loss. She literally did not know how to do a single thing.

When Tim asked her to draw up a household budget, she found she couldn't do it, and this made her feel inadequate. Going downtown to select a carpet for their apartment was a nightmare for her. She couldn't make up her mind which one she wanted. In the end, Tim had to do it for her. Even such a simple thing as ordering groceries for the week was a terrifying prospect.

She felt helpless and was ashamed at the way she was behaving, but she couldn't help it. She'd burst into uncontrollable crying jags, and nothing Tim did seemed to help. Eventually, his patience snapped, and they began to quarrel. Finally, after one monumental scene, Tim said he was no longer interested in living with a child bride and walked out. Shortly after that, they obtained a legal separation and divorce proceedings were instituted.

4. **Have you ever traveled "on your own" or with a friend your own age?** Some people are born homebodies and are content to settle down. But in nearly everyone's life there comes a time when he or she is bitten by wanderlust. To these people, the surroundings seem stale, their minds feel dull. They must get away and see new sights, meet new people. They're itchy and restless. It's best to get that feeling out of your system *before* you are tied down by a new house, and, possibly, the responsibilities of a new family. Sure, two weeks on the Jersey shore in the middle of summer is fine. But as you sit in the sand looking out across the Atlantic Ocean, you're wondering what's on the other side. "What's France like?" you muse to yourself. Some people have all the luck—Paris, the French Riviera, Monte Carlo. What do you have? You've got a couple of kids with running noses and a beach cottage that has a screen door that won't close properly. Life, you decide, is just not fair. We're sorry you feel that way, but you had your chance.

5. **Can you spend a day, or, even better, a week, alone without being bored and without someone else to organize your activities?** We said it earlier in this book: If you can't live with yourself, you can't live with any-

one. A wife who is totally dependent upon her husband is a dead weight. She'll eventually sink the marriage.

6. **Do you have a pretty good idea of what you want your life to be like twenty years from now?** Think about that for a moment. Is it running around to art galleries in the afternoon and keeping up with the theater at night? Maybe that's the kind of life your man is interested in, too. If so, you're in luck. But cold reality will probably tell you that what life has in store for you is a home in the suburbs and a houseful of kids. Your art appreciation will likely consist of admiring the crayon drawing of a cat made by your six-year-old daughter. And your big theatrical thrill of the year will be watching your ten-year-old son play the Third Wise Man in his school's Christmas pageant. You may think that twenty years is a long way off, but it isn't.

Review the list we've just made out for you carefully. If you can honestly answer "yes" to most of the questions we've put, you're ready for marriage. If you can answer "yes" to all of them, why aren't you married?

Are the two of you ready?

Now, for the other part of our two-part question: Can the two of you make it together? To try to get at the facts, we've gone around and shamelessly borrowed advice from all the married people we know. The following is a kind of checklist for success based on their accumulated experience. Used effectively, it should be the basis for a joint exploration of compatibility. There are no passing or failing grades, but after going over it together, the sum total of your impressions should tell you—if you care to listen to your feelings—how good a chance you have of making it together.

1. **Go through an imaginary day in the life of a married couple you know.** Detail all their responsibili-

ties and daily chores, including cleaning, cooking, laundry, child care, income-producing work and so forth. That alone may be enough to discourage you. If not, proceed. Which of you would do what? Do you agree? Does he flatly refuse *ever* to do the dishes? It's best to find out now. How willing would you both be to assume the other's responsibility either wholly or in part? Actually, the best way to do this exercise is to sit down with a married couple you know very well, and ask them what their routine is. Pick a pair about your own age. Uncle Sid and Aunt Mabel have been married thirty-five years and have grown children. Their problems will not be yours.

2. **How do you both feel about your families?** Your own? Each other's? You may think that the two of you will retire to some private love nest, but in-laws *do* expect to be invited for dinner occasionally. Also, when the baby comes, they'll be proud grandparents and will find almost any excuse to drop in and visit you and little Merton. We know in-law jokes are legion, but it's no laughing matter. You must think about your relationship with the older generation. Otherwise, you may find yourself living in a family situation that is made uncomfortable by bitterness and resentment.

3. **How does he feel about women in general?** We don't mean you. We mean the female sex as a whole. Does he feel women have a role to play and that straying from it is improper conduct? You can get hints of how a man feels about women by listening to the way he talks about women drivers, women in business, women in politics. If his references are always downgrading and if he's uneasy about women competing in what he terms a man's world, then the chances are you have an incipient male chauvinist pig on your hands.

4. **How do you feel about men in general?** Are you angry at male attitudes? Do you find masculine be-

havior coarse and vulgar? Do *you* think that men have a role to play? Would you be embarrassed to see him cry? Would you consider it unmanly for him to bake a cake? If so, then you've got a lot of thinking to do, my girl, and maybe he's got a castrating bitch-witch on his hands.

5. Are you realistic about one another? Ask him to define your personality as he sees it. Have him list your strengths, weaknesses, likes and dislikes. Do you consider the portrait accurate? This one can be quite an eye-opener. A friend of ours, Eloise, claims it saved her marriage.

"I'm the extremely practical type," Eloise told us. "I like working with my hands. I adore building things and I could happily spend hours at a carpenter's bench. I dislike sentimental stories, and I'm probably the only female in America who didn't wet a handkerchief when seeing *Love Story*. I loathe fancy French restaurants where they're either snotty or patronizing. If I had my choice, I'd live in the country any day. I've known these things about myself ever since I was a child, but you should have heard Stan describe me. I listened and I couldn't believe my ears. He was talking about a total stranger. I wondered there for a moment if he was engaged to another girl, someone I didn't even know. Then it dawned on me that Stan was projecting his own private romantic fantasies of what his ideal woman should be like. He was so in love with his personal version of the perfect female that he had attributed all her qualities to me. I told him, 'Whoa, there, buddy, you and I have got a few things to straighten out.' I finally managed to shake the stardust out of his eyes and take myself off the pedestal where he'd put me. He did it very reluctantly, I can tell you that. But, at least, when we got married, he knew what he was marrying. And *that* saved a lot of confusion and heartache."

6. Are you sexually compatible? Mutual attraction should be present from the first, but real sexual pleasure may take months to develop. If you haven't got it, don't get married.

7. What are your attitudes toward money? How much does it matter? How much do you need? Who's responsible for getting it? How much should be saved? For what? How do you feel about living on credit? Or borrowing? If you had a spare fifty dollars in your pocket and no bills to pay, what would each of you do with it? Remember this, disagreement about financial management is the single, most common cause for marital quarrels. Money, not "that other woman," is the most frequent cause for divorce. So, our suggestion to you is that you reach a basic understanding about how money will be handled in your house. If he expects an exact accounting of every penny you spend, you'd better know about it now. Otherwise, once a month, you'll be in for a steaming row when he tries to balance the family checkbook and it doesn't come out right.

8. How do you see yourself in the future? Ten years from now? Twenty? How does he see himself at those times? What are your goals and his? Be as specific as possible. Don't just say, "I want to be rich and live in a big house in the country."

9. If you could live anywhere in the world, where would you choose? This is a fun question you can both play with for hours. What sort of life would you choose?

10. How do you both feel about children? Ask him to describe his childhood. Then describe yours. How many kids do you want? What would be your method of raising them. A friend of ours once told us that she was seriously considering marrying a man until he informed her that he'd like to raise his children on a remote island somewhere in the Mediterranean where they could run around all day, naked, in the sun, and never be burdened by a formal education. Upon closer examination, he revealed himself to be an incorrigible romantic. In fact, so Byronesque was he that she decided she could never live with him.

11. What's his idea of a perfect friend? If he says it's Adolf Hitler, you may have some trouble. What qualities does he most dislike in others? What qualities do you most dislike in others?

12. What are his politics? Do they differ markedly from yours? We're not saying that a marriage between a Democrat and a Republican is doomed to failure, but it would be nice to have shared prejudices. We still remember the story of an old Vermont couple who hadn't spoken to each other for years. She was a lifelong Republican, and he was an equally staunch Democrat. She was so incensed by his political persuasion that one election day, she hid his pants and refused to tell him where she put them. This prevented him from going out to vote and he never forgave her.

13. How does he spend his leisure hours? Before he met you? When he's not with you? Is he mad for bowling while you think the game is a bore? How do you spend your spare time? What activities do you enjoy together? No, not that, dummy!

14. How much conflict exists between you, either on or below the surface of your relationship? This is a tricky one to answer because you both must be extremely honest and objective. But being entirely frank with each other on this point can make an enormous difference to a marriage.

15. How often do you laugh together? A minor point, you say, but we disagree. The ability to laugh at something together is a sign of a healthy, happy relationship.

16. **To whom does he tell his troubles?** To whom do you tell yours?

17. **What are his aesthetic values?** What, in his opinion, is the most beautiful thing in the world? The ugliest? How would you answer these questions?

18. **What triggers his emotions?** What makes him mad? What makes him sad? What makes you mad? What makes you sad? When things go wrong, what is his reaction? Yours?

19. **How does he react to a compliment?** How do you?

20. **How often do his words differ from his deeds?** Yours?

21. **How do you both react in a crisis?**

22. **Do little things about him annoy you?** If he hums, sings or whistles frequently, is he on key or off? Do you care?

23. **What books has he read lately?** If he's engrossed in *Tarzan of the Apes,* he might be a bit retarded.

24. **How long does he spend in the bathroom?** Does he have any special feelings about the need to replace the cap on the toothpaste tube? Does he squeeze the tube from the top or roll it up carefully from the bottom?

25. **What does he do with his clothes when he takes them off?** Does he just step out of them and leave them in a rumpled pile on the floor? Do you mind living with a messy man? On the other hand, is he fussy? Does he straighten pictures on the wall as he passes? Does he fluff up the pillows on the sofa. "I cannot stand a pillow patter," our friend says. "It's a dead giveaway he'll turn out to be a fussbudget."

26. **Is he lazy or energetic?** When you're traveling a short distance, does he ride or walk? If he uses the car to go down to the corner to buy a dozen eggs, you can bet he'll be overweight within ten years.

27. **Does he spend hours polishing the car?** This might mean that he'll take better care of his automobile than he will of you. Challenge him on it.

Our friend has one final, but important hint. See how his face looks when he's asleep. Do the lines go up or down?

And now our final bit of advice. Be as honest as you can with each other. Examine your own motives, and his. Take your own taste into consideration. No matter how practical and correct a certain man may seem to you, don't discount any feelings from deep inside that you may not share a real bond, spark or dream.

Charles was a good-looking, hard-working young lawyer, obviously on his way up. When Alice met him, she found him charming. They discovered a mutual interest in many activities. His manners were impeccable, he was cordial to her family and her friends. He was expert and considerate in bed. Everyone told Alice that she'd found the perfect man. Theirs would be an ideal marriage. Alice was forced to agree. Yet, when Charles finally did propose, Alice turned him down. "Why?" her friends wanted to know. "What was wrong with him?" Alice couldn't tell them. She herself didn't really understand what made her say no. The best she could do was tell herself that she had this feeling she couldn't explain. It was a feeling that the marriage wouldn't work. Alice subsequently married Fred and is blissfully happy. She still can't explain why she refused Charles. "Maybe," she says with a smile, "because I knew Fred was coming into my life. I don't know."

So, listen to that small, still voice inside you. Sometimes, it's the most reliable advice a girl can get when she's considering the scary, wonderful step of marriage.

CHAPTER XIII

"That's no lady, that's my wife."
—ROBERT ORBEN

"Go to Bed with Me? We're Married!"

Mother, it seems, let you down after all. She told you how to behave as a little lady. She told you all about boys. She told you about the birds and the bees. She told you how it would be when you finally met Mr. Right. She told you how grand and glorious your wedding day would be. But she forgot to tell you what it would be like after you were married. Maybe she didn't want to. Maybe she didn't want to discourage you, destroy your dreams and wreck your innocent, childhood fantasies. That's too bad, because you sure could use some advice. For instance, does everybody experience a letdown?

Well, yes, they do. But why must the magic vanish? Why must romance always die? This is the anguished cry you hear so often from the lips of overweight, middle-aged ladies who read gothic novels, are addicted to soap operas, and cry sweet, slightly hysterical tears at every wedding they attend. These women don't really want an answer. For them, it's all academic. The romance is long dead, far beyond their power to recall it. Only the dreams remain and, strangely enough, they are the same dreams they had years ago when they were sixteen.

What is romance made of that makes it so fragile? In varying proportions, romance consists of mystery, solitude, imagination and suspense. The romance you remember most vividly in your old age may be the one that was shortest in length. One friend cherishes a twenty-minute bus ride during which she was seated across the aisle from the most perfect man in the world. Not one word was exchanged, but it was the romance she'll never forget. Sometimes, she regrets her shyness, more often, she doesn't. She knows, as we all know once we've passed the age of twenty, that romance is 95 percent illusion.

Will passion, too, fade away? Sadly, yes. For all of us except the dyed-in-the-wool middle-aged soap-opera addict, who is most alive when she is dreaming of the racing heart, the sleepless nights, the idealization of the beloved, this knot of romantic love disappears from most marriages almost entirely.

But the word *almost* is important, for evidence seems to indicate that the real success of all marriages depends on the remainder of some portion of romantic love, but in a slightly calmer, more mature fashion. And, filling the void left by the death of passionate young romance, comes real friendship, real affection, real sharing. Sex becomes a mutual act of love, less urgent, but more deeply meaningful. It becomes an exploration, a speaking without words, an exchange and a joining.

The entire key to a deepening sexual relationship in marriage is this: Do you care enough about him and yourself to struggle against laziness and habit? Do you work to keep your sexual relationship varied and interesting? This means using all the techniques we suggested in the preceding chapters, plus all those you can dream up by yourself.

But sex after marriage presents its own peculiar problems. For example, no longer will your evenings consist of music and moonlight, dancing and kissing and the slow gradual build-up of delicious sexual tension. After a year or so of marriage, your husband is more likely to spend the evening with a book or a plumbing leak. You may be washing your hair, ironing or maybe even reading with him. Then it's time for bed. You lie there together, and your husband reaches out for you. He may be disappointed in your response—and so may you.

Are you both still searching for the perfect orgasm? Don't let it become your goal, your obsession. Every woman dreams of the moment when she cries out in perfect passion, sees brilliant lights, feels like an erupting volcano. This idea is thrilling, but the search, like the search for *perfect* joy, *perfect* peace, *perfect* happiness, is pointless.

Also, beware of using sex as a weapon. Trouble, hostility or disappointment in a marriage can often be felt first in the sexual relationship. Sex—the greatest and most personal give and take—frequently comes to be used as a weapon or as a prize given in return for some payment.

Finally and most disconcerting, you may find you're bored by sex. Everyone remembers his or her wedding night but who remembers the thousandth night? Repetition of anything, sex included, tends to produce a levelling off of excitement. In a sexual relationship, this can lead to "not tonight" and finally to "why bother."

This, in turn, often leads to an affair. In terms of conditioning, women are more monogamous than men. But everyone, women included, has a curiosity about extramarital sex. It may be that women don't go in search of an affair as often or as actively as men. By and large, women content themselves with vague, romantic dreams, a favorite soap opera or a good cry over a bad novel.

Of course, many of them go a step further and play flirtation games with other people's spouses. The woman who tells you "I hope you don't mind, but I adore your husband," could be expressing dissatisfaction with her own marriage. But don't let it concern you. That type isn't playing for keeps.

The list of games goes on and on. Most often, though, they lead to nothing. And, statistically, it seems as though it is the woman who usually puts an end to them. Why?

Because a woman quickly loses interest in an affair which provides her with nothing more than an orgasm. And she shies away from allowing the relationship to become deep or meaningful. It could take the place of her marriage. Most women know this. They know they can't handle a love affair and a fairly healthy marriage at the same time.

Yet, in some circles, the affair has become the standard adventure, even a status symbol, and women willingly embark on them. Why? To feel beautiful again. To feel wanted again. To make a real contact, to touch, perhaps even to love again.

Between the ages of thirty-five and forty, when marriage has become routine, often dull, when husbands and wives find themselves drifting in different directions, the women most frequently try an affair. In the absence of any other ambition or aim, she may become a middle-aged flirt. Such a woman wants much more than an orgasm in return for her trouble. She wants a reason to continue living.

Is it realistic to expect to find satisfactions within the average marriage that will make extramarital affairs unnecessary? Opinions vary, but most experts agree that, in the long run, it is the healthiest and most satisfactory course to try.

It is the boredom, the lack of things to do, that drives many married women into the arms of a lover. Perhaps a safer outlet might be to resume working, but this can present a problem, especially if there are children.

For many women, a career means challenge, stimulation, fulfillment. It also means real complications in the married woman's role as wife, mother and housekeeper. As our society is presently constituted, each person must weigh the personal advantages and disadvantages of working against not working at every period of her married life. A decision reached at the age of twenty-eight may not be the same one you arrive at when you're thirty-eight.

Naturally, for the woman with no children, or the woman with older children, having a job is less complicated than for those with infants or youngsters. But, in many cases, a serious career is fatally damaged by a ten-year maternity leave.

Look at what happened to Sandra, a highly trained microbiologist who left her profession to have three babies in a row. "That was four years out of my professional life right there," she points out. "Then, of course, I didn't want to leave them when they were infants, so I waited until the littlest was three years old. That was another three years gone. Finally when I went back to work, people were talking to me in a language I didn't understand. And they, in turn, thought I'd come right out of the Stone Age. There had been so many advances in the field of microbiology in the seven years I'd been away, that I simply couldn't contribute anything any more. I couldn't cut the mustard. I was pretty desperate until a colleague advised me to go back to school and take some courses over again. I felt like an idiot sitting in lecture halls with people ten and twelve years younger than I was, but I stuck it out. I had to. It was the only way."

Sandra's dilemma points out a common source of frustration. Our goals as a woman are often not compatible with our goals as a person. Let's hope, however, that human liberation—not women's liberation—will change all that.

As things stand now, a woman will function best if she can accept several roles in her lifetime, and juggle them with good humor, if not with ease. If her mate can do the same, and they can interchange roles when the need arises, it might some day be possible to be both a woman and a complete person.

"Maybe," you mutter darkly to yourself, "but my problem is now, and nobody seems to understand that." Oh, yes, we do. Here's what's troubling you.

You haven't learned the techniques for efficient housekeeping. There *are* books on the subject, you know. Many of them are helpful, and some are downright amusing. Try one.

You try to do a good job, but hate the job you have to do. Why do you have to do it all by yourself? Have a heart-to-heart talk with your husband. In fact, why didn't you have that talk *before* you were married?

You have many ambitions as a human being, but you're afraid they may complicate or even destroy your marriage. We don't buy that one. You're not afraid of that at all. You're afraid of failing. It's been so long, you've gotten rusty at your trade. Come on, brace up. You can do it. Ever hear the old saying, where there's a will, there's a way?

You use all those labor-saving devices and still you feel puzzled and sometimes bitter that they don't seem to increase your free time. Ever hear of Parkinson's law? Activity increases to fill the time available. Parkinson is saying that no matter how much time is available, a businessman will always fix it so there's not enough. It's the make-work principle. Don't let yourself get caught in that trap.

Your life is hectic and fragmented. So what else is new? You think you're somebody special?

Your standards are impossibly high. Your house must be immaculate, your family perfectly groomed. Now, sit down for a minute and think *that* one over. Aren't you being just a tiny bit obsessive about it?

You live in what's known as a "nuclear family," which means there is no other adult to depend upon to share your responsibilities. This is an interesting point, and currently the subject of lively debate. There are those who stoutly defend the traditional family unit. Others present equally strong arguments against it. The kind of life they propose is a sort of a loose confederation of young families living together. Perhaps there are six families with fourteen children among them. Each child has its natural mother, of course. At the same time, he is also the responsibility of the five other mothers. That way, say the ones urging change and responsibility-sharing, the old mother-fixation problem is neatly avoided, and each mother has more time to do her own thing. Interested? Groups are forming today all across the country.

You have great difficulty in justifying a day, or even a few hours, off to pursue your own interests. What are you feeling so guilty about? You're a person, too, you know. You'll also be a more interesting and effective mother and wife if you occasionally get involved in something more stimulating than polishing the silverware.

You need to juggle the roles of wife, lover, adviser, playmate, confidante, companion, mother, maid, cook, nurse, laundress, chauffeur, wage earner and plain human being, and then you'll be expected to keep on smiling. Right on, sister. So you do. But, then, so does your husband have to juggle his roles of husband, lover, adviser, playmate, confidante, companion, father, carpenter, plumber, electrician, handyman, garbage man, wage earner and plain human being and keep on smiling. Say, why don't you two have a good talk about all this?

Most important of all, be a little tolerant with yourself. It's a very hard job. But do watch out for the health of your marriage. Here's a checklist of possible problems. Consult it often. Your marriage may be in trouble IF:

1. You cannot, in the past month, remember *one* romantic moment between your man and yourself.
2. You do not often feel proud of him, either how he looks or what he says when others are present.
3. You don't think he feels proud of you under the same circumstances.
4. You feel it is necessary to lie, pretend or hide your feelings from him.
5. You are bored or repelled by the idea of lovemaking.
6. You've allowed yourself to become fat, sloppy and careless about your appearance.
7. Your housekeeping has become so important that it has wiped out other aspects of yourself you once believed necessary to your happiness.
8. You are so involved with your children that your husband has taken a back seat as far as your attention and affection are concerned.
9. You've had to give up all your personal goals for the "good" of your marriage.

Those are the clues to failure. What are the keys to success? Over and over again, the same words crop up. Companionship. Equal status. Maturity. Real interaction. Admiration. Esteem.

Maybe all these words are dimensions of a concept we've all heard of, but few understand in its fullest sense—the concept of love.

Epilogue

We've been chattering and nattering at you, telling you how to look, what to wear and how to behave for a long time now. We've talked about the first stirrings of romance, and discussed what to expect from that first great night together to the day the blahs finally hit a marriage. What more, you wonder, can we possibly say?

Just this. If there's one theme that runs consistently through this book, it's the message to "be yourself." Don't do *anything* that isn't completely free and natural. The rules of conduct that once seemed so important don't really matter now. The New Morality means we have an opportunity to explore the world around us, and to make a place for ourselves that is uniquely our own, and not dictated by rules or custom.

Of course, the fundamentals of decent human behavior still apply. If we sock somebody over the head with our purse just because we feel like it and don't like the way he looks, we'll deserve all the trouble we get. If we cheat and lie and pretend to be somebody we're not, we may get what we're after, but then the world will probably leave us alone to enjoy our prize. Because *things* aren't considered especially valuable by the New Morality. It's the way we live that counts. It's the way we share our life that matters. Think about it.

We've thought about ways to end this book. We thought perhaps we could bow out most gracefully by saying, "May you find happiness." Or, "May you find love." But then we thought of a better ending.

May you find . . . yourself.